Native
Religions
and
Cultures
of Central
and South
America

From the Series Anthropology of the Sacred
Edited by Julien Ries and Lawrence E. Sullivan

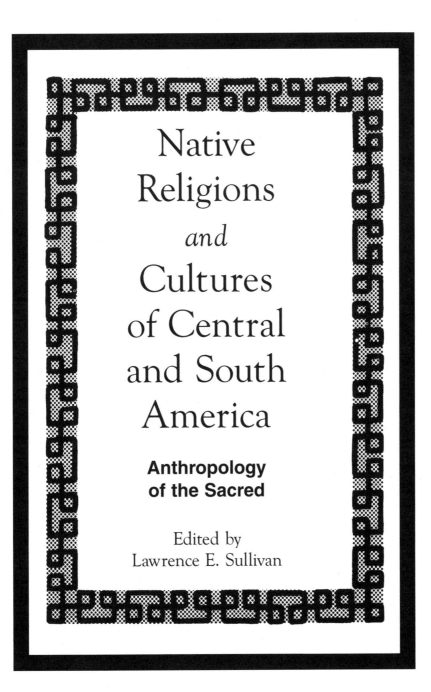

Native
Religions
and
Cultures
of Central
and South
America

**Anthropology
of the Sacred**

Edited by
Lawrence E. Sullivan

Continuum · New York and London

2002

The Continuum International Publishing Group Inc
370 Lexington Avenue, New York, NY 10017

The Continuum International Publishing Group Ltd
The Tower Building, 11 York Road, London SE1 7NX

Originally published as *Culture e Religioni Indigene in America Centrale e Meridionale*
© 1997 Editoriale Jaca Book spa, Milano

English-language edition copyright © 2002 by The Continuum Publishing Company.

Printed in the United States of America

Library of Congress Cataloging-in-Publication Data

Culture e religioni indigene in America centrale e meridionale. English
    Native religions and cultures of Central and South America / edited
by Lawrence E. Sullivan.
        p.   cm. — (Anthropology of the sacred)
    Includes bibliographical references and index.
    ISBN 0-8264-1119-3
    1. Indians of South America—Religion.   2. Indians of Mexico—
Religion.   3. Indians of Central America—Religion.   I. Sullivan,
Lawrence Eugene, 1949-   II. Title.   III. Series.

F2230.1.R3 C8513 2001
299'.8—dc

                                                            2001028379

Contents

Introduction

Lawrence E. Sullivan

"To write is to weep," cried the native Quechua chronicler Felipe Guamán Poma de Ayala. As one of the first native literati, he set down in writing the tragic events of the Conquest of Peru in his *Primer nueva corónica y buen gobierno*, the first full history of his own people. In it he wept for one thousand pages and sketched three hundred ethnographic drawings to depict the despair and calamity of the Andes. The book is actually a letter of lament addressed to King Philip III of Spain. Guamán Poma views the Spanish king as the sole remaining messianic figure and metaphysical principle capable of restoring cosmic order, now that Tupac Amaru, the last reigning royal Inca and center of the Inca universe, has been annihilated in a public beheading. That center no longer holds, and all is collapsing around it; evidence is supplied on every page of the chronicle.

Ever since the execution of Tupac Amaru in 1572, chaos has been unleashed by supernatural forces of destruction. Guamán Poma's view is a religious one: he is an eyewitness to the final *pachacuti*, the destruction that occurs at the end of a world cycle as described in Quechua mythology. There have been four previous universal destructions, each one destroying a mythic world—through fire, darkness, flood, or petrification. The current one is the fifth and final devastation; it will be a total dissolution.

Guamán Poma styles himself as the official spokesperson (*auki*) interceding with the king. His nom de plume indicates that he speaks on behalf of all the peoples of the Andes, for the name unites both of the two halves (or ritual moieties) of the population: *guaman*, the falcon, is the emblem of the sky (*hanan*) and upper moiety; *poma*, the puma, dwells on the earth (*hurin*) and presides over the lower moiety. Consonant with Guamán Poma's new-found awareness of the

1

power of the written word, his pen name joins heaven and earth in that fusion and immanence that signal the end of the world.

By providing a summary account of the chaos for which "there is no remedy" in this world, his book is intended to play the efficacious role of a scripture: provoking the messiah into salvific action and bringing on the culminating, cleansing catastrophe of flood and darkness. After that will dawn the new social order (*buen gobierno*) and a new physical universe, one that will be an everlasting source of bounty and well-being.

In the book-based (literally, biblical) culture of modern literacy, a writer or reader could only hope as much for any book, especially one describing the fantastic religious realities of South America and Mesoamerica. In fact, the hope that writing will communicate an important message that transforms readers and their world draws its inspiration and model from sacred scripture. And yet the fate of Guamán Poma's work offers writers a sobering lesson. Though he tells us the heart-rending personal costs of describing the malaise of his day—"Reader, this book cost me thirty years of labor and poverty. Leaving behind me my child, my house, and my property, I worked by mingling with the poor"—for hundreds of years, there was never a trace of his book anywhere in the historical record. As spokesman for humans and the cosmos, Guamán Poma poured out the history of atrocities and laid bare what he took to be the last hopes of his people. History leaves no indication that his letter was ever read by the king or by any living soul. There exists no mention of a response from any source until after the work was found in an archive in Copenhagen in the twentieth century. Since that time it has been known mostly to a small circle of scholars specializing in its study.

We often find ourselves reading other people's mail when we try to understand the religious life of South and Mesoamerica. The fate of Guamán Poma's lost manuscript teaches us that the accounts of religious life among native peoples are scattered throughout notes addressed frequently to people other than us: administrative reports to colonial governors, marginalia on the natural histories written by explorers to their sponsors, dissertations written to fulfill university requirements for a career advancement, and letters of lament to the king. Treatment of religion is frequently a by-product of other purposes intended by writers largely unprepared to study religion in the first place. The ironic result of all this indirection is that a central concern important to native peoples of the Americas, namely, the religious evaluation of their existence in time and the rich religious imagery they conjure to handle their experiences, often remains marginal to our concern and remote from our understanding. Though the first European contacts with the Americas were with native peoples of South and Mesoamerica, the indigenous religions of these areas remain little known. In spite of the attempts of indigenous writers to underscore the centrality of religious experience to their worldview, from Guamán Poma to the recent Nobel Peace Prize winner Rigoberta Menchú of Guatemala, the religious ideas and practices they point to receive insufficient attention, are filtered through inadequate and unhelpful categories such as "superstition" "animism," or "syncretism," or become lost altogether in exhaustively political and economic analyses.

We are fortunate to have in this volume the writings of specialists who have dedicated their professional lives to understanding on its own terms the religious life indigenous to the Americas. (A companion volume to this one gathers essays on the religious life of native North America.) As described by these experts, the religious worldviews of native peoples prove startlingly coherent, comprehensive, and critical. The ongoing creativity of these communities defies centuries of deliberate eradication as well as decimation by microbial shock waves of disease, and it testifies to the reflexivity of communities confronting the real threat of cultural extinction. Native peoples have suffered the ravages of modernity. "Historians have been able to estimate with reliable plausibility that in 1500 around 80 million inhabitants occupied the New World. By 1550 only 10 million natives were alive. In Mexico there were close to 25 million people in 1500. By 1600 only 1 million native Mesoamericans were still alive."[1]

Against the prevailing tendency to regard indigenous thought as inherently archaic or "primitive," the ethnologist André Marcel d'Ans declares:

> In am convinced of the historical value and of the modernity of our Amazonian contemporaries. They are not . . . the ancient vestiges of an overthrown past. In an epoch concretely dominated by the effects of western thought, they are moving witnesses to a different way of apprehending the world and others. . . . That is no doubt why they

---

[1] Carrasco 1990, 129.

pay such heavy tribute to a History from which, not having been its accomplices, they stand to gain no benefit.[2]

The native religious viewpoints presented in this volume reflect on life at all levels of existence, from the personal to the social and cosmic, and they offer penetrating critiques of the destabilizing predicaments of modernity.

No attempt has been made to offer a complete treatment of religious life in South and Mesoamerica. The linguist Juan Adolfo Vázquez once estimated that there could be as many as 1,500 different South American native languages present or extinct. Even in the multivolume encyclopedias describing cultures in South and Mesoamerica, no attempt is made to describe exhaustively the rich religious lives in all these cultural groups.

This volume chooses instead a few cases in order to illustrate something of the range of religious concerns and practices. The aim is to select cases that are exemplary of a variety of beliefs and activities rather than pretend to provide coverage that is exhaustive. As a result, the reader will find descriptions of the religious views of the Aztec, Maya, and Inca civilizations, dating to the time before contact with Europeans. It must be remembered, in this connection, that when the soldiers of Hernán Cortéz entered the Aztec-Mexica capital of Tenochtitlán set in the Valley of Mexico in 1519, they were stupefied at the sophisticated level of civilization they encountered and could not decide whether, in fact, they were dreaming. They stood within the largest urban settlement in the world of their day. One of them, Sergeant Bernal Díaz del Castillo, recorded this memoir of that first sighting:

> When we saw so many cities and villages built in the water and other great towns on dry land and that straight and level causeway going towards Mexico [City], we were amazed and said that it was like the enchantments they tell of in the legend of Amadis, on account of the great towers and buildings rising from the water, and all built of masonry. And some of the soldiers even asked whether the things that we saw were not a dream. . . . And all was cemented and very splendid with many kinds of stone (monuments) with pictures on them. . . . I say again that I stood looking at it and thought that never in the world would there be discovered other lands such as these, for

---

[2] D'Ans 1978, 22.

at that time there was no Peru, nor any thought of it. Of all these wonders that I then beheld today all is overthrown and lost, nothing left standing.[3]

In addition to these important examples from the history of first contact onwards, the volume includes select contemporary cases from all the major cultural-geographic areas of the subcontinent of Latin America, from the contemporary Andean highlands, to the forests of the Amazon (both in the northwest and in the gallery forests of the southern tributaries), to the plains of the Argentine Chaco, and the mountainous regions of northeast Guerrero in Mexico. No attempt is made to impose uniform treatment on each society. On the contrary, each contributor was asked to shape an original essay around the distinctive religious profile of the culture in question. In some instances, therefore, emphasis falls on the long-term religious calendar or on some particular ritual celebrations within the calendar. In others, stress is placed on the mythology of creation. In still others, focus is sharpened on shamanic practice or architecture. To supplement the historical and geographic sampling, a third kind of analysis is also provided in the form of extended comparative studies of exemplary themes (such as myth and apocalypse).

The contributors to this volume form an international group of outstanding authorities focused on the study of religion but trained in a variety of disciplines such as archaeology, history, cultural anthropology, sociology, linguistics, musicology, political economy, and art history.

We hope that readers will find this book rich in description and provocative in interpretation of religious ideas rarely gathered in one place. The indigenous religions of the Americas—their construals and misconstruals—lie at the foundations of the New World in which we find ourselves. This is a New World that came into being in the encounter with the religions of South and Mesoamerica. The spiritual histories of various indigenous cultures play an increasingly important role in the formation of New World horizons. In understanding and evaluating the world in which we live today, it is fitting and perhaps even necessary that the long-enduring and creative agency of South American religions plays a fundamental role.

---

[3] Díaz del Castillo 1956, 191; cited in Carrasco 1990, xv–xvi.

References

Carrasco, Davíd. 1990. *Religions of Mesoamerica*. San Francisco: Harper & Row.

D'Ans, André-Marcel. 1978. *Le Dit des vrais hommes: Mythes, contes, légendes et traditions des indiens cashinuhua*. Paris.

Díaz del Castillo, Bernal. 1956. *The Discovery and Conquest of Mexico*. New York: Farrar, Straus & Giroux.

Guamán Poma de Ayala, Felipe. 1966. *El Primer nueva corónica y buen govierno* [1584-1614]. Lima.

Ossio, Juan M. 1973. "Guamán Poma: Nueva Corónica o Carta al Rey: Un Intento de aproximación a las categórias del pensamiento del mundo andino." In *Ideología mesiánica*, edited by Juan M. Ossio, 155-213. Lima.

Sullivan, Lawrence E. 1988. *Icanchu's Drum: An Orientation to Meaning in South American Religions*. New York: Macmillan.

Wilbert, Johannes. 1995. *Mystic Endowment*. Cambridge, Mass.: Harvard University Press.

———. 1996. *Mindful of Famine*. Cambridge, Mass.: Harvard University Press.

Part One
Central America

1

Aztec Religion: Sacred Cities, Sacred Actions

Davíd Carrasco

Tenochtitlán: Center of the Aztec World

The formation of Aztec religion was accomplished between the fourteenth and sixteenth centuries C.E. in the capital city of Tenochtitlán,
located in the central Basin of Mexico. Throughout the Aztec world,
sacred spaces, whether in the form of household shrines, local temples, burial sties, statues of deities, colossal pyramids, monumental
ceremonial centers, or capital cities, and extensive *ritual actions* associated with them provided human populations with profound and
varied forms of religious orientation and access to the gods and powers of the cosmos. The Aztec religious tradition combined and transformed a number of ritual, mythic, and cosmological elements from
the heterogeneous cultural groups who inhabited the central plateau
of Mesoamerica. Seldom has a capital city fit the category of "center
of the world" more completely than Tenochtitlán. While the high
plateau of Mexico was roughly the center of Mesoamerica, the Basin
of Mexico was the heart of the plateau. Interconnected lakes formed
the center of the Basin, and Tenochtitlán was constructed near the
center of the lakes.[1] From the beginning of the common era, when
the great imperial capital of Teotihuacán (the "Abode of the Gods")
was organized into four great quarters around a massive ceremonial
center thirty miles to the north of the heart of the Basin of Mexico,

I would like to acknowledge the assistance of Scott Sessions in preparing this
article for publication.
    [1] Eric Wolf, *Sons of the Shaking Earth* (Chicago: University of Chicago Press,
1959), 1–20.

through the period of Toltec dominance centered in the kingdom of
Tollan during the tenth, eleventh, and twelfth centuries, the central
highlands had been the dominant cultural region of central Mesoamerica. Even though Mesoamerican civilization had periodically
fragmented, its reintegration was controlled by cities located, in part,
at the top of the geographical pyramid. Between 1300 and 1521 all
roads of central Mesoamerica led into the lake region of the Basin,
from which the magnificent capital of the Aztecs rose.[2] Archaeologists
and historians of religions have determined that the four-quartered
city was a massive spatial symbol for the major cosmological conceptions of Aztec religion.[3]

When the Aztec precursors, the Chichimecas ("*chichi*" meaning
"dog" and "*mecatl*" meaning "role" or "lineage"), migrated into the
lake region in the sixteenth century, the area was organized by war-
ring city-states constantly competing for land and tribute.[4] This fragmented world was partly the result of the twelfth-century collapse of
the Toltec empire, which brought waves of Chichimecas and Toltec
remnants into the Basin of Mexico, where they interacted with different city-states and religious traditions. These migrants also
brought powerful religious cosmologies and ritual practices with
them and impressive amalgamations began to develop. The Chichi-
mec group, who called themselves Mexicas, settled Tenochtitlán
around 1325 C.E., and within a hundred years organized a political
unit with the capacity to dominate an expanding number of cities
and towns in central Mexico.[5] Two major urban traditions, the imperial capital of Teotihuacán and the ideal settlement of the great Tollan formed the religious and ideological background of the evolving

---

[2] For a vivid, impressionistic description, see Lawrence E. Sullivan, "Reflection
on the Miraculous Waters of Tenochtitlán," in *To Change Place: Aztec Ceremonial
Landscapes*, ed. Davíd Carrasco (Niwot: University Press of Colorado, 1992),
205-12.

[3] Johanna Broda, Davíd Carrasco, and Eduardo Matos Moctezuma, *The Great
Temple of Tenochtitlan: Center and Periphery in Aztec Religion* (Berkeley: University of
California Press, 1987).

[4] For a more extensive description of the social geography of the Aztecs, see
Alfredo López Austin's excellent, *The Human Body and Ideology: Concepts of the
Ancient Nahuas* (Salt Lake City: University of Utah Press, 1988), especially chs. 1,
11, and 12.

[5] Friedrich Katz, *Ancient American Civilizations* (New York: Praeger, 1972), especially ch. 10.

Aztec tradition. Before outlining the cosmovision of the Aztecs, we will review some of the most influential myths and symbols from these two cultures.

Teotihuacán: The Imperial Capital[6]

Known to most people as "the pyramids," Teotihuacán, which means the "Abode of the Gods," is the most frequently visited archaeological site in the Americas. At its height it was populated by over 200,000 people who shared in the prestige of a capital that influenced and integrated many cities and towns within and beyond the central plateau. Surprisingly, Teotihuacán (which developed between 100 B.C.E. and 700 C.E.) began in a cave.[7] The greatest of classic cities, with its immense towering pyramids, elaborate ceremonial courtyards, and residential palaces, began underground at the mouth of a well. Recent excavations have revealed that directly under the Pyramid of the Sun lie the remains of an ancient shrine area which was the sacred center for rituals and perhaps the goal of pilgrimages. A natural tunnel, 103 meters long, formed by subterranean volcanic

---

[6] Following the remarkable *Urbanization at Teotihuacan, Mexico: The Teotihuacan Map*, ed. René Millon, Bruce Drewitt, and George Cowgill (Austin: University of Texas Press, 1973), which rejuvenated and redefined Teotihuacán studies, there has been a new wave of insightful works. See especially Esther Pasztory, *The Murals of Tepantitla, Teotihuacan* (New York: Garland, 1976); Rubén Cabrera Castro, George Cowgill, and Saburo Sugiyama, "El Proyecto Templo de Quetzalcoatl y la práctica a gran escala de sacrificio humano," in *La época clásica: nuevos hallazgos, nuevas ideas*, ed. Amalia Cardós de Méndez (México: Museo Nacional de Antropología, Instituto Nacional de Antropología e Historia, Mexico, 1990), 123-46; Saburo Sugiyama, "Burials Dedicated to the Old Temple of Quetzalcoatl at Teotihuacan," *American Antiquity* 543, no. 1 (1989): 85-106; and Alfredo López Austin, Leonardo López Luján, and Saburo Sugiyama, "The Temple of Quetzalcoatl at Teotihuacan," *Ancient Mesoamerica* 2 (1991): 93-105; and *Art, Ideology, and the City of Teotihuacan*, ed. Janet Berlo (Washington, D.C.: Dumbarton Oaks, 1991); and *The Classic Heritage: Teotihuacan and Beyond*, ed. David Carrasco, Lindsay Jones, and Scott Sessions (Niwot: University Press of Colorado, forthcoming).

[7] Doris Heyden, "An Interpretation of the Cave underneath the Pyramid of the Sun in Teotihuacán, Mexico," *American Antiquity* 40, no. 1 (1975): 31-47. Also see Karl Taube, "The Teotihuacan Cave of Origin," *RES* 12 (1986): 51-82. The distinguished urban archaeologist Linda Manzanilla continues to investigate various caves at Teotihuacán.

activity, led into a series of small chambers shaped like a flower. Like the city that was to spread out above it, this cave was artistically reshaped and decorated by the *teotihuacanos*, who used it until around 450 C.E., three centuries after the pyramid was built over it. The tunnel was reshaped, roofed, plastered, and divided into thirty sections, which ended at the ceremonial chamber containing the spring. There can be little doubt that the ancient shrine had a profound religious significance in the early development of Teotihuacán. The place glyph for Teotihuacán, found in the *Codex Xolotl*, was two pyramids over a cave. Clara Millon, who has worked intimately with the Teotihuacán Mapping Project, said about the cave, "This may have been the beginning of everything."[8]

The cave's specific religious character may be represented by its shape, which resembles a four-petaled flower. In some of the later primary written sources, the Mesoamerican cosmos is symbolized by a four-petaled flower representing the division of cosmic space into four cardinal regions and a center. It is possible that the cave was Teotihuacán's earliest *imago mundi*, or sacred image of the cosmos. The symbolism of cardinal-point orientation and the center are duplicated in the city that developed above and around the cave.

The city's hundreds of residential, ritual, and craft buildings followed a grid pattern that was organized by two main avenues, the Street of the Dead and the East–West Avenue, which crossed at right angles in the center of the city dividing the urban space into four great quarters. Along this grand passageway were situated scores of impressive architectural structures including the grand Pyramid of the Sun and the exquisitely designed plaza of the Pyramid of the Moon. It is important to note that a number of natural features were altered in order to conform to this grid scheme; a river was canalized and some landscape structures were altered. This axial design, reflected in the city's original underground shrine, conformed to a series of precise observations of celestial bodies and natural features. At least in its central ceremonial area, the city was constructed as and considered to be a cosmic image.[9]

One of the most outstanding creations of Teotihuacán religion was expressed in the Temple of Quetzalcoatl. Located close to the axial

---

[8] In *Urbanization at Teotihuacan*, 139.

[9] For the debate on the overall design of Teotihuacán, see López Austin, López Luján, and Sugiyama, "Temple of Quetzalcoatl."

center of the capital, the Temple of Quetzalcoatl served as the shrine that integrated the geographical, political, and religious dimensions of the empire. Its special character is revealed in its architectural distinctiveness. H. B. Nicholson writes of this innovation: "With almost dramatic suddenness one of the greatest tours de force of monumental stone sculpture in world history appears as a massive decorative frieze in all four sides of the six stages of the pyramidal substructure known as the Temple of the Feathered Serpent."[10] The frieze, which is the subject of renewed study and controversy, consists of alternating giant stone heads of creator deities—perhaps Quetzalcoatl and an early version of the rain god, Tlaloc. Quetzalcoatl appears as a monumental head jutting out of the headdress of Cipactli, the earth dragon who represents the creation and passage of time. Quetzalcoatl's open jaws display white curved teeth beneath obsidian eyes. The head and headdress are joined to a thickly stylized serpent body undulating horizontally along the temple over and under various shell and aquatic figures. It may be that this entire temple is dedicated to the creation of cosmic time and the multiple destinies of gods and humans!

Its monumental magnificence, precise spatial order, exuberant craft and market systems, and sacred prestige helped make this city the center of an expanding, pulsating empire. Although its position of absolute dominance over many other cities appears to have lasted for less than two hundred years, its status as the center for the Mesoamerican world cannot be limited to the time when its art styles were imitated. For Teotihuacán was the first true capital, the first great place in central Mexico where a fully integrated, harmonious, rich, and well-fed society operated under the authority of supernatural forces and cosmo-magical formulas.

The Great Tollan: An Ideal Type

One of the most prestigious and widespread sacred histories that influenced Aztec society focused on Quetzalcoatl, the Feathered Ser-

---

[10] H. B. Nicholson, "Major Sculpture in Pre-Hispanic Central Mexico," in *Handbook of Middle American Indians*, ed. Robert Wauchope, Vol. 10, *Archaeology of Northern Mesoamerica, Part I*, ed. Gordon F. Ekholm and Ignacio Bernal (Austin: University of Texas Press, 1971), 197.

pent, and the fabulous kingdom he ruled called Tollan, Place of Reeds. According to extensive research into the surviving pictorial and ethnohistorical tradition carried out by H. B. Nicholson and others, it appears that Aztec schools taught the life story of a great ruler of a prosperous kingdom that was the source of all the arts and technology of human culture.[11] It appears that after the collapse of Teotihuacán, "the Great Tollan" was formed consisting of twenty settlements centered in the capital of Tollan. At the heart of this new kingdom were two Quetzalcoatls: (1) the creator god Quetzalcoatl, who was revered as the personification of the high god, and (2) his human representative Ce Acatl, Topiltzin Quetzalcoatl, or One Reed Our Young Prince the Feathered Serpent.[12] The Great Tollan, we are told, was inhabited by the Tolteca, "who were wise. Their works were all good, all perfect, all wonderful, all miraculous, their houses beautiful, tiled in mosaics, smoothed, stuccoed, very marvelous." This world of excellence was supported by the fruitful agricultural endeavors of the Toltecs, whose fields were full of large squashes, huge ears of maize, cotton of many colors gleaming beneath the songs of beautiful birds. Within this superabundant agricultural world, the Toltecs developed technological excellence and artistic perfection, becoming the greatest feather workers, jewelers, miners, and makers of "all the wonderful, precious, marvelous things." Added to this was their ability to discern the orbits of the stars, construct the calendar, and invent the divination of dreams.[13]

---

[11] H. B. Nicholson provides a meticulous record of primary evidence about the Toltecs ("Topiltzin Quetzalcoatl of Tollan: A Problem in Mesoamerican Ethnohistory" [Ph.D. diss., Harvard University, 1955]).

[12] The sacred history begins when the young prince Quetzalcoatl was miraculously born after, in one text, his mother swallowed an emerald. The mother dies while giving birth to One Reed or Ce Acatl. The motherless prince was adopted by the earth goddess, who raised him in a royal manner. While growing up, Ce Acatl undergoes seven years of penance, during which he bleeds himself and seeks divine aid for becoming a great warrior. He is successful as a war leader and renowned for his piety, which results in his ascension to the throne of Tollan, where the Toltecs achieve magnificent works of construction and art.

[13] David Carrasco, Quetzalcoatl and the Irony of Empire: Myths and Prophecies in the Aztec Tradition (Chicago: University of Chicago Press, 1992); Miguel León-Portilla, "Quetzalcoatl, espiritualismo de México antiguo," Cuadernos americanos 105 (1959): 127-39; and Michel Graulich, Quetzalcoatl y el espejismo de Tollan (Antwerp: Instituut voor Amerikanistiek, 1988).

All this abundance and creativity were structured by a ceremonial center consisting of a great pyramid surrounded by four temples facing in the cardinal directions. This pattern of the center and quadripartition was paralleled in the landscape of Tollan, which contained four named mountains where Quetzalcoatl carried out autosacrifices and the great central peak "Crying Out Mountain," from which Quetzalcoatl sent out the laws to all parts of his kingdom. Into this kingdom came Quetzalcoatl's arch-rival, Tezcatlipoca, whose magic leads him to ruin and the collapse of the society. Heartbroken over his failure, Quetzalcoatl decides to leave Tollan with a retinue of followers, resulting in the waning of Tollan's glory and its collapse. Quetzalcoatl flees to the seashore, where he either sails away on a raft of serpents or cremates himself and turns into the Morning Star. This tradition of an ideal city with the paradigmatic priest king inspired the Aztec rulers and priests to emulate the Toltecs and gain access to their royal lineage.[14]

The Aztec Cosmovision

The general attitude toward the Aztec position in the cosmos appears in a poetic fragment about the capital:

> Proud of Itself
> Is the city of Mexico-Tenochtitlán
> Here no one fears to die in war
> This is our glory
> This is your Command
> Oh Giver of Life

---

[14] For a fine introduction to the religious conceptions associated with the Toltecs, see Miguel León-Portilla, *Aztec Thought and Culture* (Norman: University of Oklahoma Press, 1963) and the more specific detailed work by Nigel Davies, *The Toltecs Until the Fall of Tula* (Norman: University of Oklahoma Press, 1977). The best synthesis of archaeological research appears in Richard A. Diehl, *Tula: The Toltec Capital of Ancient Mexico* (London: Thames & Hudson, 1983); and Leonardo López Luján, Robert H. Cobean T., and A. Guadalupe Mastache F., *Xochicalco y Tula* (Milan: Editorial Jaca, 1995). For a new interpretation of the interactions between Tula and Chichén Itzá, see Lindsay Jones, *Twin City Tales: A Hermeneutical Reassessment of Tula and Chichén Itzá* (Niwot: University Press of Colorado, 1995).

Have this in mind, Oh princes
Who would conquer Tenochtitlán?
Who could shake the foundation of heaven?[15]

The image of the capital city as a military citadel transformed into
the foundation of heaven, which the Aztecs conceived of as a vertical
column of thirteen layers extending above the earth, points to the
cosmological conviction underpinning Aztec religion that there
existed a profound correspondence between the sacred forces in the
universe and the social world of the Aztec empire. This correspondence between the cosmic structure and political state was anchored
in the capital of Tenochtitlán, where fearless warriors followed the
dictates of the high god.[16]

In his important summary of religion in pre-Hispanic central Mexico, H. B. Nicholson has outlined the "basic cosmological sequential
pattern" of the Aztec cosmogony that is found in the myths and historical accounts associated with the Mexicas. A summary view
reveals that Aztec life unfolded in a cosmic setting that was dynamic,
unstable, and finally destructive. Even though the cosmic order fluc-
tuated between periods of stability and chaos, the emphasis in many
myths and historical accounts is on the elaborate ritual strategies to
overcome or forestall chaos, which repeatedly overcomes the ages of
the universe, divine society, and the cities of the past.[17]

This dynamic universe appears in the sixteenth-century prose
accounts *Historia de los mexicanos por sus pinturas* and the *Leyenda de
los Soles*. In the former, the universe is arranged in a rapid, orderly

---

[15] Miguel León-Portilla, *Pre-Columbian Literature of Mexico* (Norman: University
of Oklahoma Press, 1969), 87.

[16] For a general description of the social formation related to the Aztec capital,
see Pedro Carrasco, "The Peoples of Central Mexico and their Historical Traditions," in *Handbook of Middle American Indians*, ed. Robert Wauchope, Vol. 11,
Archaeology of Northern Mesoamerica, Part II, ed. Gordon F. Ekholm and Ignacio
Bernal (Austin: University of Texas Press, 1971), 459–74. A more recent and complicated description appears in Rudolph van Zantwijk, *The Aztec Arrangement: The
Social History of Pre-Spanish Mexico* (Norman: University of Oklahoma Press, 1985).

[17] Nigel Davies presents a good overview of the rise of the Aztec state (*The
Aztecs: A History* [London: Macmillan, 1973]). Some of the best interpretations of
the religious dynamics of the Aztecs appear in Inga Clendinnen's *The Aztecs: An
Interpretation* (Cambridge: Cambridge University Press, 1991); Leonardo López
Luján, *The Offerings of the Great Temple of Tenochtitlan* (Niwot: University Press of
Colorado, 1994); and López Austin, *Human Body and Ideology*.

fashion after the divine pair, Ometeotl, dwelling in Omeyocan, the Place of Duality, at the thirteenth level of heaven, generates four children: the Red Tezcatlipoca (the Smoking Mirror), the Black Tezcatlipoca, Quetzalcoatl (the Plumed Serpent), and Huitzilopochtli (Hummingbird on the Left). They all exist without movement for six hundred years, after which the four children assemble "to arrange what was to be done and to establish the law to be followed." Quetzalcoatl and Huitzilopochtli arrange the universe and make fire, half the sun, "not fully lighted but a little," the human race, and the calendar. The four brothers reassemble and create water and its divine beings. Then the gods set about creating and destroying the cosmos four times.

Fortunately, we have an image on the famous Aztec Calendar Stone that refers to the Aztec view of these repeated creations/ destructions. In the center of the stone we see the carved image of the five "ages" or "suns" through which the universe passed prior to the great migration of the Chichimecas. According to ancient wisdom recorded in Nahuatl texts about the stone image, the First Age or Sun had its beginning over three thousand years ago and was called 4-Jaguar. The age lasted 676 years, during which the different gods did battle to gain ascendancy, until ocelots descended on the peoples and devoured them in a ravenous battle. The First Sun was destroyed and the cosmos was in darkness. Then the Second Sun, called 4-Wind, was created and lasted 364 years. The gods battled again before huge winds came and destroyed the homes, trees—everything—and the Sun was also carried away by the storm. Then the Third Sun was created and called 4-Rain, which really meant rain of fire. Again there is a dramatic confrontation among the gods, and the people were destroyed again, this time by fire that rained for a whole day. The Sun was also burned up and the cosmos was in darkness once again. Then the Fourth Sun, called 4-Water, was created, and it lasted for fifty-two years before the heavens collapsed and the waters swallowed up everything including the mountains. Finally, the Fifth Sun, the age in which the Aztecs dwelled, was created, and it was called 4-Movement, which meant two things. On the one hand, the name 4-Movement meant that the Sun would move in an orderly fashion across the heavens. On the other hand, it meant that the age would end when the earth moved violently. It was feared in Aztec times that their age would be destroyed by colossal earthquakes.[18] The dynamic, unstable cosmos is vividly portrayed in the climax of the myth of the creation of the Fifth Sun.

The world was dark and without movement at the end of the Fourth Sun when the gods gathered around a fire in a place called Teotihuacán, or the Abode of the Gods, to contemplate how to re-create the sun. It was decided that one of the gods must hurl himself into the fire out of which the sun would be born. The gods debated among themselves about who would make the ultimate sacrifice. Two gods, Tecuzztecatl and Nanahuatzin, threw themselves into the fire. The gods sat for a long time looking in all directions as a reddening of dawn appeared everywhere. Quetzalcoatl and Xipe faced east and the sun rose in the east, "When it appeared, it was flaming red . . . no one was able to look at it: its light was brilliant and blinding; its rays were magnificently diffused in all directions."[19] The Sun did not move but rather "kept swaying from side to side." Faced with this partial sunrise and the crisis of no heavenly movement, the gods decided to sacrifice themselves. They cast themselves into the fire but still the sun did not move, until Ehecatl, the wind god, "exerted himself fiercely and violently as he blew" the sun into motion across the sky.

In other sources, we find that following the creation of the Fifth Sun, warfare was established so that human beings could be captured and sacrificed to nourish the sun on its heavenly and nocturnal journey. Typically, a god such as Mixcoatl created four hundred human beings to fight among themselves in order for captives to be sacrificed in ceremonial centers to provide the divine food, blood, for the gods who ensure cosmic life.

The Aztec universe, had a geometry[20] consisting of three general levels: an overworld, or celestial space; the middle world, or earthly level; and the underworld, sometimes known as Mictlan ("Place of the Dead"). In some cases, there was a World Tree[21] that joined these

---

[18] See León-Portilla, *Aztec Thought and Culture*, for what is still the best line-by-line interpretation of this myth. Also see Wayne Elzey, "The Nahua Myth of the Suns," *Numen* (August 1976).

[19] León-Portilla, *Aztec Thought and Culture*, 45.

[20] López Austin, *Human Body and Ideology*, especially ch. 2.

[21] Doris Heyden has written the most illuminating work on sacred vegetation: "Flores, creéncias y control social," *Religión y sociedad: cuadernos de trabajo* 17 (1976): 1–145.

three levels with its roots in the underworld, its trunk in the middle world, reaching up with its highest branches into the celestial world. In the celestial realm above the earth there were thirteen levels (some sources say nine) each inhabited by diverse gods and supernatural beings, often depicted as conjugal pairs. Each level had a certain color, power, and name. Here is a list of celestial levels and gods:

Omeyocan, Place of Duality (Levels 12 and 13)
The God Who Is Red
The God Who Is Yellow
The Place that Has Corners of Obsidian Slabs
The Sky That Is Blue-Green
The Sky That is Blackish
The Sky Where Gyrating Occurs
The Sky-Place of Salt
The Sky of the Sun
The Sky of the Skirt of Stars
The Sky of Tlalocan and the Moon

Below this celestial column of gods, forces, colors, and dualities floated the four-quartered earth in the sacred waters. And below the earth were the nine levels of the underworld:

The Place for Crossing the Water
The Place Where the Hills Are Found
The Obsidian Mountain
The Place of the Obsidian Wind
The Place Where the Banners are Raised
The Place Where People Are Pierced with Arrows
The Place Where Peoples Hearts Are Devoured
The Obsidian Place of the Dead
The Place Where Smoke Has No Outlet

These nine levels served as way stations for the soul of the dead as it passed slowly toward the bottom rung. As with the celestial world, the terrestrial levels were occupied by gods and minor supernatural forces who were capable of escaping into the earthly level and influencing daily life.

In some versions of this universe there were four other trees, giant ceiba trees which held up the sky at the four quarters of the world.

These trees were also the main entry points of the gods and their influences from the upper and lower worlds into the surface of the earth and the world of humans! These influences and forces radiated along lines of communication called *malinalli* (a revolving double helix) between the four quarters and the central section, where the old god, the lord of fire, transformed all things.

The Aztec Pantheon: Hierophanies of Nature

One of the most striking characteristics of the surviving screenfolds that present ritual and divinatory information is the impressive array of deities who animated the Mesoamerican world. Likewise, the remaining sculpture and sixteenth-century prose accounts of Aztec Mexico present us with a pantheon so crowded that a thorough study of Aztec religion includes a list of over sixty distinct and inter-related names. Scholarly analysis of these many deities reveals that literally all aspects of existence were considered inherently sacred and that these deities were expressions of a numinous quality that permeated the world. Aztec references to numinous forces, expressed in the Nahuatl word *teotl*, were always translated by the Spaniards as "god," "saint," or "demon." But the Aztec *teotl* signified a sacred power manifested in natural forms—a rainstorm, a tree, a mountain, or in persons of high distinction such as a king, an ancestor, a warrior—or in mysterious and chaotic places. What the Spaniards translated as "god" really referred to a spectrum of hierophanies which animated the world. While it does not appear that the Aztec pantheon or pattern of hierophanies was organized as a whole, it is possible to discern clusters of deities organized around the major cult themes of (a) cosmogonic creativity, (b) fertility and regeneration, and (c) war and sacrificial nourishment of the sun.[22]

Aztec deities were pictorially represented as anthropomorphic beings. Even in cases where the deity has an animal form, as in the case of Xolotl, the divine dog, or is in the form of a ritual object, as in the case of Iztli, the knife god, he is disguised with human features such as human arms, torso, legs, face, and so on. Aztec deities

---

[22] H. B. Nicholson, "Religion in Pre-Hispanic Central Mexico," in *Handbook*, 10:395–446.

dwelled in the different levels of the thirteen-layer celestial sphere or in the nine-layer underworld. The general structuring principle for the pantheon, derived from the cosmic pattern of a center and four quarters, resulted in the quadruple or quintuple ordering of some gods. For instance in the *Codex Borgia*'s representation of the *tlaloque*, the rain god Tlaloc inhabits the central region of heaven while four other *tlaloque* inhabit the four regions of the sky, each dispensing a different kind of rain. While deities were invisible to the human eye, the Aztecs saw them in dreams, visions, and in the deity impersonators called *teixiptla*, who appeared at the major ceremonies. These costumed impersonators, which included human beings, effigies of stone, wood, or dough, were elaborately decorated with diagnostic insignia such as conch shells, masks, weapons, jewelry, mantas, feathers, and a myriad of other items. While the diagnostic insignia of each deity was unique in its combination, individual elements were often shared with other deities who had similar functions and powers.

Creator Gods

The Aztecs had a supreme dual god called Ometeotl (Lord of Duality) or Tloque-Nahuaque (Lord of the Close and Near), who was the celestial, androgynous, primordial creator of the universe—the omnipotent, omniscient, omnipresent foundation of all things. Ometeotl's male aspects (Ometecuhtli and Tonacatecuhtli) and female aspects (Omecihuatl and Tonacacihuatl) in turn merged with a series of lesser deities associated with generative and destructive male and female qualities. The male aspect was associated with fire and the solar and maize gods. The female aspect merged with the earth fertility goddesses and especially the corn goddesses.[23] Ometeotl was

---

[23] Thelma D. Sullivan, "'Tlazolteotl-Ixcuina': The Great Spinner and Weaver," in *The Art and Iconography of Late Post-Classic Central Mexico*, ed. Elizabeth H. Boone (Washington, D.C.: Dumbarton Oaks, 1982). Perhaps the best treatment of feminine forces in Aztec life appears in Clendinnen's *Aztecs*. Also see June Nash, "The Aztecs and the Ideology of Male Dominance," *Signs* 4, no. 2 (1978): 349–62; Cecelia F. Klein, "Rethinking Cihuacoatl: Aztec Political Imagery of the Conquered Woman," in *Smoke and Mist: Mesoamerican Studies in Memory of Thelma D. Sullivan*, ed. J. Kathryn Josserand and Karen Dakin, BAR International Series 402 (Oxford:

more "being" than "action." It is significant that these supreme gods were rarely represented in material form. Most of the creative actions to organize the universe were accomplished by the divine couple's four offspring: Tezcatlipoca, Quetzalcoatl, Xiuhtecuhtli, and Tlaloc, all of whom received widespread representations in wood, stone, and pictorial manuscripts.

Tezcatlipoca (Smoking Mirror) was the supreme active force of the pantheon. This powerful, virile numen had many appellations and was partially identified with the supreme numinosity of Ometeotl. Tezcatlipoca was also identified with Iztli, the knife and calendar god, and with Tepeyollotl, the jaguar-earth god known as the Heart of the Mountain, and was often pictured as the divine antagonist of Quetzalcoatl. On the social level, Tezcatlipoca was the arch-sorcerer, whose smoking obsidian mirror revealed the powers of ultimate transformation associated with darkness, night, jaguars, and sha-manic magic. There are various descriptions of Tezcatlipoca's temple in Aztec communities, and it is apparent that there was an extensive cult spread throughout central Mexico at the time of the conquest.[24]

Another tremendous creative power was Xiuhtecuhtli, the ancient fire god, who influenced every level of society and cosmology. Xiuhtecuhtli was represented by the perpetual "fires of existence" that were kept lighted at certain temples in the ceremonial centers at all times. He was manifested in the drilling of new fires that dedi-cated new ceremonial buildings and ritual stones. Images of Xiuhte-cuhtli have been found in excavations throughout the Basin of Mexico and in various screenfolds from the Mixtec and Oaxacan regions. Most importantly, perhaps, Xiuhtecuhtli was the generative force at the New Fire Ceremony, also called the Binding of the Years, held every fifty-two years on the Hill of the Star outside Tenochtitlán. At midnight on the day that a fifty-two-year calendar was exhausted,

---

B.A.R., 1988), 237–77; and Susan M. Kellogg, "Cognative Kinship and Religion: Women in Aztec Society," in *Smoke and Mist*, 666–81.

[24] Thelma Sullivan, "The Rhetorical Orations, or *Huehuetlatolli*, Collected by Sahagún," in *Sixteenth-Century Mexico: The Work of Sahagún*, ed. Munro S. Edmon-son (Albuquerque: University of New Mexico Press, 1974), 79–109; David Car-rasco, "The Sacrifice of Tezcatlipoca: To Change Place," in *To Change Place: Aztec Ceremonial Landscapes*, ed. David Carrasco (Niwot: University Press of Colorado, 1992), 31–56; and Doris Heyden, "Black Magic: Obsidian in Symbolism and Metaphor," in *Smoke and Mist*, 217–36.

at the moment when the star cluster we call Pleiades passed through zenith, a heart sacrifice of a war captive took place. A new fire was started in the cavity of the victim's chest, symbolizing the rebirth of Xiuhtecuhtli. The new fire was carried to every city, town, and home in the empire, signaling the regeneration of the universe. On the domestic level, Xiuhtecuhtli inhabited the hearth, structuring the daily rituals associated with food, nurturance, and thanksgiving.

Fertility and Regeneration

A pervasive theme in Aztec society was fertility and agricultural regeneration. The entire society depended on various forms of intensive agriculture, which required well-organized planting, nurturing, and harvesting schedules and coordination among various groups. The gods of agriculture were crucial to the work and understanding of human beings. In the case of the Aztecs, a massive agricultural system of *chinampas* ("floating gardens"), which constituted large sections of the city's geographical space, supported a population of over 200,000 people. In addition, surrounding city-states were required to pay sizable amounts of agricultural goods in tribute to the various capitals or dominant ceremonial centers. While many female deities inspired the ritual regeneration of agriculture, the most ancient and widespread fertility-rain god was Tlaloc,[25] who dwelt on the prominent mountain peaks, where clouds were thought to emerge from caves to fertilize the land with life-giving rain. The Aztecs held Mount Tlaloc to be the original source of the waters and of vegetation.[26] Tlaloc's supreme importance is reflected in the location of his shrine alongside that of Huitzilopochtli at the Templo Mayor. Sur-

---

[25] For a new interpretation of Tlaloc's meaning within the Aztec tradition, see Philip P. Arnold, "Eating Landscape: Human Sacrifice and Sustenance in Aztec Mexico," in *To Change Place*, 214-32.

[26] Johanna Broda has written a series of penetrating articles on the sacred mountains that circled and animated the Aztec world. See especially "El culto mexica de los cerros y del agua," *Multidisciplina* 3, no. 7 (1982): 45-56; "Geography, Climate and the Observation of Nature in Pre-Hispanic Mesoamerica," in *The Imagination of Matter: Religion and Ecology in Mesoamerican Traditions*, ed. David Carrasco, BAR International Series 515 (Oxford: B.A.R., 1989); and numerous other works.

prisingly, the great majority of buried offerings excavated at the temple were dedicated to Tlaloc rather than Huitzilopochtli.[27] Recent research has made it evident that Tlaloc or Tlaloc-like rain gods were widespread and very ancient in central Mexican society. Tlaloc was often accompanied by a female counterpart, sometimes known as Chalchiuhtlicue, the goddess of lakes and running water represented in various forms including precious greenstone effigies.

The most powerful group of female fertility deities were the *teteoinnan*, a rich array of earth-mother goddesses, who were representative of the usually distinct but sometimes combined qualities of terror and beauty, regeneration and destruction. These deities were worshiped in cults concerned with the abundant powers of the earth, women, and fertility.[28] Among the most prominent were Tlazolteotl, Xochiquetzal, and Coatlicue. Tlazolteotl was concerned with sexual powers and passions and the pardoning of sexual transgressions. Xochiquetzal was the goddess of love and sexual desire and was associated with flowers, feasting, and pleasure. A ferocious goddess, Coatlicue ("serpent skirt") represented the cosmic mountain that conceived all stellar beings and devoured all beings into her repulsive, lethal, and fascinating form. Her huge statue, excavated in the center of Mexico City in 1790 and now displayed at the National Museum of Anthropology, is studded with sacrificial hearts, skulls, hands, ferocious claws, and a giant snake head. This image has been interpreted as a single, solid sculptural image of the layers and powers of the Mesoamerican cosmos.[29]

An outstanding feature of Aztec religion was the tutelary/patron relations that specific deities had with particular social groups whom

---

[27] The best interpretation of the burials at the Templo Mayor appears in López Luján, *Offerings of the Great Temple of Tenochtitlan*. López Luján has achieved a synthesis of fifteen years of research by the archaeologists working in Proyecto Templo Mayor. In addition, for a stunning overview of the entire site, see Eduardo Matos Moctezuma, *The Great Temple of the Aztecs: Treasures of Tenochtitlan* (London: Thames & Hudson, 1988).

[28] Doris Heyden, "Dioses del agua y vegetación," *Anales de antropología* 20 (1986): 129–45. Elizabeth Baquedano, "Aztec Earth Deities," in *Polytheistic Systems*, ed. Glenys Davies (Edinburgh: Edinburgh University Press, 1989), 184–98.

[29] A brilliant statement about the Aztec commitment to imitating celestial archetypes and sculpture appears in Richard F. Townsend, *State and Cosmos in the Art of Tenochtitlan* (Washington, D.C.: Dumbarton Oaks, 1979).

they guided during their peregrinations. These patron deities, or *abo-gados* as the Spanish chroniclers called them, were represented in the *tlaquimilolli*, or sacred bundles, which the *teomama* (godbearers), or shaman priests, carried on their backs during the long journeys. The teomama passed on to the community the divine commandments that were communicated to him in visions and dreams. These sacred specialists were considered *hombre-dioses*, man-gods, whose extraordinary powers of spiritual transformation, derived from their closeness with these numinous forces, enabled them to guide, govern, and organize the tribe during migrations and the settlement of new communities.[30] A pattern in the sacred histories of tribal groups is the erection of a shrine to the patron deity as the first act of settlement in a new region. This act of founding a settlement around the tribal shrine represented the intimate tie between the deity, the *hombre-dios*, and the integrity of the people. In reverse fashion, conquest of a community was achieved when the patron deity's shrine was burned and the *tlaquimilolli* was carried off as a captive.

The Warrior God: Huitzilopochtli

As indicated by the mythology, Aztec religion was pervaded by military themes. The best example of a war god was Huitzilopochtli, the patron of the wandering Mexicas. According to Aztec tradition, Huitzilopochtli inspired the Mexica *teomama* to guide the tribe into the Basin of Mexico, where he appeared to them as an eagle on a blooming cactus in the middle of the lake following a long and arduous journey. The people constructed a shrine to Huitzilopochtli, who instructed his people to build a four-quartered city around the shrine, which became the quintessential sacred place in the empire. Known today as Great Aztec Temple, it was destroyed by the Spaniards in 1521, when they dismantled and blew it up and carried the great image of Huitzilopochtli away. This colossal image of the Aztec god has never been found. But the mythology of this great warrior god was expressed in the song of his birth, a cosmic event com-

---

[30] Alfredo López Austin, *Hombre-dios: religión y política en el mundo náhuatl* (México: Universidad Nacional Autónoma de México, 1973).

memorated in oral tradition, pictorial images, and sculpture.[31] According to the *Florentine Codex*, Coatlicue, Lady with the Serpent Skirt, became pregnant when a ball of feathers she was sweeping out at the temple on Coatepec fell to the floor. When her daughter Coyolxauhqui heard of the pregnancy, she incited her 399 siblings into dressing for war and attacking the mother on Serpent Mountain. When Coyolxauhqui led the warriors to the top to kill her mother, Coatlicue gave birth to the fully grown and armed Huitzilopochtli, who dismembered his sister. Her body went falling down the mountain and broke into pieces. Huitzilopochtli then annihilated the other siblings. In Aztec ritual, this type of sacrifice was repeated when women and masses of captured warriors were sacrificed on top of the Templo Mayor (called Coatepec by the Aztecs) and rolled down the temple steps to the bottom. This myth is further replicated in the symmetry of the temple's architecture where Huitzilopochtli's shrine sits at the top of the stairway while the colossal stone of Coyolxauhqui's dismembered image rests at the bottom.[32]

Practice and Paraphernalia of Human Sacrifice

As the example of Huitzilopochtli's cult indicates, human sacrifice was a powerful aspect of Aztec religion. In fact, it has been called "the central fact of Aztec life . . . the nuclear cult of war, sacrifice and cannibalism."[33] While the ritual of sacrificing human beings (*tlamictiliztli*) did animate a wide spectrum of Aztec ceremonies, a major argument has developed in Mesoamerican studies concerning the

---

[31] See Gordon Brotherston, "Huitzilopochtli and What Was Made of Him," in *Mesoamerican Archaeology: New Approaches*, ed. Norman Hammond (Austin: University of Texas Press, 1974); and Yólotl González, "El dios Huitzilopochtli en la perigrinación mexica: de Aztlán a Tula," *Anales del Instituto Nacional de Antropología e Historia* 19 (1976): 175–90.

[32] David Carrasco, "Templo Mayor: The Aztec Vision of Place," *Religion* 11 (1981): 271–97.

[33] Burr Cartwright Brundage, *The Fifth Sun: Aztec Gods, Aztec World* (Austin: University of Texas Press, 1979), 196.

mystico-militaristic character of post-classic cultures. Some scholars, for example, Miguel León-Portilla have illuminated a mytho-poetic tradition that emphasizes not sacred violence but illumination through sacred words. Before viewing the Aztec philosophical and poetic tradition, the sacrificial tradition must be described.

It must be understood that human sacrifice was carried out within a larger, more complex ceremonial system, in which a tremendous amount of energy, wealth, and time was spent in a variety of ritual festivals dedicated to a crowded and hungry pantheon. This dedication is reflected in the many metaphors and symbols related to war and sacrifice. Human hearts were likened to fine burnished turquoise, and war was *teoatltlachinolli*, meaning divine liquid and burnt things. War was the place "where the jaguars roar," where "feathered war bonnets heave about like foam in the waves." And death on the battlefield was called *xochimiquiztli*, meaning the flowery death.

This crowded ceremonial schedule was acted out in the many ceremonial centers of the city and empire. The greatest ceremonial precinct formed the axis of Tenochtitlán and measured 440 meters on four sides. It contained, according to some accounts, over eighty ritual temples, skull racks, schools, and other ceremonial structures. Book 2 of Sahagún's *Florentine Codex* contains a valuable list with descriptions of most of these buildings, including "the Temple of Uitzilopochtli . . . of Tlaloc . . . in the middle of the square, . . . it was higher, it was taller . . . faced toward the setting of the sun." Also we read of "Teccizcalli: there Moctezuma did penances; . . . there was dying there; captives died there"; and "Mexico Calmecac: there dwelt the penitents who offered incense at the summit of the Temple of Tlaloc, quite daily"; and "Teccalco: there was casting [of men] into the fire there"; and "The Great Skull Rack: there also there used to be slaying," followed by "The Temple of Cinteotl: there the impersonator of Chicomecoatl died, at night only. And when she died, then they flayed her . . . the fire priest put on the skin"; and "Coaapan; there the fire priest of Coatlan bathed himself"; and for cooking "Tilocan; there cooked the [amaranth seed dough for] the image of Uitzilopochtli"; and finally for cannibalistic preparation, "Acatl Yiacapan Uey Calpulli; . . . there they gathered together the sacrificial victims called Tlalocs . . . when they had slain them, they cut them to pieces there and cooked them. They put squash blossoms with their flesh . . . then the noblemen ate them, all the high judges: but not the common folk—only the rulers."[34]

Though important variations of ritual activity were carried out at these temples, schools, skull racks, and bath houses, the general pattern of human sacrifice was as follows. Most Aztec ritual began with a four-day (or multiples of four) preparatory period of priestly fasting (*nezahualiztli*). An important exception was the year-long fast by a group of priests and priestesses known as the *teocuaque* (god-eaters) or the greatly feared *in iachhuan* Huitzilopochtli *in mocexiuhzauhque* (the elder brothers of Huitzilopochtli, who fasted for a year). This preparatory period also involved nocturnal vigils (*tozohualiztli*) and offerings of flowers, food, cloths, rubber, paper, poles with streamers, as well as incensing (*copaltemaliztli*), the pouring of libations, and the embowering of temples, statues, and ritual participants. Dramatic processions of elaborately costumed participants moving to music ensembles playing sacred songs passed through the ceremonial precinct before arriving at the specific temple of sacrifice. The major ritual participants were called *in ixiptla in teteo*, or deity impersonators. All important rituals involved a death sacrifice of either animals or human beings.

The most common sacrifice was the beheading of animals such as quail. But the most dramatic and valued sacrifices were the human sacrifices of captured warriors and slaves. These victims were ritually bathed, carefully costumed, often taught to dance special dances and sometimes either fattened or slimmed down during the preparation period. They were elaborately dressed to impersonate specific deities to whom they were sacrificed.

The different primary sources reveal a wide range of sacrificial techniques including decapitation, shooting with darts or arrows, drowning, burning, hurling from heights, strangulation, entombment and starvation, and gladiatorial combat. Usually, the ceremony, which often lasted as much as twenty days, peaked when splendidly attired captors and captives sang and danced in procession to the temple, where they were escorted (sometimes unwillingly) up the

---

[34] See especially Bernardino de Sahagún, *Florentine Codex: General History of the Things of New Spain*, Book 2, *The Ceremonies*, ed. and trans. Arthur J. O. Anderson and Charles E. Dibble (Santa Fe: School of American Research and University of Utah, 1981), appendix.

stairways to the sacrificial stone.[35] The victim was quickly thrust on the sacrificial stone (*techcatl*) and the temple priest cut through the chest wall with the ritual flint knife (*techpatl*). The priest grasped the still beating heart, called "precious eagle cactus fruit," tore it from the chest, offered it to the sun for vitality and nourishment and placed it in a carved circular vessel called the *cuauhxicalli*, or eagle vessel. In many cases, the body, now called "eagle man," was rolled, flailing, down the temple steps to the bottom, where it was dismembered. The victim was decapitated, the brains taken out, and, after skinning, the skull was placed on the *tzompantli*, or skull rack consisting of long poles horizontally laid and loaded with skulls. It is possible that beheading was a ritual offering to the earth. In some cases, the captor was decorated, for instance with chalk and bird down and given gifts. Then, together with his relatives, he celebrated a ritual meal consisting of "a bowl of stew of dried maize called *tlacatlaolli* . . . on each went a piece of the flesh of the captive."[36]

Among the most remarkable festivals was the feast of Tlaca-

---

[35] Human and autosacrifice have been the subject of a heated controversy in recent years. The now discounted positions of Michael Harner ("The Ecological Basis for Aztec Sacrifice," *American Ethnologist* 4 [1977]: 117–35) has been ably summarized and critiqued by Bernardo Ortiz de Montellano, "Counting Skulls: Comment on the Cannibalism Theory of Harner-Harris," *American Anthropologist* 85, no. 2 (1983): 403–6. See Peggy Reeves Sanday, *Divine Hunger: Cannibalism as a Cultural System* (New York: Cambridge University Press, 1986). Also see David Carrasco, "Cosmic Jaws: 'We Eat the Gods and Gods Eat Us,'" *Journal of the American Academy of Religion* 63, no. 3 (1995): 101–35; idem, "Give Me Some Skin: The Charisma of the Aztec Warrior," *History of Religions* 35, no. 1 (1995): 1–26.

[36] Sacrifice and especially the public display of human sacrifice was closely related to the intimidation of allied and enemy city-states as a means of acquiring massive tribute payments such as maize, beans, cloth, war service, and labor. An example of this use of geopolitical sacrifice among the Aztecs was the Xochiyayotl (Flowery Wars), which lasted from 1450 to 1519 and consisted of a series of scheduled battlefield confrontations between warriors of the Triple Alliance and warriors of the Tlaxcala-Puebla Valley kingdom. Aztec sources claim that the "wars" were staged primarily to provide sacrificial victims for ritual festivals and to keep the warriors in training. One Aztec political leader, Tlacalel, compared the warrior going to the Flowery Wars with a merchant going to distant markets to purchase luxuries. The god and his army went to the battlefield to purchase blood and hearts, the luxuries of the temples. In actual fact, the Flowery Wars were true wars, political expressions aimed at intimidating allies and enemies into maintaining an inferior status quo relationship with the great island capital in the lake.

xipehualiztli ("the feast of the flaying of men"), during which a prisoner of war was taken by a priest called the "bear man" and tied to a huge, round sacrificial stone, called the *temalacatl*, which was placed flat on the ground. The captive was provided with a pine club and a feathered staff to protect himself against the attacks of four warriors armed with clubs of wood and obsidian blades. When he was defeated he was taken off the stone, his heart was taken out, and he was flayed. The captor's friends and family enjoyed a ritual meal in which parts of the victim's thighs were consumed.

A remarkable festival celebrated on the first day of the month of Atlcahualo involved the paying of debts to Tlaloc, the rain god.[37] On this day, children (called "human paper streamers") with two cowlicks in their hair and favorable day-signs were dressed in costumes of various bright colors such as dark green, black striped with chili red, and light blue and were sacrificed in seven different locations. The flowing and falling of the tears of the children ensured the coming of rain.

Aztec Spirituality: The Supreme Duality

In a number of significant books and articles based on a careful analysis of Nahuatl texts, Miguel León-Portilla has illuminated an alternate religious worldview within Aztec society concerned with "truly spiritualistic wisdom." The basic philosophical position of a group of *tlamatinimi*, or "knowers of things," argued that the practice of sacrifice and conquest central to the military religion of Aztec elites could not lead the human personality to an understanding of the fundamental truths or Truth. Plagued by a series of doubts about the overwhelmingly aggressive religious practices of the majority of Aztec nobles, these philosophers developed a school of thought and aesthetic ritual during the period of 1430 to 1519. Central to their approach was a rhetorical strategy designed to overcome the spiritual crisis caused by the mystico-militaristic religion of Tenochtitlán.

It is well known that these aesthetic and rhetorical strategies to

---

[37] Anthony F. Aveni, "Mapping the Ritual Landscape: Debt Payment to Tlaloc During the Month of Atlcahualo," and Philip P. Arnold, "Eating Landscape," in *To Change Place.*

understand human nature and its relation to ultimate truth were part of a theological tradition rooted in the Toltec creativity associated with the kingdom of Tollan. But the clearest examples of its expression come from a series of texts collected in the sixteenth century by persistent Spanish friars who uncovered the poetic geniuses of such figures as Nezahualcoyotl, King of Texcoco; Tecayehuatzin, Prince of Huexotzinco, and eleven other *tlamatinimi*.

The rhetorical strategy of this school of thought was aimed at making a series of poetic inquiries "into the region of the gods above and into the region of the dead below," that is, into the reality beyond human existence. This search focused on the source of truth, which existed in the Place of Duality, or Omeyocan, referred to as "the innermost region of heaven." The problem facing humans thirsty for this knowledge was that human existence was utterly transitory, fragile, and vulnerable. Within the world where "jade shatters, the quetzal feathers tear apart," that is, where precious things decay, there was no foundation, truth, or permanence in normal language or thought. This vulnerable existence led the *tlamatinimi* to inquire, "O God you mock us, Perhaps we do not really exist, Perchance we are nothing to you?"

One of the purposes of this line of inquiry was to offer a critique of the vicious practice of incremental human sacrifice, where human hearts were transformed into food for the gods. That approach to the fundamental truths of existence ended in a pomp of pessimism. The solution to this spiritual crisis was proposed at a gathering of *tlamatinimi* who met at the palace of Tecayehuatzin, King of Huexotzinco, in the last years of the fifteenth century. In their view, the human personality, described by the metaphor "face and heart," was the arena where the spiritual quest for liberation must be carried out.

The approach to liberation through true knowledge focused on the meaning of art, poetry, and symbolic forms embedded in a powerful linguistic metaphor—*in xochitl in cuicatl*, or "flower and song." This form, called a *difrasismo* by the Nahuatl scholar Angel María Garibay K., works when two words are used together to create one special idea. In the rhetorical and aesthetic program worked out by the gathering of wisemen, a correspondence was revealed linking the human personality, poetic structures, and the divine foundation of the universe together through the use of his metaphorical device. First, the human personality was a *difrasismo* "face and heart," which achieved an authentic mode when it integrated into itself the poetic *difrasismo* "flower and song" through the creation of true words or supreme poems or aesthetic works.

> As is stated repeatedly, "flower and song" are present only in the soul of those who have learned "to converse with their own hearts." The result is a kind of deification of the innermost self which should impel the "deified heart" to undertake the "deification of things," that is the introduction of "flowers and songs" into all that exists.[38]

This aesthetic creativity linking poetry to personality reflected the third level of duality in the Nahuatl world, which had created everything. The most profound and authentic *difrasismo* created and therefore discovered by the *tlamatinimi* was the high god Ometecuhtli-Omecihuatl, Lord and Lady of Duality, who were beyond "all time, beyond the heavens in Omeyocan." Therefore, in a subtle reversal in the aesthetic project, the "heart and face" which successfully introduced true words "flowers and songs" into its existence was manifesting the fundamental structure of existence, the supreme duality that created the world. This ritual form of poetic creation combined creativity, discovery and re-creativity in one.

As we have witnessed, the history of Mesoamerican religion is embedded in the history of ceremonial cities and the ritual activities that animated them. This pattern of city as symbol was interrupted by periodic collapses, relocations of peoples and new construction of capitals. But throughout this pattern of eccentric periodicities, it was the urban center that oriented, renewed, and expressed the symbolic and social life of people. This perception is expressed at the end of one of the episodes of the *Popol Vuh*, the Book of Council of the Quiche Maya. After the "great sacrificers, . . . the wisemen . . . the great sages . . . wore their hearts out there in expectation of the sun," they went searching for a new life. The episode ends, "They heard news of a city and went there.[39]

---

[38] León-Portilla, *Native Mesoamerican Spirituality*, 134. In the last few decades, many important studies of the Nahuatl language have appeared. Among others, see the works of Thelma D. Sullivan, John Bierhorst, Frances Karttunen, R. Joe Campbell, J. Richard Andrews, William Bright, and Una Canger.

[39] *The Book of Council: The Popol Vuh of the Quiche-Maya of Guatemala*, ed. and trans. Munro S. Edmonson (New Orleans: Middle American Research Institute, Tulane University, 1971), 160.

2

Indigenous Mythology from Present-day Mexico

Alfredo López Austin

Indians of Today, Indians of Yesterday

To speak about contemporary Mexican Indians is to discuss nearly five centuries of colonial domination. In 1521 the city of Mexico-Tenochtitlán[1] fell before the arms of the Spanish. Immediately thereafter, the Spanish expanded their conquest of the indigenous tribes who occupied the territory that today belongs to Mexico. The political and economic subjugation was accompanied by cultural conquest in the broadest sense of the word. The progressive advance of the Europeans imposed a colonial regime that employed evangelization as one of its most important ideological pillars, under which the Indians suffered not only spoliation and subjugation but also the marginalization of their worldview, which was interpreted by their conquerors as an absurd and archaic notion. The natives soon fell into poverty and became a minority of strangers on their own lands. They recognized the need to establish some correlation between the two traditions that their new reality forced them to now live simultaneously. But the great differences and frequent antagonism between the two traditions greatly hindered the integration process because the natives lacked the necessary knowledge to comprehend the culture of their conquerors and could not rely on the institutional backing of their forefathers, which, being of a hopelessly lost world, had suddenly become largely obsolete.

---

[1] Capital of Mexica—the most powerful Mesoamerican people at the time. Although this is not entirely correct, these people are also known as Aztec. Linguistically, they belonged to the Nahua.

From the time the Spanish colony was established for the subsequent three centuries of its prevalence, the destinies of the indigenous populations were quite varied. Many tribes were incorporated
into the dominant society under disadvantaged conditions which
began the strong mestization that characterizes present-day Mexico
and contributed to the laggard gestation of the so-called national culture. Others, especially the hunters and gathers of the north, were
exterminated, and still others maintained their marginality and
formed belief systems that responded to their dependent situation.
The latter, who, isolated even from each other, were dominated by
the Spanish in unequal forms and methods, interpreted the teachings of the evangelizers and the cultural heritage of their ancestors to
restructure their cosmos, create new institutions, and continue their
allegiance to those gods on whom their lives, health, and harvests
depended.

Spanish political domination ended in 1821; however, the enormous transformation of the independent country did not produce
the awaited improvements for the Indians. Marginalization persisted
on all levels. Even in the present century, despite the official pos-
turing that has maintained a nationalistic position, proud of its pre-
Hispanic cultural roots and the mixed ancestry of the majority of
Mexicans, the Indians must continue the struggle to defend their
most elemental rights. Because of a large mestizo population, it is difficult to estimate the total number of Indians. According to linguistic
criteria and the official census figures of 1990, the country has
5,282,347 individuals over the age of five who speak Indian languages, to which are added 1,129,625 individuals under the age of
five who belong to homes whose head of family speaks an indigenous
language. The above gives a total of 6,411,972. Indigenous organizations, however, do not accept this figure and maintain that their population is greater. It is also difficult to identify the actual number of
indigenous languages spoken today because of variations in linguistic
criteria. Officially, there are a total of fifty-nine indigenous languages
currently being spoken in Mexico.

Colonial Indian religions comprised two currents: the pre-Hispanic
and the Christian. The pre-Hispanic had three components in dif-
fering proportions: the Aridamerican, the Mesoamerican, and the
Oasisamerican. The first includes those groups that inhabited the
arid northern lands that were unfit for cultivation. They were dispersed societies of which we have little information because their

dependence on hunting and gathering and their bellicose nature led to their reduction into sedentary communities, assimilation, or extinction under the advance of the Spanish. There are very few Aridamerican communities subsisting in Mexico today. Among them are the Seris of Sonora and a few small groups in Baja California.

The Mesoamerican tradition has a more complex history. It dates back to 2500 B.C.E.—a time when nomadic groups changed their subsistence activities to depend predominantly on the consumption of cultigens which obliged them to adopt a sedentary lifestyle. This significant change in lifestyle extended to the fertile lands and involved distinct ethnic groups and languages. The exchange of goods between villagers kept them in permanent communication. As a result of intensive interactions, the maize agriculturists shared a history and common cultural elements. In spite of the profound social transformations that occurred during the four-thousand-year history of Mesoamerica and the enormous differences among particular traditions, the common cultural nucleus remained incredibly resistant. The Olmec of the preclassical period,[2] the Teotihuacán, Zapotec, and Maya of the classical,[3] and the Toltec, Mexica, Tarasco, Huastec, Totonaco, Mixtec, Zapotec, and Maya of the postclassical[4] are only some of the distinguished examples in the complex of tribes that shared this common history. Today their descendants form the greater part of the ethnic groups in Mexico.

Sedentary societies appeared in northwestern Mexico and the southwestern United States around 500 B.C.E. With great effort and advanced techniques they cultivated maize and developed a complex culture in an agriculturally unfavorable, arid territory. These people have been generically classified as Oasisamericans. Since 500 C.E., Oasisamerica has maintained a considerable commerce with Mesoamerica. We estimate that the more important centers of one of these traditions, the Hohokam, disappeared around 1450, leaving

---

[2] The preclassical—the period of the villages and regional centers—is dated between 2500 B.C.E. and 200 C.E. The Olmec lived in the territory near the Gulf of Mexico between 1200 and 400 B.C.E.

[3] The classical—the period of the great cities—begins in 200 C.E. and ends in the beginning of the tenth century. The Zapotec and Maya traditions, which experienced great development during the classic period, are still present today.

[4] The postclassical—the militaristic period—concludes in the sixteenth century with the Spanish conquest and the establishing of the colony.

the Pápago as their Mexican descendants. Another Oasisamerican tradition, the Mogollón, had Paquimé as one of its first-ranked centers located in the state of Chihuahua. Apparently, this center fell in the fourteenth or fifteenth century. It is not known whether its inhabitants emigrated to the north, but it is believed that the possible Mexican descendants of the Mogollón tradition may be the Tarahumara, Ópata, and the Cahita (Yaqui and Mayo).

The Inheritance from Ancient Thought

Mythology is an area of indigenous social production that most clearly shows the persistence of nuclear elements from ancient religion. Unfortunately, the historic study of the Mexican myths has been difficult because of a great gap in the available data. Following a vigorous initial interest in the ritual beliefs and customs of the conquered, studies of this nature declined notably and were only renewed toward the end of the last century. With the exception of a few important accounts from the intermediate period, we have accounts from the sixteenth century and the first half of the seventeenth. On the other hand, there are the records of the last hundred years. Therefore, reconstruction of the ties between both extremes of the tradition must be made with limited information and many conjectures.

Nevertheless, the relationship between ancient and present myths is so evident that the comparison between the past and the present is highly enlightening. If we begin in the present, the variety of myths is great because the ethnographic records provide numerous elements that facilitate the understanding of the ancient documents. If we commence with the past, we will understand the narratives of our time in a cosmological context that was valid for millennia. This context, although impoverished during the colonial period, still provides some clarity to the religious beliefs and narratives.

The Persistence of the Narrative

Some of today's narratives appear to be modern versions of those that were recorded in the sixteenth century, which demonstrates the vigor of the oral tradition. A good example is the origin myth of maize as recounted by the present-day Chole of Chiapas. They tell of the god in heaven Ch'ujtiat, who informed humans of a food called maize and instructed them to search for it inside a mountain. The humans asked the woodpecker to help them locate the hidden maize. The bird struck at the rocks with its beak and discovered, by the sound, which of them contained the treasure. But its beak was not hard enough to break the rock. So the god of the heavens created White Lightning and sent him to break the rock. However, the rock only cracked under the impact of White Lightning, and the humans could do no more than spy the maize through the crevice. The humans then spoke with the black ant, whose body was so narrow that it could pass through the opening. But the insect, for being so small, could not carry the grain. So the men requested the help of the red ant. This one did have the strength to extract the maize. But it only brought out the grain, leaving the "heart" behind. The humans now knew maize. However, as they did not have the heart, they could not cultivate it in their fields. So Ch'ujtiat made Red Lightning and thrust him against the rock. But the impact of Red Lightning only served to widen the crack a bit more, not enough to allow the maize to be extracted. So the humans asked the help of the mouse. This one did fit through the crack. It managed to retrieve the maize, but it ate the grain that contained the heart. Again humans possessed maize without being able to cultivate it. Ch'ujtiat felt that humans had suffered enough and created Green Lightning. This one was able to break apart the rock, and from the opening poured the black maize, which was scorched by the lightning, followed by the red, the yellow, and finally the white. The latter, having been at the bottom, was not burned. These grains were viable seeds. Even though they had been burned, their heart remained intact because Green Lightning is the lightning of life.[5]

Now let us compare this myth from southeastern Mexico with the one recorded on the Central Altiplano during the early colonial period. The ancestral Nahua said that, after having created humans, the gods contemplated the food with which humans might nourish themselves. As the gods searched for a diet, Red Ant entered the Field of Sustenance and removed a grain of maize. The god Quetzalcóatl spied the ant and asked it where it had found the grain. At first the ant refused to reveal its secret. But later it pointed out the place.

---

[5] Morales Bermúdez 1984, 94–99.

Some of the Current Indigenous Groups

Alphabetical Order		*Numerical Order*	
Apache	9	Cucapá	1
Chantin	30	Pápago	2
Chinantec	27	Seris	3
Chole	33	Ópata	4
Chuje	35	Yaqui	6
Cora	12	Tarahumara	7
Cucapá	1	Mayo	8
Huastec	19	Apache	9
Huave	32	Kickapú	10
Huichole	13	Nahua of the Sierra Madre	
Ixil	36	Occidental	11
Kickapú	10	Cora	12
Maya	38	Huichole	13
Mayo	8	Tarasco	14
Mazatec	22	Otomíe	15
Mixe-popoluca	28	Nahua from Central Mexico	18
Mixtec	21	Huastec	19
Nahua from Central Mexico	18	Totonaco	20
Nahua from Veracruz	23	Mixtec	21
Nahua of the Sierra Madre		Mazatec	22
Occidental	11	Nahua from Veracruz	23
Ópata	4	Popoluca	25
Otomíe	15	Zoque	26
Pápago	2	Chinantec	27
Pipile	39	Mixe-popoluca	28
Popoluca	25	Trique	29
Quiché	37	Chantin	30
Seris	3	Zapotec	31
Tarahumara	7	Huave	32
Tarasco	14	Chole	33
Totonaco	20	Tzotzil	34
Trique	29	Chuje	35
Tzotzil	34	Ixil	36
Yaqui	6	Quiché	37
Zapotec	31	Maya	38
Zoque	26	Pipile	39

A Few of the Now Extinct Groups

Alphabetical Order		*Numerical Order*	
Hohokam	2	Hohokam	2
Mexica	18	Mogollón	5
Mogollón	5	Toltec	16
Olmec	24	Teotihuacan	17
Teotihuacan	17	Mexica	18
Toltec	16	Olmec	24

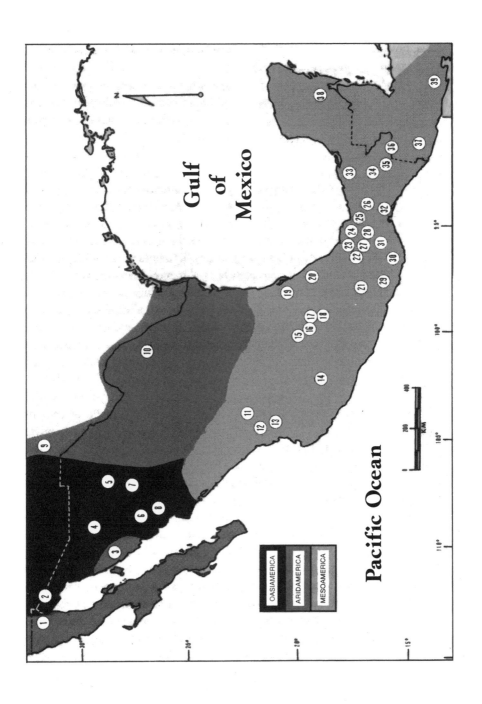

Gulf of Mexico

Pacific Ocean

OASISAMERICA
ARIDAMERICA
MESOAMERICA

Quetzalcóatl transformed into Black Ant and accompanied Red Ant in order to extract the grain. The god took the maize to the Place of Creation, where the gods tasted the maize and found it to be good. Quetzalcóatl bound the Field of Sustenance with rope to carry it away on his back. But he could not lift it. The gods Oxomoco and Cipactónal also tried their luck but came to the conclusion that only Nanáhuatl would be capable of carrying off the field. The gods of rain prepared themselves—the blue, white, yellow, and red gods. Nanáhuatl beat the field with a stick until it broke apart. From it there came the white, black, yellow, and red maize, the bean, the amaranth, and the *chía*. The gods of rain lorded themselves over all these foods.[6]

In other cases, this myth could vary from those found in the ancient documents, but it does reproduce some of the more attractive adventures. George M. Foster, who studied the Popoluca traditions in the state of Veracruz in 1940 and 1941, notes that the episodes in the maize origin myth are very similar to those of the ancient mythology in the *Popol vuh*.[7] Foster was correct. The adventures of the Quiché myths are very similar despite the fact that they do not narrate the origin of maize, but rather that of Sun and Moon.

The Persistence of Actors

Continuity can be perceived also among the actors on diverse levels. This is most evident when the gods conserve even their names, as in the case of the goddess Tonantzin in the Western Sierra Madre[8] or in that of Nanahuatzín in the region of the Gulf of Mexico.[9] But even without the name, the twin actors of the astral gods frequently refer to the brothers Hunahpú and Ixbalanqué in the ancient Quiché myths.

The substitution of figures from the religion of the conquerors for ancient actors does not necessarily imply a significant variation in their mythic performance. The Jews or the devils that now frequently appear in the narrations and rituals occupy the place of the stellar or

---

[6] *Leyenda de los soles*, 121.
[7] Foster 1945, 194.
[8] Preuss 1982, 173, 227, etc.
[9] Díaz Hernández 1945, 64.

aquatic gods. Similarly, Jesus Christ is often substituted for the solar god; the Virgin for the earth goddess, and the devil for the master of the animals and owner of the subterranean riches. This is why, among distinct indigenous groups, the figure of Jesus Christ appears with actors that seem very strange to those unaware of the mythical solar antecedents of Mesoamerica. This also explains why among the Tzotzile and the Mixe-popoluca, Christ is cross-eyed, with acne, pustules, and abscesses, bad body odor, or even covered with flies.[10] In the pre-Hispanic myths the actor who transforms into Sun frequently appears as an individual covered with pustules. Ancient Maya iconography also describes Sun as being cross-eyed.

The Persistence of Mythical Context

A third area that can show the continuity of the Mesoamerican religious tradition is that of mythical context. Below I will describe the peculiarities of the moment of creation. Here I have transcribed a Chole description of a time in which the world had still not witnessed the transformations resulting from the adventures of the gods:

> Before . . . Before, but long before, there was nothing—nothing at all. The world did not have heart. Neither did the coffee, the cedar, nor any other tree. There was nothing. Not even the monkey, nor the *tepescuintle*.[11] Not one animal lived—the *lucum*,[12] the *tacuatz*,[13] the birds. No one had a nest, hideout, nor cave. There was no earth, no sky, or water. Only a void. Everything was a void, dark, dark . . . darkness. Black! But Ch'ujtiat was there. He who made himself, he who always lived and will be forever. He of great heart, he of great power. The master of the sky.[14]

This text can be compared with the passage from the *Popol vuh*:

---

[10] Holland 1963, 264, 283; *Seis versiones del Diluvio,* 37; and Münch Galindo 1983, 160–62. It is also recorded in Guatemala, among the Ixile; see Colby and Colby 1983, 167.

[11] A large rodent with long feet, reddish fur with beautiful white spots, and delicious meet (*Cuniculus paca*).

[12] Generic name for snakes.

[13] *Tlacuache* or *zarigüeya.* A marsupial of distinct species among which is *Didelphis marsupialis.*

[14] Morales Bermúdez 1984, 67.

This account reveals that everything was motionless. All was calm, in silence; everything immobile, quiet, and the skies were empty.

This is the first account, the first narration. There was still not a single man, nor animal; birds, fish, crabs, trees, stones, caves, cliffs, herbs nor forests. Only the sky existed.

One could not see the face of the earth. There were only the calm sea and the all-covering sky.

There was nothing to make a sound. Nothing moved nor stirred. Nor was there a sound in the sky.

Nothing was standing; only the calm water, the calm sea, alone and still. There was no life.

There was only immobility and silence in the darkness, in the night. Only the Creator, the Former, Tepeu, (the Gucumatz)—the progenitors—were in the water surrounded by light. They were hidden under green and blue feathers. That is why they call them Gucumatz.[15]

A similar pattern appears in descriptions of mythical places such as the World of the Dead, to which actors of myths, stories, and legends frequently journey. Ancient and modern narratives alike mention opposing attitudes toward food. That which is considered food in the "celestial" world is held as disgusting on earth. On the different levels, the trials of travelers, the rivers, and the sources of the cold world of the dead conserve their old characteristics in the imagination of the modern-day believers. An example is the terrible freezing wind that, according to the pre-Hispanic Nahua, blew in the underworld. According to the descriptions, Mictlan was a dark place, full of spiny plants, where the wind beat on the souls as if with knives of obsidian. Today the Cora say that, in this place, the winds are very strong; blowing dirt and spines that can injure the eyes of travelers.[16]

The Persistence of Mythic Premises

In an earlier work I referred to "theme" as that which assumes the object of expression. In the communicative context, it is considered the presentation of a thought, the manifestation of a feeling, or a communication of a speaker to alter the thought or the feeling of the

---

[15] *Popol vuh*, 23.
[16] Jiménez Suárez 1994, 18.

listener(s). In the same work I also defined the "pneumonic themes" of the myth as those that refer to the cosmic laws underlying mythical narratives.[17] It is noteworthy that even today the ancient mythical and pneumonological themes have been preserved.

The above manifests the character of indigenous religions. They are not mere groups of disarticulated elements, but complexes of beliefs and customs with which to understand the cosmos and the movements therein. Beliefs and customs are interrelated through the congruence of a system that has as its foundation the concept of a universal norm that includes all that exists—be it natural or social, mundane or divine. Consequently, we can understand the reflections of authors such as William L. Merrill, who confronts indigenous thought: "When I began to analyze the material I discovered, as do most anthropologists, what first appeared as variations in the initial stages of the investigation resulted to be fragments of a larger and essentially coherent system."[18]

The mythical belief comprises a global taxonomy. Robert M. Zingg, while studying Huichole myths, emphasized the great cultural importance of the opposition of two complementary principles: the aquatic world of the goddesses governed by Nacawé (the goddess of rain) and the igneous world of Tatewarí (Our Grandfather the Fire) and Tayaupá (Our Father the Sun).[19] In principle, there is a great opposition between the rainy season and the dry season, which divide the year into two almost equal parts. But in a deeper sense, the confrontation of the two sides refers to a dual relationship of all that exists.

Today this duality is expressed as the pair God/devil. In fact, according to the Popoluca and the Nahua from the isthmus of Veracruz, God and the devil are brothers.[20] This same concept explains the comments recorded by Carlos Navarrete from the central lowlands of Chiapas: "There are saints aligned with God and saints aligned with the Devil. . . . It is not certain whether they (God and the Devil) are enemies. On the contrary, they carry on well together and stage the conflict before us so that, what is written, is carried

---

[17] López Austin 1990, 342–45 (in the English version, 1993, 247–50).
[18] Merrill 1992, 36.
[19] Zingg 1982, passim.
[20] Münch Galindo 1983, 161.

out."[21] The Nahua of central Mexico say that this was a law that predates God. Obliged to obey, God created his complement, the devil.[22]
They are two opposing sides. Consequently, the feminine is separated from the masculine, the darkness from the light, the low from
the high, the cold from the hot, the lesser from the greater, the
terrestrial-bound animals from the birds, death from life, and so on.
Over the entire Mexican territory the myths constantly refer to these
two interacting sides. Beyond this region, to the north, the Apache
Chiricahua interpret the alliance of the birds with light and day,
while the terrestrial animals are associated with night and darkness.
In El Salvador to the south, the Pipile associate birds with the sky,
light, and feathers, while terrestrial animals are affiliated with the
underworld, bones, and darkness.

The "division of opposites" law is completed by the inverted preeminence which is repeatedly expressed in Mesoamerican myths. It
was the basis for the alternating of opposite and complementary
forces of the cosmos in a strong cyclic perception of the passing of
time. Light and darkness, periods of waters and periods of drought,
or the course of time in its most ample aspect, were—in ancient
thought—ludicrous games of the gods that transformed the world into
a battlefield. One of the clearest examples is found in the Náhuatl
myth describing the origin of the sun in Teotihuacán. Tecuciztécatl,
a wealthy god, is commissioned by the other gods to transform himself into the sun. But, just in case, they also named a second actor as
an alternate. The alternate was Nanahuatzin, a poor and ill god,
whose body was covered with pustules. Tecuciztécatl was to be the
first to lunge upon a bonfire. But fear stopped him four times.
Nanahuatzin, however, did so on his first attempt. Embarrassed,
Tecuciztécatl also threw himself among the flames. The difference in
the order (and valor) transformed the poor god, sick and despised,
into Sun, and the rich and honorable god into Moon.

After studying the present-day solar myth of the Tzotzil, Gary H.
Gossen was the first investigator to recognize the law of the reversal
of the preeminence. He showed how the mother, superior to the son,
became his servant when he transformed into the sun and she
became the moon.[23] The beginning is now clear in many myths.

---

[21] Navarrete 1968, 61-62.
[22] Madsen 1955, 124-25.
[23] Gossen 1979, 60, 63-64.

Among them is the myth told by the Nahua of the Sierra Madre Occidental concerning the older brother and the younger brother. The older brother loses rank and becomes the evening star, while his younger brother becomes morning star.[24] The modern Mazatec emphatically agree: "Before the Moon was the older brother, but the Sun took the light and became greater."[25]

The Persistence of Mythical Themes

It is interesting to show how indigenous societies maintained many of the thematic threads in their myths in the face of evangelization and how there is a notable likeness among the modern indigenous myths in spite of differences in ethnic background, linguistic affiliation, and development under the colonial regime. The attention of narrators is focused on the sun and the moon, the discovery of maize, and the acquisition of fire, and so on. Among the surviving myths, two are distinguished and often told in succession to form a unit: the first is the account of a man who saved himself from the flood inside of a hollowed tree trunk; the second is an origin myth of humanity which began with the union of this particular man and a bitch that accompanied him inside of the trunk. I will refer to both below.

The Diverse Types of Myths

Among the indigenous traditions of Mexico exists a notable similarity in form and content among the accounts explaining the creation of beings of this world in original times. This likeness makes it prudent to group the accounts and beliefs that sustain them under the common denomination of *myths*. The term is limited to that area which refers to the divine processes through which, in another timespace, the gestation of individual beings, the classes, and the processes of the world inhabited by humans took place.[26]

---

[24] Preuss 1982, 75–81.

[25] Portal 1986, 56.

[26] For more about my definition of the myth of Mesoamerican tradition, see López Austin 1990, 481–82 (English 1993, 354).

Despite the likeness between the accounts, not all narrate the appearance of life on the world in the same manner. Classifying the myths according to the methods of creation used by the gods could help to provide a general idea concerning this subject. I do not pretend to offer an exhaustive classification. Rather I will present only a condensed guide.

Creation from the Capture of the Divine Matter

The creation process that rests on the most profound mythic conception is, without doubt, the one that shows how the gods remained enclosed in heavy matter. According to this concept, all that exists in the world is composed of two types of substances: one is heavy and perceptible; the other is subtle and imperceptible. The second is a vital force. It is a spirit capable of giving to each earthly being its essential characteristics. Each type of being has its own spirit. For example, according to the Tarahumara, the spirit of fish permits them to live under water but impedes them from breathing beyond this medium.[27] This spirit is given the name "heart." In ancient times they spoke of the "heart of the sky," the "heart of the sea," the "heart of the earth"—always referring to the subtle part, the divine, that gave power and peculiarity to the being. To cite only one case, the modern Chatin believe that in the bell tower resides the "heart" of the village; it is their center, the most sacred place.[28]

The invisible substance is divine, but how did it penetrate the beings of the world? The myths refer to a time when all was in a state of darkness because the sun and the moon did not yet exist. Within the darkness lived beings that in the accounts appear as gods, humans, or animals. A characteristic of all was the capacity of speech. This happened "many years ago, but many years ago"—say the Cora—"when the animals understood each other."[29] In a strict sense, these entities were the divine seeds of mundane beings. Still lacking their definite attributes, they debated in the "formation adventures." For example, in the beginning the deer did not have horns. It robbed them from the rabbit. Because of his crime, both animals acquired

---

[27] Merrill 1992, 142.
[28] Durand 1986, 115, 178.
[29] Jiménez Suárez et al. 1994, 20.

their final attributes. The deer remained with the horns and the rabbit without them.[30]

There came a time when all forms became fixed. The adventures suddenly end with the first rising of the sun, with the primeval aurora. The world crystallized. The rays of light hardened all the formerly malleable beings, who lost forever the use of their human voices.

In the ancient myths Sun initiates his rule over the world with a cruel mandate. He condemns all gods to death. The sacrifice was necessary in order that the new lord might reconnoiter the firmament. The concept of the massacre persists today. It is said that the mythic beings transformed into animals or stones (in some cases they took the forms of the ancient gods), or they hid beneath the earth, inside the mountains or beneath the waters. The Tzotzil say that these original beings, the "fathers-mothers," were eliminated because they did not honor the gods. This occurred while the world was beginning. St. Vincent and St. Casper blew the whistle and beat the drum. The two saints told the fathers-mothers: "Here we are providing your feast because you are to die." The souls of all were collected and, after a strong thunder, the "fathers-mothers" transformed into animals.[31] In other cases the myths mention a generalized violence, borne from fights between the animals, or simply the slaughter of the mythical characters at the moment in which their characteristics are crystallized. According to the Chuje: "In these times many animals, tapirs, deer, goats were killed and animals fooled one another. That is why many animal skins were collected. God gave the animals their qualities."[32] The same myth, but in the version told by the Chuje of Guatemala, opens with an episode that does not appear to have anything to do with the account: "It was a god who sent the rabbit to kill all of the animals, because if he did so, he would bestow power on him."[33]

The above should be interpreted as the transformation of the original divine essences of the imperceptible substances of things. The beings in the myth were trapped by the other substance, that of death—the heavy substance. There they find themselves confined,

---

[30] Schumann G. 1993.

[31] Arias 1990, 19–21.

[32] Schumann G. 1993.

[33] Buenrostro 1993.

giving their particular attributes to each being. With the divine substance within them, the types were fixed at the beginning of creation.
When an individual dies, his "heart" leaves to become part of a new
being of the same type. That is how the types persist beyond the
destruction of the individual.

To these myths belong those narratives that tell of how, during
primordial times, the beings of today were formed from the bodies
of some gods. For example, the ancient Nahua relate that from the
dead body of the god Cintéotl were born distinct food plants important for humans.

Creation from the Mixing of the Divine Substance

The gods are many and very different from each other. The light substance that constitutes the "heart" of beings is not homogeneous. If
it were, there would be no types because all would have the same
characteristics. Since the great dual opposition, distinct proportions
of the dark and the light, of the humid and dry, of the below and the
high are integrated in all beings. These groupings belong to that sector of the cosmos which corresponds to their predominant element.

To Madsen we owe the pioneering studies with respect to the
indigenous taxonomy since the discovery of the opposition of pairs.
He demonstrated how the Nahua of central Mexico employed the
pair cold/hot to classify the components of the cosmos and deduce
from the attributed qualities the manner in which humans should
behave before that which exists.[34] It obviously refers to the cold or
hot nature of things and not temperature. The Maya of Quintana
Roo speak of "charges," using the word *cuch*, which has a sense of
destiny. Accordingly, they call *ziz u cuch* that which has a cold quality and *chocó cuch* that which has a hot quality.[35]

In practically all human activities—in nature and in society—one
must account for the nature of things in order for the action to be
effective. The practical utility of the taxonomy derived from the great
division established at the time of the myth is notably expressed in
food and medicine. Among the foods is sought the equilibrium
between hot and cold. Medicine divides disease among those that

---

[34] Madsen 1955; 1960.
[35] Villa Rojas 1978, 307.

FIRST PERIOD DIVINE LEISURE	SECOND PERIOD MYTHICAL ADVENTURES	TIME LIMIT MOMENT OF CREATION	THIRD PERIOD WORLD OF CREATURES	
	The gods (germinal and playable beings) divide the cosmos and invent the elements of their mechanism;	The sun rises for the first time, consolidating the cosmic mechanism,	The Sun is the governor of the world of creatures. The gods wander this world along the routes of the cosmic mechanism.	MYTHS OF THE INSTALLATION OF THE COSMIC MECHANISM
	combine substances to form new beings	killing the germinal beings, that is, crystallizing their forms, enclosing them in the heavy matter and the mortal (in other words, converting them into the "hearts" or essences of the mortal creatures)	The creatures have heterogeneous divine material, which explains their diversity. This material gives specific characteristics to the types.	MYTHS OF THE MIXING OF THE DIVINE SUBSTANCE
The divine exists without creating			The characteristics do not vary nor do they end, in spite of the death of the individuals, because they pass from generation to generation	MYTHS OF THE CAPTURE OF THE DIVINE SUBSTANCE
	and fight among themselves to acquire the characteristics that will be definitive in the time/space of the creatures.	or sending them to the underworld, where they will be stored as "hearts" or powers that pass a time in their subterranean enclosure and another time on the earth, in the world of the creatures.	through the recycling of the powers and "hearts" that emerge from the underworld.	EXTRACTION MYTHS

originate from the land of the dead (cold) and those that descend
from the heavens (hot). In each case it prescribes remedies of opposite natures. Therefore it should not be surprising that the myths
refer to the subject of the original combining of substances, which
they resolve with the adequate divine adventures. It is here where we
find the hierogamy.

Creation from the Installation
of the World Mechanism

According to the great conceptual framework of the myth, many gods
were trapped inside the world, surrounded by the heavy matter of
death, from where they give rise to those beings of the time-space of
humans. However, heaven and the underworld continue to be
inhabited by gods. They visit the world of humans, penetrating it
periodically to transform all that exists. The ancient Mesoamerican
cosmovision gave enormous importance to these arrivals and paid
special attention to the order of the divine powers that made their
journey in the form of time. For example, every day a god was formed
through the combination of two other gods. This is how the joining
of the gods Ik (wind) and Hun (one) produced the day god of the calendar (Hun-ik). According to the rigid geometry of the cosmos, this
god as well as the other twelve gods named Ik, supposedly arrived on
earth via the north tree. The geometry, in synthetic form, was based
in the composition of three great levels (the sky, the world of
humans, and the underworld). The gods communicated with each
other through five cosmic trees, of which one was the great world
axis, and each of the others was assigned to a particular corner of the
world. The gods lived in heaven and the underworld. They came to
earth one at a time through the trees.

Today, almost five centuries later, the cosmic trees continue to
occupy a preeminent position in indigenous religions. Whether as
columns, gods, or saints, they are differentiated (as in ancient times)
by their particular color and continue to be present in indigenous
beliefs, narratives, and rituals. The belief in the four lords of the corners of the world is not limited to Mesoamerican descendants. Of a
very different septentrional tradition, the Kickapú mention the four
grandfathers who reside in the corners of the world and act as
guardians and intermediaries between humans and the supernatural

beings.[36] As is the case with other indigenous groups, the Kickapú assign four colors to the four quadrants of the cosmos and believe that the white maize came from the north, the black from the south, the yellow from the east, and the red from the west.[37] On occasion it has been convenient to modify the concept of the trees to adapt them to modern times. As a result, the Tarahumara believe that they are great columns of iron.[38]

Creation by Extraction

There are myths, however, whose adventures do not conclude with the crystallization caused by solar rays. On the contrary, the presence of beings in the world is initiated during the reign of Sun. This is how the Chole begin one of their narratives: "The days are already illuminated by Iijtzin [Sun]. Every night Ch'ujnia [the moon] appears when he comes to visit every night. As a result one can measure the days and time, and morning and afternoon. . . ."[39] They continue with a myth in which the being that will occupy a place in the world of Man will be extracted from another time-space to be placed in this one.

They had to bring many things in order that humans might adequately live. The Yaqui of northwestern Mexico and the American Southwest, explicitly refer to the necessity of having to bring from the other world what was necessary for human existence in this one. The great temporal division was the first Christmas, and the hero, the first man, Jesus. "Before the birth of Jesus there were no dances, harps, or *pascolas* [dancers]. Everything was in the earth and had to be extracted. Jesus knew how to accomplish this and he did so."[40]

Why did these beings stay in the other time-space? Various narratives from ancient Mesoamerican mythology refer to gods who were thrown onto the earth and into the underworld. Today the same is

---

[36] Latorre and Latorre 1991, 266.

[37] Ibid., 357.

[38] González Rodríguez 1984, 402-4.

[39] Morales Bermúdez 1984, 94.

[40] Rosamond B. Spicer, "The Easter Fiesta of the Yaqui Indians" (M.S. thesis, Department of Anthropology, University of Chicago, 1939), 72, cited in Olavarría 1990, 66.

reconfirmed when they say that when the Sun rose for the first time
many of the gods went to live in subterranean sites. This is why they
believe that these gods are the "hearts of the mountains."[41]

We know that the gods who remained on the earth function as
the "hearts" of everything that exists in this world. But what did
those do that went below the surface, inside the mountains or under
the waters? To understand this we should reflect on the cycles of life
and death. Within the great cosmic mountain there is an enormous
kettle, the recipient of "hearts." The treasure belongs to the mother
gods as well as the cold and humid gods who are in charge of the
rains and the dead. Each year, at the onset of the rainy season, the
lords liberate from their enclosure the spirits of plants, the forces of
growth as well as the winds and the waters in order that they may
cover the surface of the earth with vegetation. Then, at the onset of
the dry season, when the powers of heaven and heat take over, the
gods of rain collect their treasures and store them once more within
their enclosures.[42]

The extraction myths describe the origin of mundane beings but
refer mostly to confinement and liberation.

The flora paradigm includes all that exists, even the human being.
The cosmic mountain has its replicas in the mounts throughout the
world. Each indigenous group has its mount, and in each there lives
a patron. He is the "heart" of the inhabitants of each community
because he formed them from his essence as a great common ancestor. He also distributes over his people the waters, forces of growth
as well as "hearts" of children, animals, plants, and money. When
individuals die, their "hearts" return to the great storage vault to be
cleaned and to give origin to new beings of their type.

Among these myths appear narratives describing several types
that were lost because the "hearts" or "fathers-mothers" had fled the
region. This is what the Otomi say of the tropical plants: "originally
these plants lived on the altiplano, but their 'hearts' migrated
towards the warmer lands of the Huastec and no longer grow at the
higher elevations."[43] The Chinanteco believe that because of envy

---

[41] Durand 1986, 173.
[42] For a more extensive discussion, see López Austin 1994.
[43] Galinier 1990, 489-90.

and sorcery the father and mother of cotton, and the father and mother of a fish called *bobos* left the territory. That is why these no longer exist in the region.[44] Below we will see several examples of these forms of creation.

The Capture of the Gods

This archetypical form of creation comprises the most simple of myths—almost infantile stories that narrate how the animals and plants were created—and also more complex accounts. Among the latter one finds several astral myths, because as the Sun himself established his reign over the earth, he also became tied to the world of humans. It must be warned that Christianity has influenced these myths, establishing as a limit between mythical and human time not only the pristine birth of Sun, but also the birth of Christ, the crucifixion, or the beginning of evangelization. For this reason many Indians believe that the pre-Hispanic era corresponds to the period of divine adventures for which the images of the gods are those gods transformed during the first twilight.

The Armadillo and the Tepescuintla

The Chinantec tell that two women of ancient times embroidered their blouses in order to don them when the Sun arose. The *tepescuintla* finished her work on time, but the armadillo did not. When the Sun rose, the armadillo had no option except to don the cloth still attached to the weaving frame. As a result, the swift woman ended up with the beautiful markings of flowers on her back while the slow woman appears as if her back were stepped upon.[45]

The Waves, the Sole, the Crab, and the Starfish

Previously, in the Huave territory, they honored only Mijmeor Kaan —the Stone Virgin. But one day a priest arrived at the Temple

---

[44] *Relatos, mitos y leyendas*, 91, 129–30.
[45] Ibid., 76.

Within the Mountain, and Mijmeor Kaan fled to the sea. The movements of her flowered cape created waves and foam. All of the animals fled with her. The Virgin stepped on the *popoyote* fish. In doing so she created the sole fish. The jaguar stepped on the crab and left his mark forever on his back. The birds rose up in flight and abandoned their aquatic nests, and from these nests were born the starfish.[46]

Sun and Moon

I chose the Mazatec myth of the origin of the Sun and Moon because different versions of this myth are repeated by many groups of Mesoamerican descent. The Mazatecs say that an old woman was working in her garden when she heard a noise in a nearby mountain. On the mountain she found two eggs the size of goose eggs among the branches of a tree. She carried the eggs to her home and placed them in cotton and she waited for them to hatch. Months later, as she was returning home, she found her house full of garbage and became furious. She searched but could not find the culprit. Days later the event recurred. On a third occasion she returned from the garden and heard sounds of children playing. Entering in silence, she surprised a small boy and girl, who ran to hide under the table. The children escaped through a window. The old woman discovered the empty egg shells and immediately understood that these children had been born from the eggs that she had cared for. She left the house, overtook the children, and forgave them for their mischief. They lived together for a long time until the children decided to leave in order to see the world. The old woman asked that they take her with them. They agreed, but when they crossed a bridge the children threw her into the river, transforming her into the mother of the mountain animals. As the old woman fell into the river the *tepes-cuintla*, the rabbit, the deer, and many other animals emerged on the banks. The children continued on their path until an old man warned them of a dangerous giant eagle. The children constructed a cage, climbed inside, and waited for the bird to attack. The eagle

---

[46] Ramírez Castañeda 1987, 66.

came but could not harm them. So it took the cage in its talons and carried it to its nest on the summit of a mountain, which was covered with human bones and very skinny children waiting to be eaten by the monster. The boy who was born from the egg cut the hair of the captive girls and used it to braid a rope. Later he and his sister lassoed the eagle around the throat and strangled it. In order to descend from the summit the two siblings asked the animals for assistance. The bat found a solution. He ate prickly pear fruit of the *amate*[47] and proceeded to defecate on the side of the mountain. In his excrement were the seeds of the prickly pear. Suddenly, there arose a fronded tree adhering to the rock, which the children used to climb down. At the base of the mountain the children found the eyes of the eagle. The girl took the right, more brilliant eye, and the boy took the left eye, which was weaker. Soon the boy wanted to exchange his eagle eye for the one possessed by his sister, saying that he had had a greater role in the death of the monster than she had. But he could not convince his sister. Later, however, she became thirsty and demonstrated her weakness. Her brother had prohibited her from drinking water from a particular pond, but she disobeyed his instructions. She was punished by her brother, who obliged her to exchange the eagle eyes with him. He then beat her with a rabbit that became stuck on her face. Both children ascended into heaven. The boy with the more brilliant eye became Sun and the girl transformed into Moon.[48]

The unfolding of the myth seems to have an extra element: the episode with the rabbit, which in other narratives is employed to explain not only the weakness of the lunar light but also the shape (image) seen on the face of the moon. It is an unnecessary episode because the rest of the adventure not only explains the difference in light intensity but also the inversion of powers. The predominant power, originally in the hands of the girl, who possessed the more brilliant eye, is passed on to the boy, who proved to have a greater resistance than his sister.

---

[47] A fronded tree whose pulp is used in the production of paper (*Ficus involuta, F. involuta*, etc.).

[48] Portal 1986, 49–54.

The River and the Sea

Near the Colorado River and the northern coast of the Gulf of California live the Cucupá, who through a long narrative, rich in adventures, explain that in the time of the giants, a boy went to see the world in the company of his dog. He searched for the feared monster that terrorized his fellow countrymen. After much walking, the boy and his dog arrived at the lair where the beast—large, black, very ugly, and covered with foam—slept placidly on his back, snoring and exposing his enormous testicles. One testicle was blue, the other red. The boy carefully approached with his harpoon. When he was close enough, he quickly pierced the blue testicle of the monster. He immediately did the same to the red testicle. The beast roared with pain and from his severed scrotum poured two streams of liquid that flooded the region. The blue liquid formed the ocean and the red, the Colorado River. The agonizing monster sank into the salt waters, where he became a god.[49]

Edible Plants

When the first chief died, the Kickapú did not know of many edible plants. The plants emerged from his buried body. From the head came the pumpkin; from his teeth, corn; and from his fingers, beanpods.[50]

The Mixing of the Divine Substance

The complexity of the myths of the origin of Sun and Moon allow us to identify the distinct forms of creation. One of them is the mixing of divine substances, for Sun and Moon are the children of Father Sky and the earth goddess. This is evident in the pre-Hispanic myth describing the birth of Huitzilopochtli, the solar god and patron of the Mexica. Huitzilopochtli was born to the goddess Coatlicue, who, while sweeping, saw falling from the heavens, a white feather, which

---

[49] Ochoa Zazueta 1982, 188–97.
[50] Latorre and Latorre 1991, 358.

she put between her breasts. Later, when she went to find the feather, she noticed that it had vanished and she felt pregnant.

The Trique myth that I present below has the same hierogamic sense. It is a cruel myth in which grandchildren assassinate their grandfather, the deer, and rape their ancient grandmother. To understand this myth better I have included two versions because the first refers to hierogamy but does not end with the ascension of the astros. The second, however, does not mention hierogamy but does mention the ascension of the children to the heavens. The versions complement each other. I provide a compact synthesis of the two because the individual adventures are many and complex.

First Version of the Origin of Sun and Moon

The Trique tell of a young maiden who refused to marry in spite of the fact that she had several suitors. She did not accept marriage because she wanted to become a goddess and ascend to the heavens, which would be impossible if she were to have children. Her father therefore, did not accept the petitions of any suitor in order not to compromise the desire of his daughter. But on one occasion, in the face of the insistence of one of the suitors, he said: "Rise up to the sky to be there! There is no reason for you to remain on earth." The suitor ascended to the heavens. One day, when the maiden was lying face up on the ground, the man let three drops of water fall and the woman conceived two boys. The father was furious over the pregnancy of his daughter. She did not want the boys either. The father and daughter decided to kill the newborns by exposing them to danger. In spite of many trials, however, the children were spared. Later the boys, now grown, would find themselves with their grandmother, the old one, and their grandfather, the deer. They placed a trap for the deer, which they killed. They cooked its flesh and gave it to the grandmother, who was unaware of the crime, to eat of her husband's flesh.

This version finishes abruptly without mention of the ascent of the two boys to heaven in spite of the fact that the text indicates that they were to become Sun and Moon.[51]

---

[51] Hollenbach 1977, 159–65.

Second Version of the Origin of Sun and Moon

The grandmother Ca'aj wandered about the heavens with a pine torch. But its light was not bright enough. One day she found in the water two fish, which she placed in her blouse. Later she stained her genital area with a fruit and pretended to have given birth to those beings. The children grew. One day they asked their grandmother to give them *tortillas* for their grandfather. They went to search for him in the mountains. When they saw that he was a deer, they trapped him, killed him, and cooked his flesh. Later they gave their grandmother the meat, and she cried upon consuming it. Days later the boys gave their grandmother a fruit to eat which produces drowsiness. While she was in a deep sleep, one of the grandchildren fixed a stone knife to his penis and the other fixed a piece of calcium to his. Both proceeded to rape the old woman. Afterwards they ascended to the heavens. When the grandmother awoke and saw her condition, she dammed her grandchildren. That is why the children of the Sun—who are the Trique—suffer much today in this world.[52]

The Mechanism of the World

One of the most widespread myths in the Mexican territory is that of the deluge. It is a complicated myth. It has two parts that, on occasion, are narrated independently. The first tells of the adventure of a man who, enclosed in a tree trunk, saves himself from the flood-waters. The second part continues with the story of a dog that accompanied the man in a boat. The bitch would later convert herself into a woman to become the mother of mankind. Several authors, among them Horcasitas,[53] believe that this myth is the result of the merging of two distinct myths.

In a previous work I interpreted the first part of the narrative based on a comparison of the different versions of the myth.[54] Here I convey only that the hidden meaning is the establishing of the four cosmic posts whereby the gods travel.

---

[52] Ibid., 140–45.
[53] Horcasitas 1953.
[54] López Austin 1990, 472–79; 1993, 345–51.

Below I include a Nahua version of the deluge myth, which ends with a biblical reference to Adam and Eve. It is followed by another myth in which the idea of the planting of the four posts is done within a Christian framework. I close this section with still another myth concerning the formation of the world, which refers to the extension of the solid surface over the waters and the confinement of the gods to the underworld.

The Deluge and the Bitch

The Nahua of the western Sierra Madre narrate that a man cleared a parcel of land to prepare a garden. The next day he found that the felled trees were upright once again. This happened on various occasions, which led the man to hide in order to discover who was righting the trees. He observed the arrival of an old man who proceeded to put the felled trees back in their places. "Why do you do this with my felled trees?" he asked the man. The old one explained that it was necessary to fell one tree, hollow it out, place maize in the hole together with firewood, squash, several birds, and a bitch. He should then get in as well because there was going to be a great flood. The man did so. The waters came and flooded everything up to the heavens. The hollowed trunk hit up against the heavens and stayed there for two days. Later the waters receded but the man remained in the trunk for five more days. After the fifth day he sent a heron to see if all was dry, recommending that it not eat live beings. The heron departed but did not obey the prohibition. The man sent a crow, which also disobeyed his orders. Finally he sent the *tildío*,[55] which flew over the entire region and returned with the news that all was in order. The man emerged from the trunk, beat the ground with his stick, and produced the rivers and their banks.

The bitch lived with the man. One day while returning from his fields, the man discovered that someone had made him tortillas. Intrigued, he began to spy and found that the dog would take off her skin, transform into a woman, and cook for him. The man approached cautiously, threw the skin on the fire, and the woman could no longer transform back into a dog.

---

[55] Name given to diverse cardiforms, small birds, pipers, with nonpalmated toes, a sharp and pointed beak, that live along the banks of rivers and lakes. Among them is the *chichicuilote* (*Lobipes lobatus, Crocelia alba*).

In other versions of this myth, the couple gives birth to mankind. In what I have condensed here, they say that the man formed two human figures with the ashes of the skin and red soil. The dolls transformed into a girl and a boy. The two entered the secret garden of their father and, without his consent, took two apples. The father caught them in the act and scolded them for their disobedience.

The Divine Teacher

The Totonaco say that Jesus sang and whistled so well that the children asked him to be their teacher. At first Jesus refused because he was afraid that the kings who sought him would find him out. But when his mother told him that his destiny was to be a school teacher, he could not refuse. While he was in the classroom, the king's police arrived. They did not know Jesus because all of the children had the same faces. "Let us pay one of them to betray Jesus," they said. The traitor child approached Jesus and offered him a bunch of plantains. But Jesus discovered his intentions, tore off the child's head and stuck it on his rump. As a result, the traitor was transformed into a monkey. Jesus, with a miracle, made it impossible for the weapons of the police to fire and he could therefore not be apprehended. However, because the kings persisted in chasing after him, Jesus abandoned the school and, in his flight, planted a huge tree on the side of the road. He climbed the tree, stretched out his arms and remained hanging from the same. A while later, he repeated the same event on another path. He repeated this process until he had planted four trees along the side of each of four paths.[56]

The Forming of the World and the Closing of the Underworld

According to the Kickapú, Kitzihiata, the creator god, sent his son Wisaka to make the world for humans. Wisiaka struggled against the supernatural beings of the waters, who took the shape of horned felines. His enemies sent a heavy snow, but he covered himself with

---

[56] Ichon 1973, 96–97.

a cape and slept. During a second attempt to kill him, the felines of the underworld tried to drown Wisaka by raising the waters of the sea. But he made a boat and saved himself. The voracious turtle[57] and the dove offered him their help. Wisaka submerged himself and scraped mud from the feet and shell of the turtle, kneaded the mud together with the twigs brought by the dove, and made a great tortilla. Later he extended the tortilla to enclose the felines underneath. The thunders helped Wisaka to contain the beings of the underworld, who would not be liberated until the end of the world, when they would reappear to devour humanity. Wisaka asked the spider to weave a cloth to prevent the world from falling. The spider wove, and the world was hung by its extreme north.[58]

The Extraction

The extraction myths describe the form in which the gods, hidden in the world of the dead, leave to acquire reality in the world of mankind. They refer to diverse processes such as the daily birth of the Sun with the myth that discovers a bright object in the form of an egg under a stone; the birth of fire, extracted from the beyond by the Tlacuache; the extraction of the edible seeds through the intervention of the black and red ants, and so on.

Here I give two examples: the arrival of the waters, and the parting of the maize spirit. In the second example, the maize dies but is replicated in his son. The boy journeys to the world of the dead, saves his father (the "heart" of the maize), and brings him to the surface. The "heart" carries out its generative functions by being reborn on the surface. However, afterwards it must return to the underworld. This is one of the beautiful and complex myths of present-day Mexico.[59] This synthesized version is told by the Nahua of Veracruz:

---

[57] A robust turtle, notably aggressive, also known as *tortuga nordedora* [the biting turtle] (*Chelydra serpentina*).

[58] Latorre and Latorre 1991, 261–62.

[59] For an exhaustive discussion of this myth, see López Austin, "Homshuk."

The Rains and the Fire

In Yaqui mythology there is a richness-extracting actor. It is Babok, the toad. In different myths, and because of his astute qualities, Bobok obtains goods from the other world that are indispensable for human life. In one case he takes the rains to the arid lands of the Yaqui. In another he carries fire to deposit it in the rocks or inside of sticks. Long ago stones and sticks were devoid of sparks and fire. Bobok takes as his obligation those tasks which other animals such as the blackbird, swallow, crow, dog, and roadrunner are not capable of doing themselves. The astute figure presents himself before Yuku, the god of rains, and urges him to continue sending his lightning and storms. He fools him with his hidden and dispersed croakings. And like this he guides the rain to the fields of the thirsty Yaqui. He also submerges himself in the ocean waters to steal the riches from the god of fire. He escapes a furious persecution and carries the fire to the surface of the earth. In both cases his preferred tactic is the multiplication of himself as a target, because all of his sons, like him, participate in the moment of the persecution to laugh at the aggressor gods. From the feats of Babok, the Yaqui have rain and humans can now extract fire from stones and sticks.[60]

The Venerable God-son Corn

One day an elderly man and woman, who did not have children, found two large eggs, which they took to their home to be incubated by their hen. They ate one and waited for the other to hatch. From the egg emerged a boy named Si:ntiopiltzin. Already grown, the boy would go to the fields. On the way the iguanas made fun of him, shouting "Elote,[61] elote, stunted ears, in Where the Men Dry, there is your father." With the help of his grandfather he made a trap and avenged himself of the tauntings. While he was still a boy, he learned that several old men would go on a journey to "Where the Men Dry"

---

[60] Giddings 1959, 18, 60, 63.

[61] "Tender ear of corn."

[62] Large reddish (leaf-cutter ants) that form long lines as they carry bits of leaves to their nests. The leaves are used to form beds on which grow fungi, which the ants later consume (*Atta mexicana*).

and asked his grandfather for permission to accompany them. One night, during the journey, while the boy slept, the *arriera* ants[62] ate his flesh and left only the bones. Si:ntiopiltzin captured one of them and with threats made the ants replace the flesh. The next night he again lay down on a rock. When we awoke, he found that the stone had devoured him. Only his head remained exposed. A small bird approached and told him how to free himself by urinating upon his own chest. The boy followed the advice, became free of the stone, and continued on his path. Finally Si:ntiopiltzin arrived at a place where his mother was weaving beneath the shadow of a *chicozapote*.[63] The boy approached his mother and asked for his father. "Your father died many years ago," she answered, and she showed him the place where he had been buried. The boy asked his mother to return to the house because he was going to revive his father. He warned that she not touch him or cry when she saw him. Si:ntiopiltzin resurrected his father and carried him because he was still somewhat drunk. When Si:ntiopiltzin's mother saw her husband alive she could not withhold her emotions. She began to cry and embraced the man. In this moment the father of the boy transformed into a deer and fled into the forest.[64]

Today and Tomorrow

As during the difficult times of the colonial period, the modern Indians of Mexico continue their struggle to conserve the group cohesion that protects them from the dehumanizing tendencies of the dominant society. In the past it was the colonial domination. In the present, there exists a drive that pretends to homogenize people and transform them into producers and consumers in a global economy.

During the colonial period the Indians had in their cosmovision rituals and myths a strong support to maintain a protective group unity. Today this battle is even more intense, but it is unlikely that the ancient strategies will succeed against the current assaults on ethnic differences.

---

[63] A tree of very hard and resistant wood from which chicle is extracted. It Produces a very sweet fruit (*Achras sapota*).

[64] García de León 1976, 80–84.

The future of the Indian myth is uncertain, and equally uncertain is the future of the entire indigenous culture.

References

Arias, Jacinto. 1990. *San Pedro Chenalhó: Algo de su historia, cuentos y costumbres.* Chiapas: Tuxtla Gutiérrez, Gobierno del Estado de Chiapas.

Buenrostro, Cristina. 1993. "El venado y el conejo." *Folium* 2, no. 6 (September–December): 5.

Colby, Benjamin N., and Lore M. Colby. 1983. *El contador de los días: Vida y discurso de un adivino ixil.* México: Fondo de Cultura Económica.

Díaz Hernández, Vicente. 1945. "Nanahuatzin." *Tlalocan* 2, no. 1: 64.

Durand, Carmen Cordero Avendaño de. 1986. *Stina Jo'o Kucha: El Santo Padre Sol: Contribución al conocimiento socio-religioso del grupo étnico chatino.* Oaxaca: Oaxaca de Juárez, Gobierno del Estado de Oaxaca.

Foster, George M. 1945. *Sierra Popoluca Folklore and beliefs.* University of California Publications in American Archaeology and Ethnology 42, no. 2: 177–250. Berkeley and Los Angeles: University of California Press.

Galinier, Jacques. 1990. *La mitad del mundo: Cuerpo y cosmos en los rituales otomíes.* México: Universidad Nacional Autónoma de México, Centro de Estudios Mexicanos y Centroamericanos e Instituto Nacional Indigenista.

García de León, Antonio. 1976. *Pajapan: Un dialecto mexicano del Golfo.* México: Instituto Nacional de Antropología e Historia.

Giddings, Ruth Warner. 1959. *Yaqui myths and legends.* Tucson: University of Arizona Press.

González Rodríguez, Luis. 1984. *Crónicas de la Sierra Tarahumara.* México: Secretaría de Educación Pública.

Gossen, Gary H. 1979. *Los chamulas en el mundo del Sol.* México: Instituto Nacional Indigenista.

Holland, William R. 1963. *Medicina maya de los Altos de Chiapas: Un estudio del cambio sociocultural.* México: Instituto Nacional Indigenista.

Hollenbach, Elena E. de. 1977. "El origen del Sol y de la Luna: Cuatro versiones en el trique de Copala." *Tlalocan* 7:123–70.

Horcasitas, Fernando. 1953. "The Analysis of the Deluge Myth in Mesoamerica." Master's thesis. Mexico: Mexico City College.

Ichon, Alain. 1973. *La religión de los totonacas de la sierra.* México: Instituto Nacional Indigenista.

Jiménez Suárez, Maximiliana, Abel Eduardo Castillo Valtierra, Ezequiel Navarrete Arellano y Gregoriomiranda. 1994. *Historias del pueblo cora.* Tepic, s/e.

Latorre, Felipe A., and Dolores L. Latorre. 1991. *The Mexican Kickapoo Indians.* New York: Dover Publications.

Leyenda de los soles. In *Código Chimalpopoca,* 119–64. Translated by Primo Feliciano Velázquez. Mexico: Universidad Nacional Autónoma de México, Instituto de Historia, 1945.

López Austin, Alfredo. 1990. *Los mitos del tlacuache: Caminos de la mitología mesoamericana.* México: Alianza Editorial, 1990. [English: *The myths of the opossum: Pathways of Mesoamerican mythology,* translated by Bernardo Ortiz de Montellano and Thelma Ortiz de Montellano (Albuquerque: University of New Mexico Press, 1993).]

———. 1994. *Tamoanchan y Tlalocan.* México: Fondo de Cultura Económica.

———. In press. "Homshuk: Análisis temático del relato." *Anales de Antropología* 29.

Madsen, William. 1955. "Hot and Cold in the Universe of San Francisco Tecospa: Valley of Mexico." *Journal of American Folklore* 68:123–39.

———. 1960. *The Virgin's Children: Life in an Aztec village today.* Austin: University of Texas Press.

Merrill, William L. 1992. *Almas rarámuris.* México: Consejo Nacional para la Cultura y las Artes e Instituto Nacional Indigenista.

Morales Bermúdez, Jesús. 1984. *On O T'ian, antigua palabra: Narrativa indígena chol.* México: Universidad Autónoma Metropolitana.

Münch Galindo, Guido. 1983. *Etnología del Istmo Veracruzano.* México: Universidad Nacional Autónoma de México, Instituto de Investigaciones Antropológicas.

Navarrete, Carlos. 1968. *Oraciones a la cruz y al Diablo: Oraciones populares de la depresión central de Chiapas.* México: Escuela Nacional de Antropología e Historia, Sociedad de Alumnos.

Ochoa Zazueta, Jesús Ángel. 1982. *Baja California: Socio-lingüística de la comunidad indígena.* Los Mochis, Sinaloa: Universidad de Occidente.

Olavarría, Ma. Eugenia. 1990. *Análisis estructural de la mitología yaqui.* México: Instituto Nacional de Antropología e Historia y Universidad Autónoma Metropolitana.

Popol vuh: Las antiguas historias del Quiché. Translated by Adrián Recinos. México: Fondo de Cultura Económica, 1964.

Portal, María Ana. 1986. *Cuentos y mitos en una zona mazateca.* México: Instituto Nacional de Antropología e Historia.

Preuss, Konrad T. 1982. *Mitos y cuentos nahuas de la Sierra Madre Occidental.* México: Instituto Nacional Indigenista.

Ramírez Castañeda, Elisa. 1987. *El fin de los montiocs: Tradición oral de los huaves de San Mateo del Mar, Oaxaca.* México: Instituto Nacional de Antropología e Historia.

Relatos, mitos y leyendas de la Chinantla. Documented by Roberto J. Weit-laner; María Sara Molinari, María Luisa Acevedo and Marlene Aguayo Alfaro (selection, introduction and notes). México: Instituto Nacional Indigenista, 1981.

Schumann G., Otto. 1993. "De cómo el venado se hizo de los cuernos del conejo." *Antropológicas: nueva época* 5 (January): 2nd meeting.

Seis versiones del Diluvio. México: SEP-Dirección General de Culturas Populares, 1983.

Villa Rojas, Alfonso. 1978. *Los elegidos de Dios: Etnografía de los mayas de Quintana Roo.* México: Instituto Nacional Indigenista.

Zingg, Robert M. 1982. *Los huicholes: Una tribu de artistas.* Vol. 2. México: Instituto Nacional Indigenista.

3

Ritual and Myth in
Tlapanec Life

Peter L. van der Loo

The following article on aspects of religion of the Tlapanec people of Guerrero is the result of fieldwork and visits to the Tlapanec area from 1979 to 1995, especially the village of Malinaltepec (see fig. 2).[1] The longest period of fieldwork spanned more than two years; the shortest was a visit of just a few days. Over that period the perspective of the author has changed from academic interest to the perspective of someone with friends and a place to go in a village where the vagaries of life had brought him. Consequently, the academic reasons why he originally came to that village have become of secondary importance.

Parts of the following descriptions are written in the first person in violation of the general academic custom. The first reason for that format is the change in attitude alluded to above. The second reason is the fact that the author (Dutch himself) wants to keep his audience (you) aware that the depictions below were documented not by a Tlapanec, not by an omniscient observer, but by a well-informed outsider who must take the responsibility for any inaccuracies. Yet this article has become possible through the kind help of many Tlapanec people, especially don Félix Ramírez Cantú and don Felipe Chávez Poblano.

The Tlapanec live in Mexico in the northeastern mountains of the state of Guerrero, on the border of Oaxaca (see fig. 1). Tlapanec is an

---

[1] The Tlapanec name of Malinaltepec is *Muñawiin*, which means "at the river."

Otomangue language spoken by a majority of the population with many monolingual speakers in the age group over sixty. The Tlapanecs are a Mesoamerican people with cultural features typical of the area. As with all surviving indigenous Mesoamerican peoples, their traditional religion has been influenced strongly by Roman Catholic beliefs. The result is a religion that shows a mixture of the theology, mythology, and ritualism of both religions resting on the basis of a clearly native worldview. The Tlapanec religious functionaries are aware of this mixture and manage it according to the needs of the situation. For instance, they may invoke the rain god by his Spanish saint's name (San Marcos) or by his Tlapanec name (Wi'ku), depending on what they think their audience prefers. The boundaries between the two spheres are flexible. Even though a certain ritual may be labeled as traditional and always be performed away from the church, it may still include the invocation of Catholic saints. To most Tlapanecs, unless pressed by missionaries or Roman Catholic priests, the division is not of great importance. Especially in the areas of healing, hunting, agriculture, and marriage, the native rituals remain of utmost importance. This does not preclude the fact

Fig. 1.

2

3

Fig. 2. Malinaltepec, January 1980. Looking South.

Fig. 3. *Codex Borgia*, p. 27. The rain god is divided over cardinal points and time, each one with its own prognostication.

4　　　　　　　　　　5

Fig. 4. Félix Ramírez C. is ready to start a ritual against evil. In the bowl are bundles, flower chains, eggs, and copal (incense).

Fig. 5. The bundles of 6 and 9 have been placed in a rectangle. The other bundles will be placed within it or on top of it.

Fig. 6. Felipe Chávez Poblano counts bundles in a healing ritual.

6

7

8

Fig. 7. The Ndikaa Wi'ku on his way with his helpers to perform the ritual for rain god.

Fig. 8. The bundles for Wi'ku are cut and counted.

9

10

Fig. 9. The flower chains for Wi'ku are counted.

Fig. 10. The *tecorale* for Wi'ku on the mountain top.

that most Tlapanecs, if asked to what religion they belong, would answer immediately, "We are Catholics."

An interesting feature in Tlapanec traditional religion that is no longer commonly found in Mesoamerica is the performance of rituals in which pieces of reed, sticks, or long pine needles are counted out and bundled in specific numbers and put down according to prescribed patterns to achieve the rituals' goals. We find these rituals also in some of the pre-Columbian pictorial manuscripts, specifically the codices Cospi, Fejérváry-Mayer, and Laud. We will give special attention to those types of rituals as we look at a selection of myths and rituals in the religious practices and beliefs of the Tlapanecs of Malinaltepec.

First we will examine some of the beliefs concerning the origin of people, and especially of the Tlapanec. One story asserts that humans were created in "Seas 13 and 14," a mythical place where all larger animals come from and also important spirits both good and evil. Seas 13 and 14 are an interesting concept that I have encountered only among the Tlapanecs. When I asked where those seas are located, the answer was usually a vague gesture to the south, where, of course, the Pacific Ocean is. However, Seas 13 and 14 are not equivalent to or simply part of the Pacific, but rather spiritual sea entities that produced life at the beginning of time and continue as the home from which certain spirits come and to which particularly evil spirits can be forced to return through the performance of ritual. There seems to be a connection with the Mesoamerican concept of a layered world (as shown, for instance, in *Codex Vaticanus* 3738, an early colonial manuscript), in which there are thirteen layers of upper world with the two highest levels occupied by important creative forces. Those two upper layers are heavens numbers 12 and 13.

Given the division of the Mesoamerican calendar in a round of 13 times 20 days, the number 13 commonly appears to indicate fullness and completion. Why then do the Tlapanecs use a number 14? The partial answer may lie in the historically documented use of the Mesoamerican calendar by the Tlapanecs. A sixteenth-century Tlapanec codex, *Codex Azoyú*, uses in its calendar numbers from 2 to 14 rather than 1 to 13. According to some scholars, this feature ties the Tlapanec calendar to Teotihuacán.[2] Whatever the case may be, it is

---

[2] See Edmonson's introduction (p. 13) to Vega Sosa 1991.

important for us that the numbers 13 and 14 in the Tlapanec tradition correspond to 12 and 13 in general Mesoamerican tradition. Consequently, it is reasonable to assume that the levels 12 and 13 of the heavens, correspond to the Seas 13 and 14 of the present-day Tlapanec. The function is similar: In *Codex Vaticanus* 3738, the upper celestial layer is comprised of both levels 12 and 13.[3] In a similar way, we see that Seas 13 and 14 are always mentioned together. In *Codex Vaticanus* 3738, the upper level is a place of creation, where the god of duality resides. Also among the Tlapanecs, Seas 13 and 14 are places of creation that possess a duality in the sense that both good and evil arise from them. This particular tradition concerning creation places humans as one group among the more important living beings who populate the earth and asserts their provenance from a place of duality that carries both good and evil.

In Mesoamerica, as in many other traditions, we commonly find more than one mythical theme that is concerned with the creation of humans. The Tlapanec are no exception. The following myth tells about the creation of humans after the world had been destroyed by a flood.

> After the flood there was only one man left and his white she-dog. The man had to work very hard—first on the land to grow corn and other food and then, when he came home, to do all the housework and prepare the food. The little dog felt very sorry for her master and asked the Sun to change her into a woman. The sun agreed and during the day, while the man was away she took off her dog skin and became a beautiful woman. From then on, when the man came home in the evening he would find the house clean and warm tortillas ready, but there wouldn't be a human around, just his little dog. After a while the man became so curious that he sneaked back to his house in the middle of the day to see who did the house work. There he saw a beautiful young woman sweeping the floor and grinding the corn for tortillas. When she was done with her work, well before the hour that he usually would come home, she took the white skin of a dog from a hiding place in a jar. She put it on, and behold, she changed back into his little white dog.
>
> This went on for several weeks, then the man decided that he would try and keep the woman from changing back into a dog. He sneaked home again during the day, took the skin from its hiding

---

[3] For further discussion of the levels of heaven and earth in Mesoamerica, see López Austin 1984, 61 ff.

place and burned it while the woman had gone to the river to fetch water. When she came home she started to cry over what he had done because now she could not change back into a dog anymore. He explained that was exactly what he wanted, because he wanted her to be his wife. This idea was attractive to her, so they lived very content as wife and husband and became the mother and father of all Tlapanecs and also of all other people in the world.[4]

This myth begins with reference to a flood that destroyed the world. In the present-day Tlapanec religious understanding this flood is usually equated with the Old Testament flood. On a historic level it is probably the remnant of a typical Mesoamerican myth of the creation of the world in different stages, where subsequent worlds are created and destroyed, each leaving its particular inheritance to the next one. The fact that humans were born from a human who was married to a dog is a common theme throughout the Native Americas. It gives a more direct etiological explanation for the existence of humans, while at the same time also placing them in intimate relationship with other important living beings. This last aspect is similar to the assertion of the theme concerning Seas 13 and 14.

A third theme has more to do with the physical presence of the Tlapanecs in their homeland. Often Tlapanec people have affirmed to me that the earth of their land is red because of all the Tlapanec blood that has flowed on it, while conversely, their blood is so red because it is nourished by that same red earth. One man illustrated his statement by pouring some *pulque* (a sacred drink; see below) on the ground. Pointing at the resulting red mud, he said, "That is our blood."

The Tlapanec tradition tells that the first inhabitants of what is now their homeland came there by long travel first through great woods and then for long stretches underground. They came up in several places, but finally chose their present homeland after a struggle with earlier inhabitants.

This mythical theme may remind the reader of the Old Testament wandering of the Jewish people. However, it is also a common theme in Mesoamerica. In the Aztec tradition of wandering, the "Place of the Seven Caves" is important for the origin of different ethnic entities. The Tlapanec story does not mention the origin of different

---

[4] Told by Félix Ramírez Cantú, December 1979.

groups in caves but does stress the fact of underground travel to reach their homeland. It is interesting that this migration is not put in a mythical beginning of time, but in actual historical time. When asked for an estimate of how long ago the migration occurred, those who would venture a guess put it around five hundred to six hundred years ago. This theme and its related issues place the Tlapanec people firmly and rightfully on their land, with which they have an intimate, mutually nurturing relationship.

In their cosmogonic myths, the Tlapanecs preserve a tradition concerning the origin of the sun and the moon that contains several Mesoamerican themes. In the Tlapanec myth an old woman found two eggs in the field. She took care of them until they produced two little boys, whom she brought up as her children. The two boys grew up very rapidly and involved themselves in mischief. First, they made a terrible disorder out of the weaving tools and materials of the old woman. Later they killed the deer who was her husband and to whom she used to bring food daily. The boys stuffed the skin of the dead deer with bees. When the old woman came with her husband's food she became very angry with him because he wouldn't talk to her. Finally she hit him, which set off the bees who stung her terribly. She made it home in great pain, where the boys prepared the first sweat bath for her. But instead of letting her just cure herself in the bath, the boys blocked the entrance of the bath and killed her with the heat, promising that because of her death she would become the goddess of the sweat bath. From then on, all people using the sweat bath must pay homage to her. We shall continue the story, slightly abbreviated, in the words of Mr. Félix Ramírez Cantú.

> It was their task then, to go to a lake to kill a monster that lived in there. They slew the monster with their arrows. After that they had a race to pull out the eyes of the monster. He who acquired the right eye was to become the sun, the one with the left eye the moon.
>
> They continued their way until they came to a mountain so high that it reached to the sky. They started to climb and climb that mountain. Halfway up they noticed that the weather was turning bad and a tremendous storm was to be expected. So they hurried to build a firm shelter. While they were building, an old woman met up with them. She actually had hopes of becoming the sun or the moon. After hearing about the coming storm she too started building a shelter, but it wasn't as sturdy as the boys'. She asked them where they

were going, but they just said, "Oh, just looking around at what there is to be seen."

When the storm burst the boys were safe in their shelter, but the wind and rain destroyed the shelter of the old woman. Completely drenched she ran over to the boys and begged to be let in. They said, "Come on in." She came in and sat by the fire to warm up and to dry her clothes until she fell asleep.

When it was time to go, the Sun said, "Well Moon, let's go." But the Moon didn't want to leave yet.

"Stay if you want to, Moon," said the Sun, "I'm going."

The Moon answered, "Look at the old woman, she is half naked, I am going to do something bad to her."

"Do as you please, Moon, but I am going." The Sun left.

The Moon took two sharp stones and started shaving off all the pubic hair of the old woman, while the Sun went ahead. Then a sudden dawn with sun rays streaming over the mountain side took the Moon by surprise. The Moon said, "He has left me behind, but I will still follow."

The Sun was already high in the sky and the Moon had also risen from the top of the mountain, when the old woman finally woke up. When she saw that the boys had left her behind and what they had done to her, she started to curse them. She took the pile of hairs that the Moon had left behind and threw them up into the sky where they became the stars of the Pleiades.[5]

There are several Mesoamerican themes in this myth. The old woman who is stepmother to two boys who become the sun and the moon is common, and so is the fact that her husband is a deer who is killed by the boys. Interesting in the Tlapanec myth is the clear connection of the old woman with the art of weaving and the sweat bath. This identifies her as the Mesoamerican goddess we know as Tlazolteotl in the Nahuatl tradition. In the pictorial manuscripts of the so-called *Borgia Group* this goddess often appears in conjunction with the sweat bath, and some of her standard adornments are spinning spools worn in her headband.

Another common theme is that the moon stays behind because of some involvement that has to do with his sexual desires. In Mesoamerica the moon is often male and altogether too much of a Don Juan. In several traditions it is pointed out that he is pale

---

[5] Compiled from two versions of the myth told by Félix Ramírez Cantú in 1979 and 1984.

because of his many exhausting affairs, or, as in the case of the Tlapanecs, always late because of his pursuit of women.

When asked, the storyteller explained that the first old woman is
identified with the sweat bath, but that the second old woman is
entirely different from her and has no specific name. Even though
the second old woman does not become Sun or Moon, at least part
of her still gains a place among the celestial bodies.

In general, the elements of the story, with the two boys who
become Sun and Moon and the old woman who has a deer for a
husband, show that the Tlapanec people shared a fundamental
Mesoamerican view of the cosmos.

In many Mesoamerican cultures the opossum appears as a trickster and also as a culture hero. As a religious phenomenon, those two
are different sides of the same coin. They both tend to be active in
creating or acquiring certain important goods or customs, only the
trickster obtains the goods by accident or as the result of an error,
while the culture hero consciously acquires the goods. Among the
Tlapanec we find the opossum definitely in the role of culture hero
more than trickster. He actually gave the people fire, that most
important element providing light, heat, and cooked meals. He also
gave the people *pulque*, a very important sacred drink.

We will first look at the myth that concerns the acquisition of the
fire. The story contains references to "dead souls" and the Tlapanec
marriage ritual. We will further discuss those after the story.

> The people lived in darkness and ate everything raw, until somebody
> —we don't know his name—said there was fire on a high mountain
> peak guarded by seven tigers. The people tried to go to the place
> where the fire was, but the mountain was too steep. Nobody could
> climb it, and those who tried fell down into the river and drowned.
>
> Now, in those days all animals could speak, and the people said to
> the opossum, "Why don't you climb up that mountain, you can do it."
>
> "All right," said the opossum and he left. He went into the river
> and got himself completely wet. Then he climbed up the mountain,
> where the tigers saw him coming.
>
> "Ah, there comes meat, let's eat him," they said.
>
> "Hold on, hold on," said the opossum. "I am all wet, let me dry
> myself by the fire first, then you can eat me."
>
> "All right," said the tigers and they all sat down by the fire. Then
> the opossum put his tail in the fire and started swishing it back and

forth, which caused sparks and fire to land on the tigers. The sparks flew into their eyes and they started jumping around in anger and pain. The opossum grabbed the fire and ran down the mountain. Halfway down, he set the trees on the mountain slope on fire which caused the pursuing tigers to burn to death.

The opossum went to the people, who had already prepared four stacks of wood, which they lit with the fire the opossum gave them. All the people then gathered, bringing squash and beans and corn, which they put on the fire to cook. But some people were impatient and took the food out again before it was fully cooked. Eating that half-raw food caused many people to be sick and to die right there at the fire.

Now, when somebody cries or is very sad while looking at the fire, the souls of those dead will grab him, and he or she will be very ill. To satisfy those dead souls and to avoid the illness they might bring, we now perform the ritual of the burning of the firewood at a wedding.[6]

The "tigers" in the story are mountain lions or ocelots, which are often referred to in Mexican Spanish as *tigres*. The dead souls that remain in the fire are a major negative force in the Tlapanec worldview. In all rituals they are always remembered and receive an offering to be appeased.

"The Burning of the Firewood" is the name of the traditional Tlapanec wedding ritual. The burning of the wood appeases the dead souls that reside in the fire and is of the greatest importance when a new household is about to be set up. It is a complex ritual that takes long to prepare. In Malinaltepec it is usually done outside of the village on a remote spot. The specific reason to go to a hidden place is that the Roman Catholic priests used to forbid the performance of the ritual. Now finding a remote area for the ritual has become part of the tradition.

The families of the bride and groom gather on the specially prepared ground, each family on its own side of the center area where the firewood is placed. A religious specialist (*ndikaa wi'ku*) performs the ritual, which involves the counting out of many bundles of reed cut in approximately finger-length pieces. When part of the bundling is completed, the firewood is lit and the bride and groom kneel in the center of the ground in front of each other. The *ndikaa wi'ku* con-

---

[6] Told by Félix Ramírez Cantú, December 1979.

tinues the counting ritual and blesses the couple. Afterwards there is a great feast, where the families leave their assigned sides, mingle with each other, and exchange gifts to assure the continuation of good relationships between the families.[7]

This ritual is performed separately from the wedding in the Catholic church and will often take place at a much later date, in many cases not until one or more children have been born. Many consider the financial burden caused by the preparations and execution a problem. Nevertheless, it is one of the traditional rituals that is considered necessary by all. If the new couple experiences excessive health problems, or if the two families do not get along well, this ritual is considered the only remedy. Many have assured me that it is a very effective one.

Another myth involving the opossum concerns the acquisition of *pulque*. *Pulque* is a sacred drink prepared from the juice of the agave plant. The very sweet, clear juice is taken from the heart of the plant and allowed to ferment. The result is a lightly alcoholic drink that, in moderation, is very healthful and refreshing. For the Tlapanecs *pulque* is a sacred drink that can be enjoyed socially but always with the observance of some ritual. We know from pre-conquest pictorial manuscripts and early colonial sources that even then *pulque* was a sacred drink. Then as now it was to be enjoyed in moderation, because there were severe punishments for inebriation. Only old people were allowed to imbibe to their hearts' desire. In present scholarly thinking these strict rules concerning the use of *pulque* are often seen as an attempt to control what supposedly must have been a problem with excessive alcohol consumption in pre-conquest times. This may be the case, but it is also useful to look at it from another perspective, less functionalist and less based on reactions to problems that plague our Western societies. *Pulque*, as a sacred drink, establishes a contact with the world of spirits and gods. This contact may never be taken lightly, and if people enter that state of contact with the sacred world for purely frivolous reasons it may endanger the whole community in its relations to the spirit world. One clear example of this way of thinking in Mesoamerica can be found in the

---

[7] For a description of this ritual in Malinaltepec in the 1930s, see Schultze-Jena 1938, 149–51, 188–95. For a description of this ritual in the neighboring Tlapanec village of Tlacoapa in the 1970s, see Oettinger and Oettinger 1975.

reports of the Mazatec healer María Sabina, who insisted that the frivolous use by outsiders polluted the power and the spirit of the hallucinogenic mushrooms she employed for her healing trance.[8]

Be that as it may, in present-day Tlapanec society drunkenness is a common social disease. As among so many colonized peoples, it is a reaction to the oppression, but it only leads to more suffering. Contrary to popular thinking, excessive drinking is not an accepted practice among Mesoamerican peoples in general or the Tlapanecs in particular. I have often heard the assertion that a good man "works hard and doesn't drink."

Apart from this there are ritual customs that need to be taken into account. Religious specialists will ritually become inebriated on certain occasions, as, for instance, during the great ritual for rain, which we will discuss later. Inebriation still carries an aura of sacrality, even if done too often and inappropriately. People will treat an intoxicated person with care, even if the person will be scolded later. Drunkenness is usually achieved with beer and distilled liquor, not with the far less potent *pulque*.

Let's now look at the myth concerning the acquisition of *pulque* and, after some commentary, at the ritual way of consuming this sacred drink.

One day the people wanted to have a feast, but they didn't have water that inebriates.

"Where are we going to find water that inebriates?" they asked.

"Well," said Mr. Opossum—in those days all animals could speak— "I know where to find water that inebriates." He knew that San Marcos [the Christian name for the rain god] and his wife had seven pots with drinks somewhere on a mountain. They had *pulque* and *chicha* and *aguardiente* and Don Pedro [brand name of a Mexican brandy] and who knows what else.

Mr. Opossum showed the people where the pots were and he appointed seven men. "You, you and you, go and bring the pots with the drinks." That's what they did and there was a huge feast, but afterwards many people died, they had a bad drunkenness.

"I know what happened," said Mr. Opossum. "Four days from now it will be my feast." The opossum knew that San Marcos was angry because he didn't know who had stolen the drinks.

"Now I go," said Mr. Opossum. He went to the first pot, opened

---

[8] See Estrada 1977, e.g., chap. 18.

it just a little bit and drank with a straw until his stomach was completely filled. He went back to the people and deposited it all in a pot.
He did the same with the second pot and the third and so on until
the seventh.

Then his feast began. He said, "The people died because they did
not ask permission from Holy Mother Earth, San Marcos' wife. You
should know that *pulque* is her milk. That is why we must first ask permission from Holy Mother Earth when we drink pulque.

Thus we were taught by Mr. Opossum.[9]

It is clear, especially at the end of the myth, that the actual concern is about *pulque* and not so much about the other alcoholic
drinks. The storyteller added those into the beginning to account for
their existence. The San Marcos mentioned in the story is the rain
god. His Tlapanec name is Wi'ku. The story clearly stresses that
pulque must be drunk with the correct ritual observances, because
people will suffer dire consequences otherwise.

My first encounter with this ritual was an interesting lesson for a
foreigner. I hadn't been in Malinaltepec very long when, returning
from bathing in the river, I saw a group of men standing in a circle,
drinking something. When I passed by, they invited me over and
asked if I wanted some *pulque*. I accepted and one of the men
handed me a plastic bowl that must have contained approximately a
third of a liter. This seemed a bit much to me, but by the etiquette
that I was brought up with, I felt I had to finish what was offered
to me. With long gulps I emptied the bowl. This caused great laugh-
ter and an old man patted me on the shoulder and said, "You cer-
tainly know how to drink, son. That must be why you're so tall." I
soon found out what a big mistake I had made, but nobody was
angry or explained to me what was wrong. Simply by observing I
soon learned the correct manner of drinking *pulque* in Malinaltepec, which is as follows.

The men stand in a circle and one of them purchases a bowl of
pulque from the vendor. The one who bought the *pulque* is also the
first to drink, unless he wants to pass his right, as a sign of esteem,
to the man on his left. Whichever the case, the first man to drink
pours out a libation to María Santísima (the same as Holy Mother
Earth) before actually drinking. The one pouring the libation must
also drink first. The bowl is handed around the circle; each man

---

[9] Told by Primitivo Ramírez, April 1984.

drinks and usually the bowl is empty when returning to the first drinker.

Pouring the libation in the beginning is done solemnly. The perpetrator prays silently, and one only hears four times "María Santísima," while he drops a little bit of *pulque* on the earth. Then he says, "Let's drink," immediately followed by, "I am going to drink in the presence of all of you." After drinking he hands the bowl to the left and says, "Accept this and drink, sir." The next man accepts with the words, "Thanks to God, for what you have given me." These phrases are repeated with the exception of the very first ones, until the bowl has made its way through the circle. The last man gives the empty bowl back to the first one saying, "Here is your bowl, sir." While the drinking goes on the men talk, sometimes seriously, sometimes lightheartedly, but the formal ritual sentences and gestures are repeated without fail.

The ritual for drinking *pulque* in Malinaltepec undoubtedly shows an old traditional way to enjoy the drink while curtailing some of its potential dangers. The sentence said by all, "I drink in your presence," tells all present that they are expected to accept a responsibility for each other's well-being during the drinking. At least, possible inebriation is placed within a sacred context, which is not the case with other alcoholic beverages.

We referred above to the Tlapanec rituals with counted sticks or other objects. In those rituals the *ndikaa wi'ku* carefully counts out bundles of pine needles, sticks, or cut pieces of reed (see fig. 6). The numbers used for the bundles all have a specific meaning, but that meaning can change from one *ndikaa wi'ku* to another. The tradition of this bundle making is also in evidence among other Meosamerican peoples, especially the Mixe and the Tequistlatecs, both in the state of Oaxaca. It is also shown in pre-conquest manuscripts, namely, in the *Codex Fejérváry-Mayer, Codex Laud,* and *Codex Cospi.*[10] As can be seen in fig. 11, in the codices the bundles are placed in a pattern. The Tlapanecs will also often use a pattern in which four bundles of six and four bundles of nine are put in the corners of the offering area. These are the bundles that are offered to placate any evil forces,

---

[10] For a further comparison of bundle rituals in the codices and among the present-day Tlapanecs, see van der Loo 1982; Anders, Jansen, and van der Loo 1994, 289–330.

so that the actual offering that is placed within the rectangular area formed by the sixes and nines can serve its function undisturbed (see figs. 4 and 5).

For instance, in a ritual to protect and augment one's livestock the following bundles are used:

2 bundles of 14	for the Seas 14
2 bundles of 13	for the Seas 13
2 bundles of 12	to complete the offering
2 bundles of 11	to complete the offering
2 bundles of 10	to complete the offering
4 bundles of 9	for the souls without faith
4 bundles of 6	to ward off evil

The "souls without faith" are a large group of malevolent souls that include the "dead souls" we saw before in the myth about the acquisition of fire. Other groups of souls in this category are those who died in the mountains, fell into ravines, or drowned. They are malevolent because there is nobody to take care of them, and they must be placated to prevent them from doing harm. We have also seen Seas 13 and 14 before when discussing creation. It is appropriate that the offering be directed at these entities because livestock originates from those places.

The numbers 10 through 12 serve as a completion. When asked, the *ndikaa wi'ku* explained that one could think of it as a staircase that must be climbed to reach the important numbers, which in this case are 13 and 14.

The placement of the bundles corresponds to the general pattern described above. The sixes and nines are placed in a rectangular pattern, the other bundles are then placed in a row within the area that has thus been formed (see fig. 12).

This particular ritual is performed in the mountains at a so-called Green Cross, which is a tree that grows in a more or less crosslike form with the arms of the cross pointing approximately north to south. The performer of the ritual stands facing east in front of the cross and first places chains made out of cotton string with flowers tied into them on the tree. On each arm of the cross a chain of 150 flowers is hung. At the east side of the cross a chain of 69 is placed on the ground. The number 150 belongs to "the Father the Son and the Holy Spirit." The number 69 again serves to ward of evil influences. In addition, a turkey egg and a chicken egg are buried under

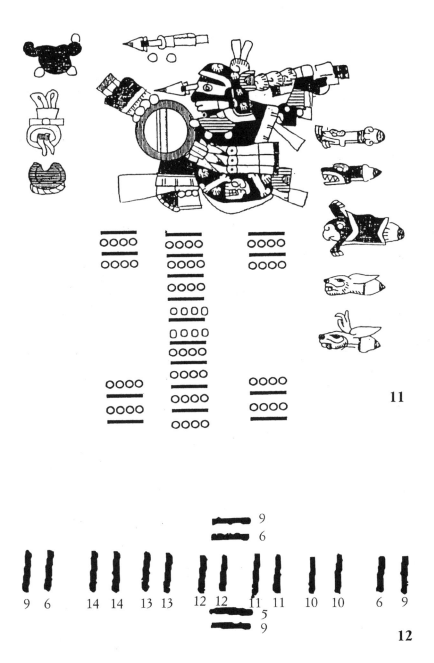

Fig. 11. *Codex Cospi*, p. 30. The black Tezcatlipoca appears with an offering of counted bundles. The number in all bundles is 9 (a bar equals 5, a dot equals 1.

Fig. 12. The pattern of the bundles in a ritual at a "Green Cross."

each arm of the cross. The favorite days for this ritual are Wednes-
days and Saturdays. It is considered especially auspicious to ward off
or heal any illness of livestock.

Perhaps the most important ritual with counted bundles is the ritual for the rain god. It is performed on the eve of April 25, lasting
through much of the night. The preferred locations are on a mountaintop or in a cave. In Mesoamerica in general, high mountains are
thought of as the abode and water reservoir of the rain god. This is
also true in the Tlapanec tradition, where the rain god can be
addressed by his Tlapanec name, Wi'ku, or by the saint's name he has
acquired, San Marcos. Probably he received this name because the
feast day of St. Mark in the Catholic calendar is the April 25. In rural
western European traditions St. Mark is petitioned at that time for a
good growing season. Undoubtedly, the Tlapanecs combined the two
because of the similarity in associated date and function between that
saint and their rain god. The ritual for Wi'ku could then be presented
to the Catholic priests as an offering to St. Mark.

The Tlapanec myth about the origin of Wi'ku/San Marcos is as
follows:

> An old woman was married to Fire, but they had no children. One
> day the old woman found four little children in the field. The couple
> brought these four little boys up as their own.
>
> Fire had a very powerful sister, she could grab anything she
> wanted. Fire wished to limit the power of his sister and he also
> wanted to give something of it to his sons. He went to his sister and
> asked what it was that made her so powerful. She explained that her
> secret was that she could grab anything with her fiery tongue. She
> showed how she could reach out with her tongue and make things
> catch fire, thus making them hers. Fire asked her to demonstrate once
> again. When she did, he pulled out his machete and chopped off her
> tongue. She was furious, but he said that he wanted to limit her power
> because she used it for evil purposes. He said that from then on peo-
> ple would bring her offerings, for the sacrifice she had made, but her
> powers had come to an end.
>
> At home, he cut the tongue in four pieces and gave one piece to
> each of his sons. These four pieces of tongue changed into four pow-
> erful weapons, which they could use to fly.
>
> Of the four children one is jealous and wants to do harm, the other
> three are benevolent. The three benevolent ones make rain in a quiet

useful way, but the fourth makes rainstorms with thunder and lightning. Each of the four lives in one of the cardinal points, but we don't
know where the malevolent one lives.[11]

The division of the deity into four entities over the four cardinal
points is typically Mesoamerican. The pre-conquest *Codex Borgia*
shows on its page 27 the division of the rain god over the cardinal
points with different colors, time periods, and predictions for each
particular aspect of the deity (see fig. 3).

The sister of Fire is an old woman, who in Tlapanec has a name
that can be translated as "First Old Devouring Woman." She is
thought of as an aquatic monster somewhat similar to the crocodile.
When one hears this myth in Malinaltepec in the late twentieth century, it is interesting to see the theme depicted in the pre-conquest
Codex Fejérváry-Mayer. On page 4 of the codex the rain god appears,
standing on the back of a scaly water monster, holding the fiery
tongue that protrudes from the monster's mouth (see fig. 13).

In this myth Rain is the son(s) of Fire. There is another Tlapanec
myth in which Fire appears as the son-in-law of rain. To me as a foreign observer this seemed a glaring inconsistency when I first heard
the two stories. I asked a *ndikaa wi'ku* if we were still talking about
the same Rain, or if there were different rain deities. His answer was
a shrug of the shoulders and a dry, "it's the same Rain, but another
story." This simple occurrence showed me that religious stories are
not necessarily concerned with consistency—something I had been
taught before, but had never sufficiently realized. Religious stories are
concerned with the why and how of our existence. This is also the
case with the two myths involved here. The one told here about the
origin of the rain deity explains the power and ambivalence of Wi'ku,
who by coming or staying away dictates abundance or starvation for
the people.

The ritual on April 24 is performed in an attempt to ensure the
coming of the rain. It takes place on the highest mountaintop in the
surroundings of Malinaltepec, La Lucerna, which is a brisk five-hour
march from the village. A *ndikaa wi'ku* ascends the peak with helpers
and a group of people who want to attend the ceremony, and per-

---

[11] Told in Tlapanec by Felipe Chávez Poblano and translated by Félix Ramírez
Cantú into Spanish, January 1980.

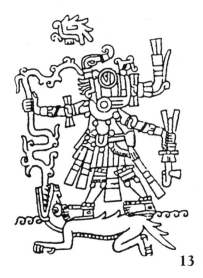

Fig. 13. Codex Fejérváry-Mayer, p. 4.
The rain god stands on a water-
monster, holding its fiery tongue.

forms the ritual known simply as "pray to Saint Mark," or "ask for
the water" (see fig. 7) They leave on the 24th, stay overnight for the
ceremony and come back in the morning of the 25th.

In 1984 I was allowed to participate in this short pilgrimage.[12] To
obtain permission I had to petition the mayordomo in charge of organizing the ceremony.[13] He chooses the right ndikaa wi'ku and super-
vises the gathering of materials necessary for the ritual. He also can
grant or deny any person permission to attend the ceremony. He
must make sure that nobody will go with intentions that may bring
harm to the community in the crucial matter of the season's rain.

The mayordomo, on granting his permission, imposed rules and
regulations on me accordingly: I had to follow all the instructions of
the ndikaa wi'ku; any malevolent act on my part could endanger the
village and would be dealt with accordingly. I had to do my share in
carrying supplies. I had to promise never to use any knowledge
acquired on the trip in a harmful way. The "acquired knowledge"
was not simply witnessing the ritual but also the possible knowledge
that might come to me through dreams or visions while being in a
place of great sacredness at its most sacred time.

We arrived at the top of La Lucerna in the late afternoon, and the
whole group immediately went to work on the preparations for the

---

[12] For a more detailed description, see van der Loo 1991.
[13] For a description of the mayordomías in the Tlapanec area, see Dehouve 1990.

ceremony. Reed that had been brought up was cut in finger length pieces, counted out in the right numbers and bundled (see fig. 8). The chains of flowers were made and also counted out and cut in prescribed numbers (see fig. 9). The place, or *tecorale*, where the offerings were to be put down was carefully cleared out (see fig. 10). A *tecorale* is an area formed by stones piled up in the form of a horseshoe, creating an area within the horseshoe used for placing offerings. *Tecorales* can be of different sizes; the one for Wi'ku is quite large with a diameter of approximately four meters. It also has a large wooden cross in it.

The *ndikaa wi'ku* started with preliminary prayers before nightfall, but the actual ritual did not start until it was dark, at approximately 19:30. With intermissions it lasted until 3:30. During this time the *ndikaa wi'ku* put down the bundles, placed the chains, and put with the bundles eggs, bottles of liquor, and cigarettes, some of them personal gifts to Wi'ku from specific villagers. A turkey was killed and its blood was sprayed on the bundles. The *ndikaa wi'ku* and his helpers then stood by the offering reciting prayers while the *ndikaa wi'ku* drank with Wi'ku. This means that he took regular drinks of an alcoholic beverage, but for each of his drinks he poured a greater amount on the ground as an offering to Wi'ku. The purpose is to out-drink Wi'ku and to convince the deity to bring good rain in the coming season.

The bundles used in this ritual are as follows.

4 bundles of 4	to complete the offering
4 bundles of 6	to ward of evil
4 bundles of 7	for the souls of the living people
4 bundles of 8	as thanksgiving
4 bundles of 9	for the souls without faith
4 bundles of 12	for the help of a good spirit
4 bundles of 13	for the help of a good spirit
4 bundles of 14	for the help of a good spirit
4 bundles of 24	for Fire
4 bundles of 50	to defend ourselves
4 bundles of 53	against enemies
4 bundles of 69	for Lady Seven Corn Plants, who lives in the Seas 13 and 14
4 bundles of 169	for the village
4 bundles of 269	for the whole world and its propagation

The bundles are put down in accordance with the model previously described. The meaning of the numbers we have seen before speaks for itself. Comparing the numbers with previously described rituals clearly demonstrates that numbers can have different meanings in different ceremonies.

Fire appears again in this ritual for Wi'ku. This is not surprising, because Fire is considered a necessary presence at any ritual. For that reason Fire will often receive his own number (24 is common, but not exclusive) and bundles within the ritual itself.

Lady Seven Corn Plants is a supernatural woman from the Seas 13 and 14. The following myth is about her.

> She fell in love with a human man and lived with him in this world. Whenever she went to the cornfield, she would just walk through and when she came out her basket would be filled with corn. The people liked her very much, but her husband became jealous and did not treat her right. As a result, she left and returned to the Seas 13 and 14, and now it is hard work to grow and gather corn.

Even though she has returned to her home, this corn woman must be petitioned as part of the rain ritual, so that she will provide healthy corn at harvest time.

After the turkey had been sacrificed, it was cooked and shared by all those who had come to attend the ritual. The atmosphere at the campfire, a little away from the *tecorale* took on a festive note. At times only the *ndikaa wi'ku*, his helpers, and the curious foreigner were standing at the place of ceremony. All the others had gathered around the campfire, singing, eating, and drinking.

Early the next morning the group descended to the village, tired but in good spirits. When we returned many people asked me if I "had dreamt anything while up there." I had to disappoint them. I didn't seem to remember any extraordinary dream. The common response was, "Well, maybe you will remember later." All the participants in the ritual, including me, were congratulated on a job well done; we had gained some status in the community.

The rainy season should start a little over a month after the ritual, but rain on May 15th is a preliminary sign of a good season to come. On that day in 1984 there was a day-long downpour that shorted out the electricity that had just been installed in the village. All around, however, there were happy shouts and smiles of great expectation.

Obviously there is much more to Tlapanec religion than can be dealt with in this one article. There are issues of continuity of tradition, religious change, religious and social oppression, discrimination against the Tlapanec people for being Indians with an Indian religion, and many other issues that were only hinted at here. I intended to present a picture that shows myths, beliefs, and rituals that are very much alive in Malinaltepec now and that do not show signs of being forgotten any time soon. To provide a balance I chose private functions, such as the petition for livestock, and public ones, such as the ceremony for Wi'ku.

Malinaltepec is changing—the electricity has been reinstalled and on the roofs of many adobe dwellings sit satellite antennas. During my last visit, the youngest daughter of my friend Félix Ramírez Cantú looked open-mouthed at the television where a terrifying vampire on roller blades cruised through the New York City night looking for victims. Nodding toward the little girl, I asked don Félix what he thought of the changes that indubitably are coming to Malinaltepec. He thought and said, "New things are coming, but this here is Tlapanec land and as long as we are Tlapanecs we will ask Wi'ku for rain for our crops, and we will burn the firewood for the health of our families."

References

Anders, Ferdinand, Maarten Jansen, and Luis Reyes García. 1993. *Los Templos del Cielo y de la Oscuridad: Códice Borgia.* Akademische Druck- und Verlagsanstalt, Austria, and Fondo de Cultura Económica, Mexico, and Sociedad Estatal Quinto Centenario, Spain.

Anders, Ferdinand, Maarten Jansen, and Peter van der Loo. 1994. *Calendario de Pronósticos y Ofrendas: Códice Cospi.* Akademische Druck- und Verlagsanstalt, Austria, and Fondo de Cultura Económica, Mexico.

Anders, Ferdinand, and Maarten Jansen. 1994. *La Pintura de la Muerte y de los Destinos: Códice Laud.* Akademische Druck- und Verlagsanstalt, Austria, and Fondo de Cultura Económica, Mexico.

Anders, Ferdinand, Maarten Jansen, and Aurora Pérez Jiménez. 1994. *El Libro de Tezcatlipoca, Señor del Tiempo: Códice Fejérváry-Mayer.* Akademische Druck- und Verlagsanstalt, Austria, and Fondo de Cultura Económica, Mexico.

Carrasco, David. 1991. To Change Place: Aztec Ceremonial Landscapes. Niwot, Colo.: University Press of Colorado.

Carrasco, Pedro. 1960. "Pagan Rituals and Beliefs among the Chontal Indians of Oaxaca Mexico." Anthropological Records, vol. 20 no 3.

Codex Vaticanus 3738. 1979. Akademische Druck- und Verlagsanstalt, Austria.

Dehouve, Daniele. 1990. Quand les Banquiers Etaient des Saints. Paris: Centre National de la Recherche Scientifique.

Estrada, Alvaro. 1977. Vida de María Sabina, la sabia de los hongos. Siglo Veintiuno Editores, Mexico.

Loo, Peter L. van der. 1982. "Rituales con manojos contados en el grupo Borgia y entre los Tlapanecos de hoy día." In Los Indígenas de México en la época prehispánica y en la actualidad, edited by M. E. R. G. N. Janses and Th. J. J. Leyenaar, 232-43. Leiden: Rijksmuseum voor Volkenkunde.

————. 1987. Códices Costumbres Continuidad, un estudio de la religión mesoamericana. Leiden: Archeologisch Centrum Rijksuniversiteit Leiden.

————. 1991. "Vamos a Rezar a San Marcos: A Tlapanec Pilgrimage." In To Change Place: Aztec Ceremonial Landscapes, ed. David Carrasco. Niwot, Colo.: University Press of Colorado.

López Austin, Alfredo. 1984. Cuerpo Humano e Ideología. Universidad Nacional Autónoma de México, Mexico.

Oettinger, Marion. 1980. Una Comunidad Tlapaneca. Instituto Nacional Indigenista, Mexico.

Oettinger, Marion, and Patrica P. Oettinger. 1975. "The Burning of the Firewood Ceremony: Final Consecration of Marriage in the Tlapanec Community of Tlacoapa, Guerrero." Paper presented at the XIII mesa redonda de la Sociedad Mexicana de Antropología. Mexico.

Ruiz de Alarcón, Hernando. 1953 (1629). "Tratado de las supersticiones y costumbres gentílicas que oy viuen entre los indios naturales de esta nueva España, escrito en México año de 1629." In Tratado de las Idolatrías, by Jacinto de la Serna et al., 2:17-130. Mexico D.F.

Schultze-Jena, Leonard. 1938. "Bei den Azteken Mixteken und Tlapaneken der Sierra Madre del Sur." In Indiana, vol. 3. Jena.

Suarez, Jorge A. 1983. La Lengua Tlapaneca de Malinaltepec. Universidad Nacional Autónoma de México, Mexico.

Vega Sosa, Constanza. 1991. Códice Azoyú 1: El Reino de Tlachinollan. Fondo de Cultura Económica, Mexico.

4

Sacred Forces
of the Mayan Universe

Mercedes de la Garza

All cultural creations of the Maya are based on their religious concepts of the world and life. According to their beliefs, the entire universe originated from and is permeated by sacred energies that
appear in many forms, in diverse natural beings, and determine
events according to a temporal order. The Maya believe that the
supernaturals created the cosmos for a specific goal—the maintenance of their own existence by humans, who, distinguished from
other beings because of their consciousness, became the motor and
axis of the cosmos. To that end the Maya made ritual activity the center of their existence.

The Maya expressed their religious concepts through all of their
cultural creations, of which the most distinguished are their cities, art
(generally accompanied by text), and the codices,[1] as well as the
sacred myths or histories that were preserved in books written by the
Maya at the beginning of the colonial era in their own languages
using Latin characters.

Some of the historical and religious chapters of the colonial books
were copied from the ancient codices with the intent of preserving
religious customs and traditions—in other words, to maintain self-
identity in the face of a Western cultural invasion. These books were
written in the Mayan language, which is still spoken today, and

---

[1] The *Dresden, Madrid,* and *Paris* codices are the only ones that survived the
destruction carried out by the Spanish Friars in the so-called *autos de fe.* There may
exist another Maya codex—the *Grolier*—which has not yet been proved to be authentic and therefore is not considered here.

redacted with Latin characters. They contain the Maya's own version of their history, ideas, and beliefs, revealing their concepts of the world and life. Among them are legal historical documents written for the purpose of demonstrating to the Conquerors the Maya's legitimate possession of the territory, as well as ritual, historical, and mythological texts, which we refer to as "the sacred community books," written to be read during clandestine ceremonies performed to preserve tradition, customs, and beliefs as a form of "counter-evangelization."[2] The latter prove most useful for gaining an understanding of indigenous religious thought, and the most prominent books are the *Popol Vuh* of the Quiché, the *Memorial de Sololá* (Memoirs of Sololá) of the Cakchiquel, and the *Libros de Chilam Balam* (Books of Chilam Balam) of the Yucatec Maya.

The myths contained in the colonial books not only explain how the world began (cosmogony), but also why humans and other beings are the way they are, and why they follow a determined behavior. They also describe the history of the Mayan people as part of the same process, because, for the Maya, myths represent a living history, a true history, and not one of fiction. They represent their truth and orientation, which determine their behavior in this world because they explain the existence of humans and their place within the cosmos.

For these reasons the fundamental myths of creation and the structure of the universe survived among indigenous communities into modern times. In spite of the Spanish conquest, these cosmogonic myths of the pre-Hispanic period, having suffered only minor alterations, continue to be valid among the modern Maya. One is therefore led to think that if the essential elements of the myths could survive both the colonial period and the subsequent highly acculturative events, then they are probably from the preclassical period. Indeed, we do have sufficient evidence from the hieroglyphic inscriptions, art, and the codices, that permit us to understand if not the origin at least the antiquity of the fundamental religious concepts expressed by the Indians during the colonial epoch, which may also explain and help us to understand their significance.

The survival of pre-Hispanic Mayan religious concepts of the world and life is surprising since the Spanish colonial regime and

---

[2] De la Garza 1980, Prologue.

subsequent events brought on such great change. The remaining materials contain many specific explanations concerning the particular history of each group and the great conservative drive that, through various means, fueled the struggle against the Spanish imposition. But there is another, general explanation for the common universal structures of the religious phenomena. We found that, among all indigenous groups, those myths that describe their concern and the essential events affecting human life appear to have survived.

Considering this fact, the employment of a comparative method to examine the sources of the distinct epochs in order to understand Maya religion is fundamental to this study. The comparative method has been common practice in historical investigations of Maya culture for decades. Fortunately, it was also adopted by related disciplines. Today, for example, epigraphists maintain that comparative analyses between hieroglyphic texts from the classical period and such colonial books as the *Popol Vuh* have produced many important insights that would not have come to light using the technique of isolated inscription interpretation.[3]

On the other hand, a general knowledge of symbols and religious phenomena is essential for understanding any religion, as demonstrated by the comparative history and phenomenology of religions. Thus, these methods have become basic phases of our research.

The Preclassical Manifestations of Principal Mayan Religious Symbols

The analysis of symbols representing supernatural beings and forces in classical Mayan sculpture points us to similar motifs found in various sites in the highlands of Guatemala and Chiapas (especially in Izapa) that appear to have been produced in the preclassical period by non-Mayan peoples. Bordering the discussion of the ethnic identity of the creators of this culture, called the "Izapa Culture," their sculptures reveal without doubt an essential precursor to the religious symbols and ritual practices of the Maya of the classical and postclassical periods. We therefore included a brief summary of these representations.

---

[3] Freidel and Schele 1993, 60.

On the stelae from Izapa are various deity figures represented as bird-men and dragons;[4] a man or god within the jaws of a serpent or jaguar; the serpent god of rain, ax in hand; and people worshiping the gods. These were to become the principal motifs of Mayan art.

The dragon of the Izapa style is a fantastic animal. It is part serpent, bird, jaguar, tapir, lizard, and crocodile—all animals symbolizing the sacredness of the universe and the natural phenomena on which the human agriculturist depends for his material existence. Therefore, the dragon is found generally in the context of fertility, and later among the Maya the context is celestial, terrestrial, or aquatic.

Among those representations that we might consider precursors to the classical Mayan dragon are those depicted on stela 2: a diving being (head facing downward), with the body of a human, wings with the markings of St. Andrew's cross [X] (which would become a glyph representing the sky among the Maya), and a headpiece (helmet) in the form of a serpent (fig. 1). There is also a man paying homage to the celestial deity to one side of the world axis tree. On stela 21 we identify a human sacrifice (by decapitation) performed before a great god sitting on a palanquin (fig. 3). This type of sacrifice was the most common form among the classical Maya.[5]

Converging on stela 25 (fig. 2) are various essential symbols of Mayan religious thought: the bird-serpent, the terrestrial dragon, the *axis mundi*, and the human (attending to the gods) placed in the center of the cosmos. On the inferior portion of the stela is what may be the most ancient image of the terrestrial dragon, in the form of a crocodile, head pointing downward and body in a vertical position. It transforms into a tree, on which perches a bird. Completing this concept of the *axis mundi*, in the center of the stela there is a man standing over a rectangle (possibly a symbol of the terrestrial surface), supporting a mast over which is found a resting bird-serpent.

---

[4] The term "dragon" is derived from the Greek *drakōn*, "serpent," probably derived from the verb *derkomai*, which defines the intensity of a strong and paralyzing gaze of a serpent. *Drakōn* is the equivalent of an *ophis*, snake. Dragons were the malefic serpents in medieval European mythology, the fantastic serpent-beings of Persia and other areas of Asia Minor, and the benevolent gods of China and Japan, where they merged features of snake and bird. As such, "dragon" has been converted into a universal term and closely defines this Mesoamerican symbol. One of the more notable motifs is the feathered serpent found among the more important cultures of this region.

[5] Nájera 1987.

1

2

3

Fig. 1. Representation from
stela 2 of a divine being with
the body of a human, wings
with the markings of St.
Andrew's cross, and a headpiece in the form of a serpent.

Fig. 2. Various symbols of
Mayan religious thought from
stela 25: the bird-serpent, the
terrestrial dragon, the *axis
mundi*, and the human placed
in the center of the cosmos.

Fig. 3. Human sacrifice (by
decapitation) performed before
a great god sitting on a palanquin (stela 21).

As mentioned earlier, this bird is a precursor of the Mayan bird-serpent, while the tree-crocodile is the precursor of the terrestrial dragon, the great crocodile Itzam Cab Ain, symbolic image of the earth in Maya religion. The lizard, or terrestrial crocodile, also appears on stelae 6 and 11.

The man depicted on stela 25 as a being who stands in the center of the world and sustains his axis expresses the essential anthropocentric nature of Mesoamerican religion. Here the man is another *axis mundi*. Because of his consciousness and ability to enter diverse cosmic realms, he is the being who links everything else with the gods. Through his ritual and by virtue of his own vital energy (blood), he maintains the equilibrium and existence of the complete universe.

In Izapa we also find a possible precursor of the Mayan rain-god, Chaac, represented as a dragon wielding his lightning-ax before another gigantic dragon who has also the body of a serpent. They represent the sacred forces of cosmic fecundity in dialectic play, where the dragon of fertility also becomes the symbol of death, thereby symbolizing the dynamics between death and rebirth that govern the universe.

The Spatial-Temporal Cosmos[6]

The Maya are distinguished among ancient cultures for their profoundly original concepts of time and space, even though some aspects of these concepts coincide with those held by other ancient peoples—for example, the perception of time as the order of movement (shared by eastern peoples), the perception of time periods as cyclical (shared by the Hindus and Chinese), and the temporal order of the universe alternating between periods of chaos and stasis.

As in many religious traditions, the Maya consider time to be fundamentally linked to the Sun and sky. The passing of the Sun is perceived as a circular motion around the earth which determines changes of space; therefore, time is perceived as a cyclic motion. Rather than being an abstract concept, temporality is a clear and eternal dynamic of space that gives beings multiple and sometimes con-

---

[6] De la Garza (in press).

tradictory qualities. This movement is ordered and stable, as wit-nessed in the regularity of nature and human life. For the Maya, therefore, as for many other peoples, time is order and its absence is chaos.

The Mayan concepts of time and space are present in all of their beliefs and cultural creations, but principally in their prophetic and historic texts, calendrical and astronomical knowledge, and their cos-mogonic (origin of the cosmos) as well as cosmological (structure of the cosmos) myths.

Here I will limit the discussion of time-space concepts to cos-mogony and cosmology. I must state, however, that the mathemati-cal, astronomical, and chronological wisdom of the Maya is without doubt the most advanced among the ancient cultures. They were the first to invent the positional value of symbols and the use of the zero, and their solar calendar is the most exact that has been created. Its margin of error with respect to the "tropical year" is only 17.28 sec-onds.

According to Western and conventional theory, the mathematical, astronomical, and chronological knowledge of the Maya can be con-sidered an objective science. For its creators, however, these "sci-ences" are a mechanism with which to tie into the "sacred." Astral bodies and occurrences are divine energies that have influence over the world and humans, and this knowledge has as its goal to protect humans, to help them survive materially, and to anticipate their future. As such, this knowledge forms part of religion. The sacred forces generated during each period act either to the benefit or to the detriment of humans, but humans do not passively submit to these events. Because their movement is cyclic, knowing what has occurred in the past can be used to predict what is to come and to seek ways to ameliorate this destiny. Therefore, the scientific achievements imply a creative and free attitude toward the gods who have as their primary objective, the care of human destiny.[7]

Cosmogony

The Mayan cosmogonic myths that we can actually read are those found in the colonial indigenous texts, among which the most impor-

---

[7] De la Garza 1975.

tant are the *Popol Vuh* of the Quiché, the *Memorial de Sololá* of the Cakchiquel, and the *Libros de Chilam Balam* of the Yucatec Maya. However, in the codices and pre-Hispanic art we find both representations and texts that are in agreement with these myths and confirm their antiquity.

A comparative analysis of the myths contained in the colonial Mayan texts permits us to make a synthesis of Mayan cosmogony with which to identify their later expression in the art and codices. In general terms, the origin myths describe a process of creation and destruction; a chain of cycles or cosmic eras in which modern humanity and the world were formed. According to Mayan theory, the universe is being created and destroyed in a qualitative evolution, which implies that it is infinite.

The cosmogonic myth of origins of the Quiché from Guatemala[8] is the most complete of Mesoamerican texts. It describes the creator gods as situated over a primordial body of water, undifferentiated, and in a "static time" or moment of chaos. The gods decide to create the world so that a conscious being might inhabit therein and be charged with the duty of venerating and feeding the gods. Although the gods are given distinct names, they are all *Gucumatz,* "Quetzal Serpent," symbolizing the primordial water and "Heart of the Sky"— the center of origin or primordial site from which the cosmos would arise. Through the creative energy of the *word* the deities cause the land to emerge as well as the beings that would inhabit it. Through successive stages of creation and destruction, they create humans first from mud and then from wood. But the former do not meet the expectations of the gods and were destroyed by a great deluge. The latter were transformed into monkeys, and their world disappeared under a shower of scorching resin. Finally, the gods found a sacred material, maize, which they mixed with the blood of serpent and tapir (sacred animals associated with fecundity and water) to form a new human, who is conscious of the gods and his mission on earth. In this fashion the Quiché expressed their views on the similarities and differences between human beings and nature.

In the successive stages there appear distinct Suns such as Vucub Caquix "Seven Parrots," but, like humans, they are imperfect and are therefore destroyed. Alongside the man made from maize arose the

---

[8] Contained in the *Popol Vuh* and the *Memorial de Sololá*.

Fig. 4. *Dresden Codex*, p. 74, the cosmic flood.

modern Sun and Moon, created from the apotheosis of the twin
heroes Hunahpú and Ixbalanqué, who played ball with the gods of
death. They later die and are reborn in the underworld. The stars
remain fixed in the sky until the recently created humans offer them
human sacrifices and thereby initiate motion. In other words, profane time (the story of the people on earth) begins.[9]

The ancient Yucatec Mayan myths contained in the *Libros de
Chilam Balam* are formally distinct, and only a few fragments
remain. Nevertheless, they describe the same cosmogonic concepts
and narrate cosmic creation and destruction as well as the principal
cosmological concepts of the Maya. One of these fragments, called
the "Libro de los antiguos dioses" (Book of the Ancient Gods), states
that, after various epochs of the creation and destruction of humanity, the celestial space collapsed. The Bacabe gods, sustainers of the
sky from the four cosmic directions, lifted the sky once more and
placed a cosmic cedar on each of the four paths; on the frond of each
cedar was perched a bird. Finally, the Great Cedar Mother, the green
cedar, was placed in the center of the universe.[10]

The Quiché and Yacutec Mayan myths describe the people of the
ultimate age, the men of maize, as the result of a progressive perfection (in a spiraling direction) of the human being. This perfection
was determined by the substance from which humans were created,
which also undergoes perfection to attain its final form—maize. The
people of the ultimate age[11] are qualitatively different because they
contain a different sacred substance—the blood of the gods. This new
quality is their consciousness, which reveals to them their mission:
to sustain the gods.

The version of this cosmogonic Mayan myth contained in the
Popol Vuh and the *Memorial de Sololá* is represented in the hieroglyphic texts, relief art, and ceramics of the classical period. It has
survived with few changes among many Mayan groups, for example,
the Tzotzil, the Tzeltal, the Lacandon, and the Yucatec Maya, which
suggests that the myth was common among the diverse Mayan
groups from the pre-Hispanic period.[12]

---

[9] *Popol Vuh.*
[10] *Libro de Chilam Balam of Chumayel*, 242–44.
[11] In Náhuatl cosmogony this is the fifth age, which corresponds to the fifth cosmic direction, the center of the universe.
[12] De la Garza 1987.

Among the present-day Maya as well as in the classical period, one of the more celebrated myths describes the adventures of the twins Hunahpú and Ixbalanqué, who are depicted in classical ceramics and sculptures as participating in various scenarios of the myth, such as the shooting birds with their blowguns.

Freidel and Schele assure us that the Mayan creation myth contained in the *Popol Vuh* does not differ from those that were inscribed on the stone monuments of the great Mayan cities during the sixth to eighth centuries.[13]

> We do not have a book of the Classic period equivalent to the Popol Vuh, which was written by the Quiché people after the Spanish conquest. But we have the history of Creation as written by the ruling Maya on their royal monuments.[14]

Freidel and Schele interpreted three texts from the city of Cobá revealing that the world was created in 13.0.0.0.0, day 4 *Ahau* 8 *Cumhú*. According to our calendar, this date corresponds to August 13, 3114 B.C.E. This date represented the Time Era in the classical calendrical computations.[15] The same date for the birth of the present-day earth was found inscribed on stela C from Quiriguá. The text says that on 4 *Ahau* 8 *Cumhú* "the image was revealed and the three stones were placed . . . ." These "stones" appear to be related to the three stones that the Maya place in the center of their homes, which in the cosmogonic text clearly symbolizes the center of the world.

In the background or northern portion of the stela is the image of Itzamná, "The Dragon" (supreme god of Mayan religion), in humanized form and carrying the crossed celestial bands. According to the colonial texts, he is the creator of the cosmos, which further proves that the text of stela C refers to creation.

Epigraphists have found this cosmogonic myth also on the panel from the Templo de la Cruz in Palenque. Here creation begins with the birth of the First Father (June 16, 3122 B.C.E.), who "ascended" to the center of the sky over the world axis tree. Later, on December 7, 3121 B.C.E., the First Mother was born. They call the First Father Wak-Chan-Ahaw "(Six or) Risen Lord of the Sky."

---

[13] Freidel and Schele 1993, 60.

[14] Ibid., 64.

[15] According to the Maya, for whom time is infinite, on this date ended thirteen great four-hundred-year cycles called *Baktunes*. According to the cosmogonic concept, there existed other cosmic eras, which are referred to in the myths.

In the image that accompanies this text (fig. 6) we see the world axis tree associated with Itzamná, the supreme celestial god, because it is formed by bicephalous serpents above which is the bird-serpent, which we interpret as a representation of the celestial dragon.[16] Therefore, the First Father is the true Itzamná. In Palenque they call him god "G1," and it is to him that the Templo de la Cruz is dedicated. This coincides with the fact that the deity sculpted on the northern side of stela C in Quiriguá is also Itzamná.

From the postclassic period we have a notable cosmogonic scene depicted on the famous page 74 of the *Dresden Codex*, which appears to illustrate the deluge that, according to the myths, ended the cosmic eras (fig. 4). This page of the codex is dedicated to one drawing, which describes a flooding caused by the celestial dragon, Itzamná, through his open jaws and body represented by a band of star symbols. Beneath him an old goddess with bird talons for hands and feet pours water onto the earth from a pitcher. On her skirt she wears a serpentlike headdress and crossed bones, the symbol of death. She is the old goddess "O," whom Thompson referred to as Ixchebel Yax.[17]

Beneath the goddess, with one knee on the ground, is a black god holding two darts that point downward. He could be the black Chaac of the west. He might also represent destructive rain, because his glyph was placed in the upper portion of the drawing. Above the god there is an eagle, the symbol of the solar warrior, in an aggressive position with one wing extended. Based on the multiple signs of death and destruction in the scene, this clearly refers to one of the deluges that caused the destruction of the cosmos. Thompson believes that the chocolate-like color used for the background of the scene might represent the thick resin that, according to the *Popol Vuh*, destroyed the second cosmic era.[18]

---

[16] Freidel and Schele (1993) call the bird-serpent Itzam-Ye. They associate him with Vucub Caquix, Seven Parrot from the *Popol Vuh*, the false Sun of the previous era. This interpretation differs from ours. See our analysis of the bird-serpent below.

[17] Thompson 1970, 206–9.

[18] Thompson 1972, 89.

5

6

Fig. 5. The four cardinal points (glyph from a tomb in Río Azul).
Fig. 6. Panel from the Templo de la Cruz in Palenque.

Cosmology

In general there are three fundamental religious symbols that play a central role in the Mayan concepts of space: the cross and the square (one cannot be dissociated from the other), and the pyramid. According to the colonial myths, the Maya interpret the universe as having the form of a rhombohedron, or rhombuslike prism. The upper portion represents the sky, which is divided into thirteen "great steps" or levels that give it the shape of a pyramid. In the center is the earth, which is depicted as a horizontal quadrangular plain, and below the earth plain is the underworld, composed of nine levels that replicate an inverted pyramid. The conceptualization of the sky as a pyramid was first suggested by Eric Thompson and William Holland.[19] It is possible that the celestial environment was imagined in this fashion because the physical pyramidlike structures (representing sacred mountains) on which the temples were built symbolize above all the celestial space on whose ultimate stratum resides the supreme deity.[20] Accordingly, the underworld was also perceived as a pyramid comprising nine levels, possibly conceived of as inverted.[21] The earth plain was believed to be divided into four sectors, each of which was identified with a color, a tree (cedar) on which perched a bird, a type of maize, and a type of bean. The trees and the anthropomorphic gods called Bacabe,[22] are believed to prop up the sky.

The Mayan myths also mention a great green cedar, "Great Mother Cedar" located in the center of the universe, which traverses the three plains—the celestial, the terrestrial, and underworld. This image of the "Cosmic Tree" situated in the center of the world is one of the more common motifs used to symbolize the "center."

The idea of quartering the earth occurs often in Mayan cosmology. The concept appears to be derived from the witnessing of

---

[19] Thompson 1970, 195–96; Holland 1978.

[20] Contemporary Tzotzil describe the sacred mountain on whose summit live the ancestral diviners and gods as divided into various strata with great steps that unite them—that is, in the image of a pyramid (Holland 1978, 110). This reinforces the interpretation of the pre-Hispanic concept of the sky as a stepped pyramid. The colonial texts say that in the beginning of time the gods were located in the mountains (*Título de los señores de Totonicapán*, 400).

[21] For the Maya "10" is the number that represents the god of the dead; this is why it is situated under the nine strata of the underworld.

[22] *Libro de Chilam Balam of Chumayel*, 88–89.

7

Fig. 7. Representation of the cross on a tombstone in the Templo de las Inscripciones.

natural phenomena: the rising and setting of the Sun, the line (horizon) where the sky and the earth meet, and the annual cycle of the Sun. The equinoxes and the solstices, together with the rising and setting of the Sun, determine the four seasons and the cardinal points that have been linked to the quartering of space and time. Thus we find many sacred beings represented by four different images as well as a diverse set of symbols associated with the four cosmic paths.

Based on archaeoastronomical data, Alfonso Villa Rojas (1968) published a very original and well-founded interpretation concerning the concept of "quartering" in Mayan theory. He claims that the four mentioned paths correspond to the four houses of the Sun (two in the east and two in the west). The intercardinal points are marked by the yearly extremes of the Sun on the horizon: its rising during the summer solstice, its rising in the winter solstice, its setting in the summer solstice, and its setting in the winter solstice. The zenith marks the fifth house of the Sun.[23] Therefore, the north would be the path that is "to the right of the Sun's path," and the south, the path "to the left of the Sun's path," the "four corners of the world" would be located in the northeast, northwest, southwest, and southeast.[24]

However, the "four paths" did not align exactly with the cardinal points. But even though the religious significance of east and west was of primordial importance in Mayan theory (because of the sacred character of the Sun), the north and south were not eliminated from cosmological theory, as some authors would lead us to believe.[25] Miguel León-Portilla has demonstrated that in Mayan religious thought the four cardinal points were of essential significance with east and west undoubtedly of higher rank. The importance of the four cardinal points was corroborated in 1985 when Richard E. W. Adams discovered a tomb in Río Azul, on whose walls were glyphs locating each of these coordinates in their precise locations (fig. 5).[26]

There are also two additional coordinates identified in the Mayan cosmology: the zenith, marking the center of the sky, and the nadir,

---

[23] Aveni 1980; and Villa Rojas 1994.
[24] Villa Rojas 1994, 136.
[25] See the discussion in León-Portilla 1994, Appendix 2.
[26] Adams 1996, 441–42; see also León-Portilla 1994.

identifying the center of the underworld.[27] Therefore, when we include the center of the world (terrestrial), we end up with a total of seven cosmic dimensions.

The Maya could therefore not conceive of terrestrial space without the concept of time, and both space and time are determined by the solar cycle. The Sun is therefore the sacred being par excellence. Through the four sectors and three cosmic levels "walk" the four "Carriers of the Year," as they called the day of the ritual calendar of 260 days when the year begins—thereby giving ordered movement to space, and impregnating all beings with their either positive or negative influences.

Many ceremonial sites from the classical and postclassical periods express these cosmological concepts.[28] But, in addition, each of these cosmic strata is symbolized through sculpture as a reptile-like monster that we call "dragon." The Mayan dragon is a serpent-like hybrid composed of elements of diverse sacred animals. As we mentioned earlier, this being is the supreme deity that governs across the plains and levels of the universe.

In religious symbolism, the square represents the material world—the solid, the tangible, and the perceptible. However, the square is derived from the cross ["X"] because the sacred number par excellence is not four but five. The fifth point is located at the intersection of the two lines that make up the cross and represents the center of the universe. The four sides cannot be considered without their relationship to the center. The center is the same for the sky as it is for the earth and the underworld because it is the point of union and communication of the diverse cosmic spaces. Thus the center is not only a point but an axis that joins the two poles of the cosmos.[29] And being an axis (the umbilical cord of the world), the Center is the threshold that makes it possible to travel between the different levels.

The Mayan symbols of the quadruplex and the fifth point, or center of the cosmos, inscribed within this general meaning are diverse. First, there is the glyph of the Sun represented as a flower with four petals (fig. 5).[30] It is he who regulates time and the division of space.

---

[27] See Cohodas 1974.
[28] See below, pp. 167–72.
[29] Guénon 1969, 57.
[30] Thompson 1962, glyph T544.

8

9

Fig. 8. Panel in the Templo del Sol in Palenque.

Fig. 9. Panel in the Templo de la Cruz Foliada in Palenque.

10

11

Fig. 10. Lintel 2, Yaxchilán.

Fig. 11. Façade of Temple 22 in Copán, Honduras.

Another glyph representing the geometrically quartered cosmos with its center is the *quinconce*, which is formed by four points at the extremes and one in the center (fig. 5).[31]

The cross is one of the most noted Mayan symbols of the quartered cosmos and the *axis mundi*. We find it in various classical artwork, such as that represented on the tombstones located in the Templo de las Inscripciones (sarcophagus) (fig. 7), Templo de la Cruz (fig. 6),[32] Templo de la Cruz Foliada (fig. 9)[33] in Palenque, and on lintels 2 (fig. 10) and 5 in Yaxchilán. On the former, the cross is formed by the body of the celestial dragon, who rests over a mask associated with the terrestrial dragon, above which is the bird-serpent, who is a variation of the deity of the heavens. In the Templo de la Cruz Foliada, the "cosmic tree" is a maize plant in the form of a cross resting on the large mask of the solar god which, as the terrestrial dragon, shows a bird-serpent located above the vertical axis. Therefore these works simultaneously illustrate the four paths, the three cosmic levels, and the *axis mundi*.

On lintels 2 (fig. 10) and 5 in Yaxchilán, the rulers carry scepters that form a cross with flowers on either end of the horizontal line. There is also a diving *quetzal* bird in the superior portion, which symbolizes the celestial deity at the high end of the *axis mundi*.

There are also diverse cosmological images in the codices, such as those found on pages 75 and 76 of the *Madrid Codex* (fig. 12). These depict the four cosmic paths, and in their center a tree depicting the *axis mundi*, under which is seated the supreme god Itzamná with his female partner. The tree is also a temple, which proves that, for the Maya, temples were the centers of the world where the divine energies concentrated. Located on two of the four cosmic paths we see Itzamná again with his partner. On the other two are depicted human sacrifices: one by the removal of the heart and the other by decapitation. This proves that Man sacrificed himself to the gods in order that the cosmos may exist.

Another image of the cosmos is that found on page 67b of the

---

[31] Thompson 1962, glyph T585.

[32] Freidel and Schele call it the World Tree and say that its hieroglyphic name is Wakah-chan, which literally means "Lifted to the Heavens" (1993, 53).

[33] Freidel and Schele call this *axis mundi* Na-Te'-Kán, "First–tree–precious" (1993, 54).

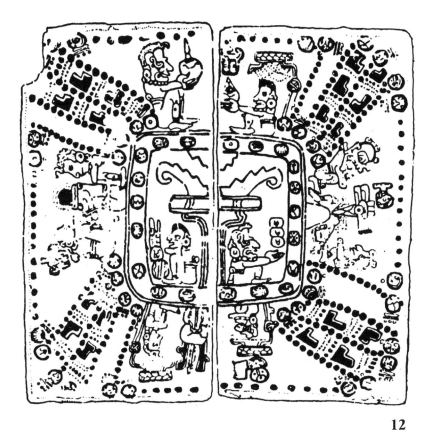

12

Fig. 12. *Madrid Codex*, pp. 75, 76: diverse cosmological images.

Fig. 13. *Madrid Codex*, p. 67b: the god of death resting on a bone.

13

Madrid Codex, where we see the god of death resting on a bone which together symbolize the underworld. From his body emerges an erect serpent (representing the earth), with its open jaws pointing upward. And from its jaws emerges the Sun, who touches an astral band that symbolizes the sky.

The pictorial art of the postclassical period reflects these same cosmological concepts. For example, in the superior portion of the Templo de los Frescos of Tulum are scenes depicting an astral band, below which are figures of sitting gods receiving offerings. On the lower level there is a band of a jaguar skin, symbolizing the earth and the underworld.

The Mayan concept of quadruplicity is not restricted to the earth, but applies also to the heavens and the underworld. The myths speak of the four regions of the sky[34] (which would be the four faces of the celestial pyramid), each of which shares the colors of the terrestrial level, and the four regions of the underworld. Even the supreme sky god, Itzamná, is simultaneously one and four because he is depicted with the four cosmic colors (those of maize), which are black, white, red, and yellow.

The pyramid is one of the universal symbols of the four-part cosmos and the center of the world. It represents the mountain and is a perfect figure: a volume oriented to its superior vertex, where the sides meet to form a union. It therefore symbolizes totality. It is marked by opposing sides that materialize the cosmic oppositions. It rests upon a quadrangular base upon the earth, with which it is identified, while its apex represents the celestial level.[35]

For the Maya the celestial pyramid symbolizes the progressive ascension from the diverse terrestrial cardinal directions toward the union, represented by the apex, where the supreme god Itzamná, "The Dragon," the vital principle of the cosmos, resides. The celestial pyramid therefore symbolizes the progressive deification of the cosmos. This supreme point is also that of the Sun because it corresponds to the zenith with which the Dragon and the Sun are identified. The deity of the zenith would be Itzamná Kinich Ahau—"Lord solar eye of the Dragon"—as cited by the written sources.

The inverted pyramid of the underworld symbolizes the descent

---

[34] *Popol Vuh,* 21; and *Cantares de Dzitblaché,* p. 373.
[35] Champeaux and Sterckx 1989, 222.

from the terrestrial quadrangle (place of multiplicity and change) to the sacred union of death equated with the end of time and earthliness. In the lowest stratum of the underworld resides the god of death, who is the dialectic complement of the supreme celestial god because he is identified with the Sun in his nadir position—the Dead Sun.

The apexes of the mirrored cosmological pyramids symbolize the two sacred opposing principles of the solar position that symbolically represent life and death and determine the equilibrium of the cosmos, whose alternations result in the existence of the earth.

The universal Mesoamerican symbols are the pyramid, or triangle with its vertex pointing upward; the mountain, rising to the sky; and the inverted pyramid, symbolizing a cavern, which is the gateway to the underworld. Accordingly, the former is a masculine and active principle, while the latter is feminine and passive.[36] The Maya equate the underworld with the womb of Mother Earth, where she stores seeds and treasures with the dead, who can originate new life.

In the minds of the Maya, therefore, the theory of quadruplicity unifies the celestial plain with that of the underworld. This unification of opposing sacred principles is the culmination of a progressive spiritualization, the abandonment of that which is material, and the solidification of the terrestrial level toward life and death.

In this concept there is an unequivocal consciousness of the cosmic unit. Although the earth, the sky, and the underworld are distinct realities, they nevertheless participate in the sacred and share a structure where the cross, the square, the triangle, and the sphere coexist. In other words, space and time constitute a unit.

The cosmological concepts as well as astronomical knowledge were used to determine the construction of the sacred spaces on earth represented by the ceremonial centers. The temples were oriented according to astral reference points[37] such as the equinoxes and solstices. They were built upon a pyramid-shaped base that only the priests could ascend during religious ceremonies while the general public remained in the plazas.

Ascending a pyramid, which represented the sacred cosmic moun-

---

[36] Guénon 1969, 186-87.

[37] This was demonstrated through archaeoastronomy, a field founded by Antony Aveni, to which Horst Hartung and John B. Carlson and others have contributed.

tain, implied ascendance into the celestial world in order to communicate with the sacred. Upon reaching the superior terrace of the
temple the priest was believed to cross over into another level,
thereby transcending the space of humans into that of the gods.

There are many architectural works and sculptures that reflect
Mayan cosmology and demonstrate that the concepts expressed in
the myths have been valid since the classical period. We will mention only a few examples.

The façade of Temple 22 in the city of Copán, Honduras (fig. 11),
is adorned with an extraordinary high-relief representing the three
vertical levels of the cosmos. At its base and below the doorway is a
frieze of skulls, and on its sides are two masks of the deity of death
symbolizing the underworld. Above them are two human (semi-
kneeling) figures that appear to be the Bacabe gods (representing the
terrestrial level), who, standing on the four cosmic paths, sustain the
sky. On their shoulders they carry a great two-headed serpent, which
represents the celestial dragon.

One of the better examples of classical Mesoamerican cosmological architecture is found in the Mayan city of Palenque in the present
state of Chiapas.[38] There we find a pyramid of nine levels symbolizing the underworld (in spite of the fact that it is not an obvious
inverted pyramid) and another pyramid of thirteen levels depicting
the sky. This further proves that these environments were envi-
sioned as pyramid-like formations.

The pyramid of the underworld, Templo de las Inscripciones,
houses the grand burial of Pacal in its lowest central point, which
symbolizes the tenth stratum of the underworld because it is below
the level of the plaza where one enters from the summit of the pyramid. This symbolizes the descent to the underworld through the
nine strata beginning at the terrestrial level through which a majority of the immortal spirits of Man had to journey after their deaths.

In the city of Dzibanché, Campeche, is the Templo del Búho
(Temple of the Owl), which was also constructed as a funerary monument. It contains various mortuary chambers and a principal burial
(not yet excavated) on the next level above the plaza.[39] Access to this
level is gained only from the top of the pyramid, as in the case of the

---

[38] De la Garza 1992.
[39] Campaña 1995.

Pacal tomb in Palenque. But the base, rather than having nine levels, has only four. Thompson mentioned that the pyramid of the underworld was formed by four stairs on one side, four on the other, and the lower level, which gives a total of nine. Therefore, this base may represent, as in Palenque, the underworld environment, to which the spirit of the dead descends.[40]

The celestial pyramid of Palenque is the Templo de la Cruz (Temple of the Cross). We consider it the best architectural representation of the sky because, in addition to being set on a base of thirteen levels, it has in its apex a space dedicated to the supreme celestial god Itzamná, "The Dragon," identified here as god G1. In addition this temple forms a triangle with respect to two others: the Templo de la Cruz Foliada (Temple of the Foliated Cross) and the Templo del Sol (Temple of the Sun). The three temples, respectively situated to north, east, and west of a plaza, symbolize the sacred cycle of maize as well as the annual and daily cycles of the Sun. They are associated with the cosmic directions, the equinoxes, and the solstices as well as with the initiation rites of rulers.[41] The three temples next to the Templo de las Inscripciones constitute a clear expression of the concepts of time and space among the Maya.

The great lord buried in the Templo de las Inscripciones was represented on a sculpted monolith which forms the lid of his sarcophagus and also symbolizes temporal space (fig. 7). The figure of the ruler, in the center, is the symbol of the terrestrial level. Above him is a cross formed by bicephalous serpents (representing Itzamná) that symbolize the sky and the *axis mundi*. Beneath is a skeleton of a bicephalous serpent; bones and the "fleshless" mask of the god of death represent the underworld. The cosmological scene is surrounded by a band containing astral symbols demonstrating the preeminence of the sky, the temporal character of the universe, and the cosmic unit.

The Gods

Those beings from the classical Mayan religion that we may call "gods" are highly stylized supernatural beings made up of elements

---

[40] Thompson 1970, 195–96.
[41] Cohodas 1974; 1976.

from diverse animals and plants that are sometimes combined with human motifs. To better understand the significance of these fantastic beings it is necessary to turn to similar figures found in the surviving codices of the postclassical period as well as to the Spanish and Indigenous colonial texts. These sources may confirm the character and the manifestations of these sacred beings and provide us with their names whose meanings allow for a better characterization. During the postclassical period, the classical images were joined by other representations introduced to the area by Nahua conquerors who arrived on the Yucatan peninsula and the highlands of Guatemala around 1000 C.E.

According to the manuscripts, we know that the Maya perceived the gods as invisible and nonpalpable energies that appeared as diverse natural phenomena (stars, rain, or lightning); powerful animals (serpent, jaguar, birds, and bats); plants (maize, and hallucinogenic plants and fungi); and minerals such as quartz. The spirits of distinguished human beings were also deified at death in the same manner.

Besides these natural beings, there were also those images of gods that were made by humans to function as incarnations of the sacred energies during rites in order that they might receive the offerings of the people.

Among other authors of the sixteenth century, Friar Diego de Landa confirms the ethereal character of the gods:

> Well they knew that the idols were of their own work and dead and without deity, in addition they were held in reverence for what they represented and because they were made with much ceremony, especially those of wood.[42]

Another characteristic of the Mayan gods is that, in spite of being superior to humans and capable of creating, they were conceived of as imperfect, mortal beings. For this reason they needed to be fed in order to survive. This concept is clearly expressed in the cosmogonic myths, prophecies, rites, and hieroglyphic inscriptions of the classical period, as in Palenque, where, according to epigraphic interpretations, the births of several gods are depicted.[43]

---

[42] Landa 1966, 48.
[43] See Freidel and Schele 1993.

These sacred beings have diverse representations and multiple names, depending on their attributes, and most importantly, according to their temporal position. For the Maya, there are no "static" beings. All is in constant motion and undergoing continuous change. Therefore the gods as well as their influences are different during each period of the year. This explains why any particular god can be both celestial and terrestrial, benevolent and malevolent, masculine and feminine, and the energy of life and of death. In addition, the gods could be both one and many. They most often became four when embarking on the four paths of the cosmos; they are thirteen as the deity of the sky (in Yucatan they are labeled Oxlahuntikú, "Thirteen deity"); and nine as the deity of the underworld (Bolontikú, "Nine deity"). This obviously resulted in diverse representations of each of the gods. Further, we have to recognize the effects of distinct artistic styles of the different regions, which makes the study of Mayan gods even more difficult. However, the deities can be identified by several symbolic elements that are constant throughout the Mayan territory and the various epochs.

Here we distinguish the fundamental features of the principal divine figures of the Maya as they were identified by Yucatec and Quiché Mayan names provided by the written documents and the letters assigned to them based on the classification made by Paul Schellhas of the gods presented in the codices.[44] The postclassical gods and their names noted in the colonial texts allow us to better identify and understand the gods of the classical period. Although their representation is distinct, they contain the same symbolic elements. We have therefore decided to employ these names.

The distinct perspectives of Mayan investigations resulted in diverse interpretations of the gods. Many interpretations coincide, yet others do not. Here we adhere to those made from the comparative analysis of the distinct sources and the indigenous sources, among which we have included the *Popol Vuh* of the Quiché, other texts of this language (Cakchiquel texts), as well as Spanish versions of texts originally written in Mayan and Yucatec Mayan such as the *Libros de Chilam Balam* and the *Cantares de Dzitbalché* [Chants of Dzitbalché].

---

[44] Schellhas 1904.

Hunab Ku

For many peoples, the celestial and creator god is an "idle god." In other words, after he had created the world he remained in the highest stratum of the sky without anything directly to do with the lives of humans. Another figure, therefore, substituted for him and became the supreme god, and it is he who maintains contact with the earth and humans. The written texts from the Maya of Yucatan mention a deity by the name of Hunab Ku, "God One,"[45] who could have been the idle creator god, and whose successor was Itzamná. They say that Hunab Ku was a unique god, alive and venerated, who could not be represented because he lacked a body. He was also called *Kolop u wich k'in.*[46] It is believed that Itzamná, who participated in the creation as a culture hero, was his son and that he transformed into the supreme celestial god in the pantheon of Mayan religion.

The Dragon

In the majority of the classical figures depicting deities we find serpent elements. Stylized serpents predominate in Mayan art, which demonstrates that this particular life form was an essential symbol of sacredness. One analysis of the symbolic significance of the Mayan serpent showed that the serpent, transformed into a dragon and enriched with elements of other powerful animals, symbolizes a universal sacred power and vital force that is the principal generator of the universe.[47] For this reason he is associated with the Sun, water, land, blood, as well as semen and maize, which are depicted as diverse deities or manifestations of the supreme sacred principle.

The dragon is primarily a composite of bird and serpent for which the Maya selected excellent representatives: the *quetzal* bird (*k'uk'* in Yucatec Kekchí, Tzeltal and other Mayan languages; *guc* in Quiché and Cakchiquel) and the tropical rattlesnake (*ahau can, tzabcan, zochch* and *cumatz*). In addition, elements and traits were incorporated from other sacred animals, such as the jaguar, tapir, lizard, crocodile, and the deer, to make of the dragon a symbol of supreme

---

[45] *Ku* is translated here as "god." Perhaps it comes from *ku', quetzal,* or vice versa.

[46] López Cogolludo 1971. *Diccionario Maya Cordemex* (1980).

[47] De la Garza 1984.

sacredness. As such, the dragon integrates the vital forces of the earth (serpent and deer), the womb of mother earth—the underworld (jaguar), the waters (tapir, lizard, and crocodile) and the sky (bird). The dragon is a multiple and polyvalent individual who is the sacred figure par excellence depicted in the Mayan art of the classical period. Thanks to several descriptions of deities found in the colonial texts that concur with the symbolic elements in the art and the images of the codices, we know the names given to them by the Yucatec Maya. Itzamná is "The Dragon," an anthropomorphic celestial god identified as god D in the codices. Itzamná Cab Ain, the "Dragon Terrestrial Crocodile" or Chac Mumul Ain, the "Great Muddy Crocodile," is depicted with features representing the terrestrial world and the underworld. In the cosmogonic myths he is also called Canhel, "Dragon," in his role as a creator god and vital principle of the sky, which corresponds to the Gucumatz "Quetzalserpent" in the *Popol Vuh* of the Quiche. Following the arrival of the Toltec to the northern Maya territory, we find him merged with the figure of Kukulcán, the "Quetzal Serpent."

In addition, there are other deities which, in our opinion, are derived from the dragon because of their serpent-like character and close relationship with him. Chicchan, god H, the Biting Serpent, is the symbol of the night sky; Kinich Ahau, god G is Lord of the Solar Eye; Chaac, god B is the god of water; and Bolon Dz'acab, New Generations, or Ka'wil, god K, symbolizes the human traits of sacred fertility, blood and semen, and is associated with maize.

The Celestial Dragon: Itzamná, God D

The celestial dragon usually depicts the harmony of the great cosmic contradictions and is represented by the animal symbols of opposing forces par excellence—the bird personifying the sky and the serpent symbolizing the earth. The dragon is depicted as bicephalous, feathered, winged—a bird-serpent; as a body formed by a band of stars; as an ancient man with facial features of a serpent; and as a man-bird-serpent. As such he represents the celestial dragon who appears in the codices and art all over the Mayan territory during the pre-Hispanic period.

The dragon as bicephalous is found on altars G and O in Copán (fig. 14). Here the feathered serpent is schematized and carries on itself symbols of water. It has the feet of a lizard or the claws of a jaguar. From the open jaws of both serpent heads there emerge anthropomorphic god figures. On altar O are two representations: on one side is the bicephalous dragon with jaguar claws, and on the other the feathered serpent with the same head of the dragon. This shows that we are dealing with the same deity.

In various works from Yaxchilán, Palenque, Piedras Negras, Tikal, Copán, and Uxmal, the dragon is represented as a feathered serpent, often bicephalous, with very stylized heads and open jaws—as depicted on lintel 3 of Temple IV of Tikal (fig. 15), on stela D in Copán, and on the panels of the Templo de la Cruz and the Templo de las Inscripciones in Palenque (fig. 7).

We found winged dragons like those on the headdress of the ruler Pacal and his wife Ahpo Hel also in the Tablero de los Esclavos (Panel of the Slaves) and over a fretwork made of stucco in the palace of Palenque.

Another form of representing the celestial dragon is with a grotesque mask (mascarón), sometimes lacking flesh altogether, on whose forehead is a glyph of the sun containing the so-called triadic symbol formed by the cross of San Andres, a glyph of the sky; a shell symbolizing origin; and a spine used for self-sacrifice representing blood. These elements, as well as the aquatic ones (circles of jade), show that the celestial monster symbolizes the fecundate energy of the sky. But at the same time, because the face is without flesh, it reveals his relationship with the earth and the underworld. This alludes to the duality of the dragon as a symbol of life and death. The glyph of the Sun over the front of the mask reveals that the star is an aspect of the dragon. Therefore we see that, in the panel of the Templo de la Cruz in Palenque (fig. 6), the mask, from whose sides extends a band containing star symbols, identifies the celestial character of this deity.

Altar 41 in Copán (fig. 19) represents the bicephalous dragon as a type of lizard with four legs and two serpent heads. Above one of them is the triadic symbol, which shows that the mask from the Templo de la Cruz in Palenque and the others that have this symbol also represent the celestial dragon. From the jaws of the other head emerges the god of maize.

Another sacred image that we have associated with the celestial dragon is the bird-serpent. In contrast to the feathered serpents, this image is dominated by the bird motif. It has stylized serpent heads over its wings and, occasionally, the head of god K with markings of

14

15

Fig. 14. Two-headed dragon found on altars G and O in Copán.

Fig. 15. The dragon as a feathered serpent on lintel 3 of Temple IV of Tikal.

the serpent. This representation appears in various forms and contexts, often associated with the figure of the bicephalous dragon, the feathered serpent, or one with a humanized aspect.

The bird-serpent with the head of god K, Bolon Dz'acab, which is another aspect of the dragon, appears on the great stucco panel of Toniná (fig. 16) and those of Palenque. In these works he is seen in profile, but there are others where he has the face of a bird, viewed from the front, with wings stretched out toward the sides over which are the heads of serpents. This is how he is depicted on the censers that were recently discovered in Palenque (fig. 22).

The bird-serpent is often placed over the serpentine dragon (lintel 3 in Temple IV in Tikal) (fig. 15). Over the ruler, who occupies its center, there is a great feathered bicephalous serpent whose body is adorned with circles of jade-water feathers. From one of his heads emerges god K, and poised over the serpent is the bird-serpent facing forward with outstretched wings. It has a headdress, ear coverings, and serpent tails under the wings. These have crossed bands to demonstrate that they are of the celestial deity.

A similar merging of these two representations of Itzamná, but in a very distinct artistic style, was found in the trapezoidal motif formed by bicephalous serpents on the building Este del Cuadrángulo de las Monjas, located in Uxmal. Over this figure is the bird-serpent, whose face is also facing forward.

Other examples are seen in the stucco relief of house E of the Palenque Palace, where the body of the bicephalous dragon, represented by an astral band, has in its center the bird-serpent, facing forward, with outstretched wings, over which is the head of a serpent. This bicephalous dragon is a clear expression of the duality of life-death and sky-underworld because one of the heads is spewing down water (as is the dragon of page 74 in the *Dresden Codex* [fig. 4]) and the other, with a fleshless face, is looking upward.

Among the principal representations of the dragon as an *axis mundi* and its identification with the bird-serpent and god K, we will present the best known figures in Palenque.

The tombstone of the Templo de las Inscripciones (fig. 7) represents an *axis mundi* with a cross that simultaneously represents Itzamná himself. The horizontal axis is a bicephalous serpent with mandibles made from flakes of jade that symbolize water and feathers. The upper end of the vertical axis ends with another serpent head and a coiled bicephalous serpent with a limber body made from

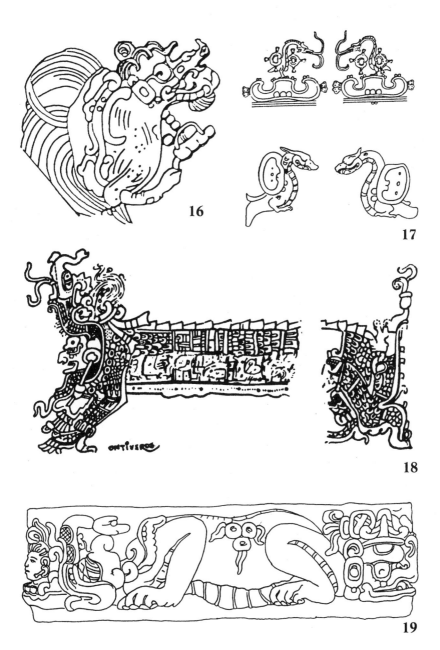

Fig. 16. The bird-serpent with the head of god K, on the great stucco panel of Toniná.

Fig. 17. Winged dragons in the Tablero de los Esclavos and over a fretwork in the palace of Palenque.

Fig. 18. Two-headed dragon with body formed by an astral band. *Dresden Codex*, pp. 4b, 5b.

Fig. 19. Altar 41 in Copán.

flakes of jade. From its jaws emerges god K. At the very top is poised a bird-serpent with the head of bird K. In its beak it holds a pestle, a sign of human power, which alludes to the sacred ruler. Over the headdress of the bird-serpent and below the tail and face are Yax symbols (blue-green-water), which are associated with the celestial deity.

The central motif of the panel from the Templo de la Cruz in Palenque (fig. 6) represents the dragon in four distinct forms. In the lower portion we see him with a body composed of an astral band (described earlier) above which arises a tree-cross-serpent whose horizontal bar is a bicephalous serpent over which is another bicephalous serpent with a limber body formed by Yax glyphs. The vertical bar terminates above with a bird-serpent almost identical to that of the Templo de las Inscripciones.

In the codices, the bicephalous dragon and the dragon are drawn with a body formed by an astral band. On pages 4b and 5b of the *Dresden Codex* is a monster with the scaled body of the serpent, adorned with blue and green transversal lines, and a type of crest of yellow and red. In addition there is a band of the same colors on his abdomen. His feet appear to be a combination of deer hooves and the talons of a bird of prey. He has two stylized heads. The dragon represented on page 4 supports spirals and streamers from which emerges the face of god D, Itzamná. This description identifies the dragon with this anthropomorphic deity.

The representation of the dragon with the body of an astral band, which comes from the classical period (stucco of House E from the Palace, and the tombstone from the Templo de la Cruz in Palenque [fig. 6]), suggests that the celestial dragon was associated with the milky way,[48] called *sacbé*, "white road." Its terrestrial representations were the network of sacred roads constructed with plaster in the Mayan cities and those that united one city with another.

One of the most noted representations of the celestial dragon with a body as an astral band is the one found on page 74 in the *Dresden Codex* (fig. 4). Here the body of the dragon contains the glyphs of Venus, the sky, the sun, and darkness.[49] The dragon is located above,

---

[48] Sosa 1984.

[49] Thompson (1962, 6) and Förstemann (1966) say that they represent Venus, Mars, Jupiter, and Mercury. Many planetary bands that appear in the *Dresden Codex* are therefore symbols of the celestial dragon (see de la Garza 1984, 168).

in the sky, and from enormous jaws it spews water upon the earth. Underneath its body are the glyphs of the Sun and the Moon, from which water also falls. Its legs end in the form of deer hooves (an animal symbolic of the Sun), which confirms the dragon as a solar deity. As mentioned earlier, the entire page denotes one of the cosmic destructions. Therefore, in addition to being the vital principle of the cosmos, the dragon is also the principle of destruction. He is the power of life and the power of death. There are many other representations of the astral band standing alone in the *Dresden* and *Madrid* codices, but we know from the image described above that it symbolizes the body of the celestial dragon.

On page 22 of the *Paris Codex* there also appears a celestial dragon with planetary markings on his body. Above him are seated two deities encircled by a rope that descends below the dragon. On pages 23 and 24 of the same codex we see planetary bands from which are hung solar glyphs of symbolic animals.

In postclassical art we did not find as many representations of celestial dragons as in the central area during the classical period. But the dragons of the postclassical period (represented as anthropomorphic figures of the celestial deity such as god D) also carry within their jaws various vases from Santa Rita Corozal and Belice. One such vase was deposited as an offering in front of Temple 1 in Chacchoben, which lay in ruins already between 1200 and 1400 C.E.[50]

In the colonial texts the dragon is identified with the creator gods during the "static time" of origin. In the *Libro de Chilam Balam* in Chumayel, the dragon, Canhel, appears as a vital principle of the sky, who, upon being pressured by the gods of the dead, initiates the destruction of the world.[51] The *Popol Vuh* suggests that Gucumatz, the "Quetzal-serpent," was the common name for all of the creator gods. Therefore, the distinct names of these gods appear to have referred to distinct attributes of the same deity.[52] Gucumatz primarily symbolizes water and is identified with the vital energy with which he transformed the world. Water later became the impulse that continuously produces life.

---

[50] Romero and Riqué Flores 1955.
[51] *Libro de Chilam Balam of Chumayel*, 88.
[52] *Popol Vuh*, 13.

The celestial dragon has an anthropomorphic representation, god D, who appears to correspond to Itzar   ntioned in the writ-ten records.[53] He is depicted as an old   1 a single serpentine eye that is large and round or square(unded angles and a curve below. He has a large rounded n   mouth that is tooth-less or with only a single tooth. He i: es drawn with femi-nine attributes, which makes him an   ous deity similar to Ometeotl, the supreme god of the N: image appears most often in the codices, but we have four   ;o in works of art.

The colonial sources reveal that Itzamn: the sky and sent rain. Friar Bernardo de Lizana noted the 1

> The ancient ones had an idol, the most c(vho was called
> Ytzamat ul, which means he who receives ar   ; grace, or dew,
> or substance from heaven. . . . they say that   1s a king, great
> lord of this earth, who was obeyed as the s   )ds: and when
> asked his name, or who he was, said no m(:se words: . . .
> I am the dew, or the substance from heavel   1s.[54]

Itzamná was also a culture hero. He invented agriculture, the writ-ten word, the calendars, and other human creations. He dictated the laws and governs through those elected by him. In the codices we see him affecting many events related to his role as a culture hero, as, for example, in ritual scenes that could be interpreted as mythical para-digms of priestly duties. We see him also writing, which shows his identification with Itzamná, the inventor of writing.[55]

This humanizing of the deity is seen also among various ceramic figures from the postclassical period, such as the censer placed as an offering in the ruins of building 2 in Dzibanché. This figure is car-rying a ball of copal in one hand and displays a spiral on its chest. From the Mayapán we have various ceramic coffins that show the ancient god carrying a censer or some other ritual object in his hands.

The identification of Itzamná mentioned in the texts, god D of the codices, and the dragon who was present in the Maya area since the preclassical period, is confirmed in various works such as altar 41 of Copán (classical; fig. 19), which shows a bicephalous dragon, one of

---

[53] Schellhas 1904; Thompson 1970, 227–28; and Taube 1992, 41.
[54] Lizana 1893, 4.
[55] Sotelo 1997.

20

21

Fig. 20. Representation of Kukulcán, doorway of the Temple of the Warriors, Chichén Itzá.

Fig. 21. Representation of "Man-bird-serpent," Temple of the Warriors, Chichén Itzá.

whose heads is that of a serpent, and the other, of god D. Positioned over both heads is the triadic symbol characteristic of the celestial dragon during the classical period. The work also shows that the anthropomorphic aspect of Itzamná is of classical origin.

Kukulcán

On the Central High Plain, the symbol of the dragon as a feathered serpent constituted the deity called Quetzalcóatl, who, when merged with the god Ehécatl, also represented the wind. In the postclassical period, Quetzalcóatl was also associated with a historic figure called Ce Acatl Topiltzin, through which he acquired a more complex significance. With the arrival of Nahua groups into the Maya area, the latter integrated the worship of Quetzalcóatl into their religion. The Maya called him Kukulcán, who is represented in the art of this region as a feathered serpent and the "Man-bird-serpent." Through this process he acquired the qualities of a warrior. In this manner the figures of the Mayan dragon, venerated since the preclassical period, and Nahuatl celestial dragons were fused.

The city of Chichén Itzá was the principal center for the veneration of Kukulcán, as evidenced by the abundant representations of this god. He appears in the form of a column in the doorways of the temples of Castillo (Castles), los Guerreros (the Warriors), and los Jaguares (the Jaguars). On these columns, his head makes up the base, the body comprises the fust, and the rattle makes up the capital (pilaster). The heads and the bodies are covered with feathers (fig. 20). Where the thin northern stoops begin in the Castillo temple, there are enormous serpent heads similar to those found on the columns. But here the body of the dragon is represented by a beam. There are also feathered serpent heads on the platforms of Venus, los Aguilas (the Eagles), and los Jaguares (the Jaguars).

All of these works are round sculptures, but there are also feathered serpents on the diverse relief art such as we see along the benches of the Ball Court and on the gold repoussé disks depicting warriors and sacrificial scenes as observed on the superior portion of disk H, where we see a serpent with snails etched on his back—which is a symbol of Quetzalcóatl.

For example, the "Man-bird-serpent" symbol is represented in the Venus Temple, the beams of the northern building of the Ball Court, the column at the foot of the Templo de los Guerreros (fig. 21) and

22

23

24

25

Fig. 22. Clay censers. Palenque.

Fig. 23. Representation of Kinich Kak Moo. *Dresden Codex*, p. 40b.

Fig. 24. Altar depicted on stela D in Coplán.

Fig. 25. Representation of Ah Puch, god A.

on the eastern walls. The motif is the body of a bird with claws, seen from the front, that has in the center the head of a serpent (which is a round relief in the Temple of the Warriors), with an exposed forked tongue, open jaws, and between them, a human face. This symbol appears to clearly represent Kukulcán. Therefore the integrated dragon is a historic figure. [56] Kukulcán is represented also in clay figures, distinguished by the snail carved on his chest, which is the symbol of Quetzalcóatl.

Kinich Ahau, God G

A deity who is also associated with the celestial dragon and could be a variation of the same, is the Sun. In Yucatan he was called Kinich Ahau, Lord Eye Solar, and Itzamná Kinich Ahau, Lord Solar Eye of the Dragon. In classical art, the solar god has eyes that are large, square, and crossed, a filed tooth or extended tongue, a curved incisor in the commissure of the mouth, and sometimes a serpent on his forehead whose body forms a figure eight.

A few images, like the clay censers of Palenque, have grotesque masks and a bird-serpent on the headdress (fig. 22), which demonstrates their relationship with the celestial dragon. Below them one sometimes distinguishes the terrestrial dragon.

Another tie between Itzamná and Kinich Ahau is that the glyph of this one is under the triadic symbol located on the head of the celestial dragon, as mentioned above, which proves the identity of these two deities. But the solar god is also associated with the terrestrial dragon, from whose jaws emerge the mornings and to whose jaws return the evenings. This is expressed in several classical works, as, for example, in a large mask of the terrestrial dragon in Toniná located at ground level, who has between its jaws a sphere that is an obvious symbol of the sun.

The animal epiphanies of the solar god are the deer, the jaguar, the humming bird, the eagle, and the parrot. In Yucatan he is called Kinich Kakmoo, Parrot-of-fire-of-the-eye-solar. It was said that, incar-

---

[56] However, there are some, like Miller and Taube, who call him Jaguar-bird-serpent, deny his relationship with Kukulcán, and consideer him a version of the serpent associated with war—an interpretation with which we are not in agreement (see Miller and Taube 1993, 104).

nated as this bird, the Sun descended to receive the offerings of humans in Izamal. In the Ball Court of Copán, the markers are in the shape of parrot heads, demonstrating that since the classical period, the parrot was associated with the Sun because, as we shall see below, the game was also symbolized with astral signs. An image of Kinich Kak Moo as a man with the head of a parrot carrying a torch is found in the *Dresden Codex* on page 40b.

In Quintana Roo a great acropolis was recently discovered that might have been part of the neighboring city of Dzibanché. It has been named Kinichná, House of the Sun, because of its reliefs alluding to the solar deity. It may have been dedicated to the solar cult.[57]

Near this city, and sharing its same style, is Kohunlich, whose principal temple is also dedicated to the solar god. Large masks of this deity flank the stairs of the pyramid. The masks have all of the distinctive symbols of the solar god and, in addition, some of them have the Chuen glyph in the eyes, which is related in many other contexts to the solar deity. The Chuen glyph signifies "monkey, artist, creator" and is identified with the Sun, not only because it is an astral deity (the brother of the Sun described in the *Popol Vuh*), but because both are associated with artistic creation. In addition, the head of a monkey sometimes replaces that of a solar god, such as the Kin symbol, which indicates a connection between the two.[58] Among many other things, the Maya saw the Sun as the patron of song and music, and this relationship with the monkey is clearly expressed on the masks of the principal Temple of Kohunlich. Below these, there is another mask of the terrestrial dragon similar to those depicted on several censers in Palenque.

The Sun was the principal deity responsible for generating temporality. His daily and annual cycles determine movement, the passing of days and nights, the four regions of the universe, and the four seasons. He is therefore the patron of the number 4, and his glyph is a four-petaled flower (fig. 5). His cycle, however, gives him an ambivalent character. As he crosses the sky he is light, life, day, order and good; a benevolent and vital attribute. But in the evening he enters the underworld, transforms into a jaguar, and becomes the energy of death. Among other classical works, these concepts are

---

[57] Nalda 1995.
[58] Thompson 1960, 80.

expressed on the panel in the Templo del Sol in Palenque (fig. 8), whose central motif is a mask of the solar god in the form of a shield with crossed arrows symbolizing lightning. On his forehead is a serpent forming a figure eight. He has the ears of a jaguar, the eyes of a serpent, and the spiraled pupils,[59] extended tongue, filed tooth, and the incisor of a serpent curled in the commissure of his mouth. Below the solar shield there is a bicephalous serpent (Itzamná, the celestial dragon) in whose center is the frontal view of a jaguar's face. This jaguar, when depicted in the Sun descending into the underworld during the spring equinox, and associated with the western direction of the sunset, corresponds to the position of the temple with respect to the plaza. Some consider him patron of temple GIII, which is precisely the Sun as the jaguar god of the underworld, the god of the dead.

As archaeoastronomical studies have shown, the solar cycle guided the construction of this temple as well as the other principal temples in Palenque.[60]

The Sun and the rain are often depicted as descending anthropomorphic gods. In the Templo del Dios Descendente in Tulum, we see the solar deity identified with the wings and tail of the eagle, diving with his head facing down.

Chaac, God B

The god named Chaac in the colonial texts is the most represented in the three Mayan pre-Hispanic codices (fig. 26). He is mentioned as the deity of the maize fields and as the manifestation of water—not only of rain but also of lakes, rivers, and the sea, which, transformed into vapor, rise to the sky to form clouds and return to earth as rain (fig. 27).

Chaac, god B, is another anthropomorphic deity derived from the dragon. He is most often represented in the codices of the postclassical period, where he is depicted with a large hanging nose, over which is an upward spiraled element. He has a serpent eye with a spiral-shaped pupil, and below the lower eyelashes there is another

---

[59] Some have called this eye "the divine eye." It is the eye of the serpent and is represented in all of the deities related to the serpent.

[60] Hartung 1987, 19; see also Carlson 1976.

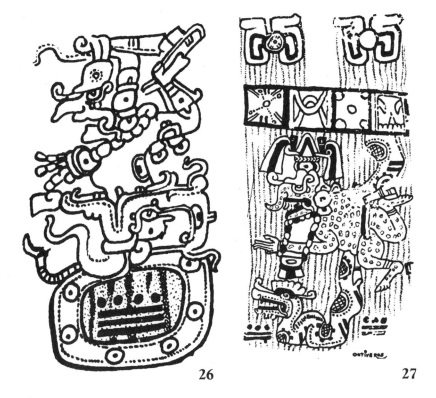

26   27

28

Fig. 26. The god Chaac. *Dresden Codex*, p. 33b1.

Fig. 27. The god Chaac as manifestation of water. *Madrid Codex*, p. 12.

Fig. 28. Mask representing the god Chaac.

spiral (similar to that of the nose) that extends over the temple of his head, and a curved incisor that projects from the commissure of the mouth. In his hand he often carries an ax that symbolizes lightning and sometimes a torch that symbolizes the dry season. On him depended the rain. We see him sitting over directional trees, animals, astral bands, and clouds; inside a frame with *Caban* signs (earth); and over the jaws of large serpents, who apparently represent temporality.

We also see Chaac on a mural painting with the same attributes as those in the Templo de los Frescos in Tulum. Sometimes, as in the paintings of Tancah, he is depicted carrying an ax and a vase containing *copal*. Other images of the god, or a priest dedicated to his cult, are found on a clay coffin in Mayapán, where he carries in his hands such ritual objects as a vase and a censer.

This deity is represented also in classical sculptures on the Yucatan Peninsula, belonging to the Río Bec, Chenes, and Puuc styles. There he appears as a large geometric mask made of a stone mosaic which decorates many of the buildings of these styles (fig. 28). The masks contain clear markings of a serpent and a large "nose," which can point either up or down, and is at times decorated with aquatic circles that symbolize an elongated upper jaw of a serpent. There are some masks that have stylized feathers or plants that could either represent Chaac, Itzamná, or Bolon Dz'acab, the god associated with maize, because all three gods are of a serpent-like character.

In the central region, where rain—and water in general—is associated with the celestial and terrestrial dragon, it is difficult to find representations that point to Chaac. But perhaps the monster named *Cauac* was a water deity who preceded Chaac. We consider him to be a representation of the terrestrial dragon because, in addition to the *Cauac* glyphs, he is presented with plant elements.

The Terrestrial Dragon: Itzam Cab Ain

In his relationship with the earth, the dragon symbolizes the terrestrial surface as well as the generative power hidden within. For this reason he is associated with the god of death who resides in the earth, and with the jaguar, the symbol of the Dead Sun, the underworld and night sky. In the classical period he was represented with a large mask, sometimes void of flesh, that carried, however, aquatic and plant symbols. Because of the presence of this glyph, which sym-

29

Fig. 29. Upper portion of zoomorph P in Quiriguá.

Fig. 30. The Cauac monster of the altar on stela M in Copán.

30

bolizes water, he is referred to as the monster of the earth or Cauac monster. Examples of the terrestrial dragon are the Cauac monster of the altar on stela M in Copán (fig. 30); the zoomorph P in Quiriguá, where he was sculpted as the Cauac monster and as a great serpent, from which he emerges as ruler (fig. 29); the mask that appears as the base of the *axis mundi* tree, with two serpent heads emerging from the commissures of the jaws, which are identified with the solar god of the panel in the Temple of the Foliated Cross in Palenque (fig. 9); and the one without flesh but with the leaves of maize and the glyph of Cauac that form the pedestal of one of the rulers represented there.

We have also seen several notable representations of the terrestrial dragon in the recently discovered site of Balamkú (Campeche), where there is a frieze with stucco reliefs called "Casa de los cuatro reyes" (house of the four kings). It has four masks of the terrestrial dragon with plant elements from whose jaws also emerge two serpents from the commissures. The terrestrial character of these masks is confirmed because above them are seated reptile figures with open jaws pointing upward from which emerge portraits of rulers.[61]

These reptile figures from Balamkú also represent the terrestrial dragon, because in much of the art in the Maya area, from Izapa as well as depictions from the colonial texts, the earth is symbolized by a great lizard or fantastic crocodile whose Yucatec name is Itzam Cab Ain, "El dragon-tierra-cocodrilo" (The earth-dragon-crocodile),[62] and Chac Mumul Ain, "Gran cocodrilo lodoso" (Great muddy crocodile). In the *Popol Vuh* we find the equivalent of this crocodile in the caiman who symbolizes the earth, Zipacná, creator of the mountains and the entire earth; son of Vucub Caquix, the imperfect sun of the period before the present.

One of the most distinguished works representing the terrestrial dragon as a crocodile is altar P in Copán and the antecedent that demonstrates the antiquity of the symbol: the crocodile on stela 25 in Izapa, which we described earlier (fig. 2).

The terrestrial dragon seen below the figure on the tombstone in

---

[61] Baudez 1996.

[62] According the the *Dictionary Maya Cordemex*, Itsam is not the name of a lizard, but rather of the deity. They consider, as we do, that he is the same Itzamná in his role as terrestrial god (p. 272).

the Templo de las Inscripciones in Palenque (fig. 7) is a large mask, devoid of flesh, within a hollow formed by bones—clearly an image of the underworld. But he is depicted with plant elements, and on his forehead he carries the glyph of the Sun with the triadic symbol of the celestial dragon. Instead of the glyph of crossed bands, however, there appears that of the dead. This image confirms that the celestial and terrestrial dragon who, as in this case, is also a figure of the underworld, represents the same sacred energy displayed in all cosmic environments.

A postclassical example of the terrestrial dragon is the figure of Lamanai, given as an offering following the Spanish conquest, which displays a crocodile with a human face between his jaws.

Ah Puch, god "A"

Often associated with the terrestrial dragon is the god who symbolizes death. He is represented as a skull, a skeleton, or a decomposing cadaver. In classical artworks he appears with a collar of rattles, and in the codices these rattles or "eyes" also appear on his head, hands, and ankles. It is noteworthy that in all of his representations he has eyes and sometimes an anus and a penis. Paradoxically,[63] in some of the figures shown in the codices, he has breasts. Therefore, as the supreme celestial god, Itzamná, the god of death, is androgynous. Representing him as a natural being demonstrates that death is not conceived of as "nothing." Rather it is an acting energy in the cosmos and necessary complement to the vital energy.[64] Next to the other gods, the god of death is drawn in the codices as affecting diverse activities; some of these are rituals such as the ceremonies of the New Year, which show his role in the life of the world.

The colonial texts refer to Ah Puch as "The Fleshless," or Kisin, "The Stinkard." He is also called Yum Cimil "Lord of Death" and Hun Ahau. He has been identified with god A in the codices. His place is the lowest stratum of the underworld, called Xibalbá in the Quiché and Mitnal texts of the Yucatec Maya. The spirits of most people come to this place when they die.

---

[63] Sotelo 1997.
[64] De la Garza 1978.

One of his most notable images is that on the great stucco panel in Toniná. There he holds the sacrificed head of a decapitated individual. The god of death was therefore logically associated with human sacrifice.

Another image of him is found in Temple XII, or in the cavern of Palenque, where he is represented in stucco on the lower parts of the doorjambs. This temple is therefore also associated with the underworld.

The altar depicted on stela D in Copán (fig. 24) shows a fleshless head of the deity. But in the place of his eyes, he has glyphs of the solar god, who, when passing through the underworld, is the god of death.

The *Popol Vuh* mentions various deities of death and disease led by Hun Camé "One Death," and Vucub Camé "Seven Death." These deities also appear represented in such works of the classical period as the "Cup of the seven gods" from Naranjo, Guatemala (750 to 800 C.E.).[65] There we see a smoking god, god L, whom Thompson identified as the jaguar god of number 7.[66] He is in a jaguar skin, seated on a trunk before six gods, who could either be several lords of the underworld mentioned in the text, or versions of the same god of death. Some of them, however, have features of the Solar god as well as jaguar skins, which associates them with the night Sun whose epiphany is the jaguar. The background is black and the principal god, who clearly corresponds to Hun Camé, Vucub Camé, is found under a crocodile who symbolizes the surface of the earth—features that demonstrate that they are in the underworld. The coincidence of the number (seven gods, gods of the number seven, and "Seven Death") on the cup and in the text, confirms the interpretation. The date inscribed on the cup is that of creation, 4 *Ahau*, 8 *Cumhú*, for which the scene could refer to the birth of the gods of the underworld at the beginning of the present era.

Bolon Dz'acab, God K

One of the serpent gods who has features, or manifestations, of the celestial dragon in the religious minds of the Maya, is god K. He is

---

[65] Reents-Budet 1994, 236; Freidel and Schele 1993.

[66] Thompson 1970, 106.

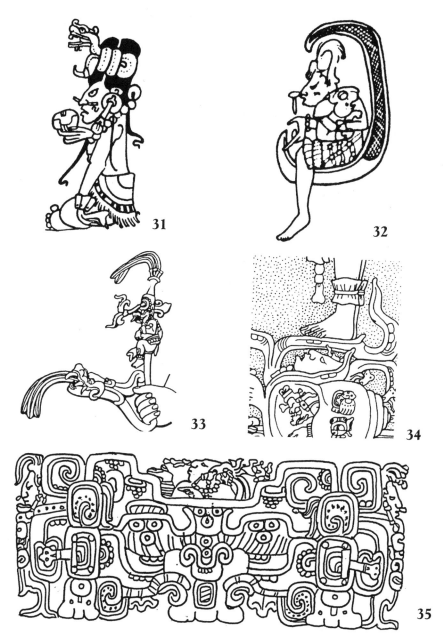

Fig. 31. Goddess of the moon. *Dresden Codex*, p. 22b2.

Fig. 32. Goddess represented as a young woman seated over a waxing moon and holding a rabbit.

Fig. 33. Figurine from altar P in Quiriguá.

Fig. 34. God K being born from a snail with corn ears emerging from his forehead.

Fig. 35. Fragment of stela 1 from Bonampak.

often identified with Bolon Dz'acab in the written sources, but especially in the references of Friar Diego de Landa and the codices.[67] In
addition, Bolon Dz'acab means "New Generations," which clearly
alludes to the illustrious lineages of the ruler; the ancestors that are
found in the underworld. Numerous classical representations
demonstrate that the deity is always linked to these figures.

Bolon Dz'acab is a serpent god, generally anthropomorphic, with
a leg transformed into a serpent. Sometimes his face looks like the
body of a bird-serpent or that of a serpent. His face is composed of a
serpent eye with a spiraled pupil and superorbital scales. He carries
the Nen glyph (mirror) on his forehead, from which emerge leaves of
maize (that sometimes end in tassels), flames, or an ax. He also has
a large bifurcated nose, which is a derivation of the superior jaw of
the serpent, and a coiled serpent tooth in the commissure of the
mouth—which also appears on other serpent deities, such as Chaac,
the god of rain,. and Kinich Ahau, the solar god.

During the classical period this god appeared on reliefs and as
individual sculptures, ceramics and figurines, canes and septum
mannequins, which sustained the rulers. In other words, these figurines are symbols of power. They have human bodies, serpent faces,
and a leg or penis converted into a serpent (fig. 33) identifying the
illustrious lineage of the ruler who displays them.

The Yucatec name for the septum mannequin is Canhel.[68] We
found it in the Chilam Balam de Chumayel designating the celestial
dragon as creator, which, in turn, identifies the two deities. In addition, the same text mentions Bolon Dz'acab participating in a cosmic
catastrophe as the deity that envelops and carries off the heart,
semen, and seeds to the sky. In other words, he is acting as the
guardian of the life of the universe.[69] On the other hand, the god of
the septum mannequin, because of the peculiarity of his leg, appears
to correspond to the hurricane "Lightning of one Leg," the Quiché
celestial god who, as rain, is the manifestation of Gucumatz. They
also call him "Heart of the Sky," which means "center or axis,

---

[67] Thompson 1970, 227.

[68] Libro de Chilam Balam of Chumayel. See the analysis of the name in de la
Garza 1984, 158-59.

[69] Sotelo 1977.

essence of sky." This is why he appears as rector over the other deities in the divine Quiché counsel.[70]

Bolon Dz'acab symbolized the offering of blood to the gods (an ascetic rite of the rulers), because in this image we can see the handles of the knives employed in the autosacrifice. Examples of these can be seen on the lintels in Yaxchilán. The septum, cane, or mannequin symbolizes the monastic rites of the offering of semen which was practiced by the ruling Maya. They appear in Yaxchilán and on the stucco reliefs in the doorway to the Temple of Inscriptions in Palenque.[71] In the codices there are drawings of figures very similar to those of the classical figures, with the eye of serpent, a large bifurcated nose curved upward (symbolizing vegetation) and a curved tooth in the commissure of the mouth.

One extraordinary image of god K was drawn on a cylindrical cup of the codex style from the region of Nakbé in Guatemala.[72] The serpent-leg of the god surrounds the voluptuous body of a woman, and from the enormous open jaws of the serpent emerges another deity, whose hands extend toward the woman. The scene makes a clear sexual allusion, which corroborates the association of god K with semen.

This god is also associated with maize, because from his forehead emerge the leaves of the plant. This relation is clearly expressed on the panels in the group from La Cruz in Palenque, where god K appears as a figurine seated facing in an easterly direction in the hands of the rulers, representing maize, whose cycle is also depicted in these reliefs. The central theme on the panel from the Templo del Sol is the maize plant that is depicted as an *axis mundi* because it celebrates his birth. We also see god K (also known by the name GII) being born from a snail with corn ears emerging from his forehead (fig. 34). All of this confirms the character of the deity associated with the maize of god K during the classical period. Because of this, he is a god closely tied to humans, who, according to the cosmogonic myth, were formed out of a dough of maize by the creator god. Taube has named him Kawil, maybe because of his association with

---

[70] *Popol Vuh*, 13.

[71] See Coggins 1988.

[72] Reents-Budet 1994. Foundation for the Advancement of Mesoamerican Studies.

maize and the fact that the word *ka'wil* means "the second maize harvest."[73]

The relationship between Bolon Dz'acab and Itzamná is evident in many images represented on the tombstone in the Templo de las Inscripciones in Palenque; on stela D in Copán; and on lintel 3 of Temple IV in Tikal, where he is depicted as emerging from the jaws of a bicephalous celestial serpent. There are other representations depicted on the stucco panel of Toniná, and the panels in La Cruz in Palenque, where his face is that of the bird-serpent, who, as we said earlier, is a variation of the celestial dragon.

All of these coincidences show that god K is a version of the celestial dragon, supreme deity of the Maya pantheon. Because he symbolizes blood, semen, and maize, god K is the manifestation of the dragon's sacred power in the human world.

God of Maize, God E

We have seen how god K is related to maize. There is another divine figure, however, showing traces of a young man without animal elements that appears be an incarnation of true maize because he carries on him the leaves of the plant and his head ends as an ear of corn. From what we have thus far identified, this image appears in art from the classical period onward and corresponds to god E of the codices.

Eric Thompson associates the god Kawil mentioned in the written sources with the god of maize because he signifies the "Abundance of our daily bread."[74] However, scholars do not agree concerning his name. Some say that he is Yum Kaax, "Lord of the Forest," and others give him the name Bolon Mayel, associated with fertility and abundance.[75] Itzamná, the supreme god, is sometimes called Itzamná Kawil, which also demonstrates that the god of maize is closely tied to the celestial dragon. The god of maize is the patron of the number 8, and his glyph is that of day *Kan*, maize.

As a classical example representing the god of maize, we can cite the well-known sculpture of Copán, a fragment of stela 1 from

---

[73] Taube 1992; *Diccionario Maya Cordemex*, 305.
[74] Thompson 1970, 289.
[75] Kelley and Taube respectively in Sotelo 1997.

Bonampak, where the god of maize emerges from the terrestrial dragon in the form of the Cauac monster (fig. 35), and various ceramic pieces depicting the deity emerging from a turtle shell.[76] As maize is the true human plant, the cosmogonic Quiché myth recounts that humans were formed from a dough made of maize, which explains why the god is represented as a human figure without animal features.

In the codices, god E is personified with a human face, an ear of corn over his head, a folded leaf on his forehead, and a vertical line that divides the face through one eye. In almost all of his images, the god is associated with the signs *Caban* (earth) and *Kan* (maize). At various times he appears with a crow, a bird much associated with maize because it feeds on maize. On pages 24c and 25c of the *Madrid Codex*, we see him seated before a lit fire-pan. Above him a dog descends from the sky with a torch, the symbol of the solar fire. The latter may allude to the obvious association of maize with the Sun. In one scene he is painted blue with one open eye—in other words, alive. In another, he is yellow with a shut eye, symbolizing maize that has already been cut.

There are various Mesoamerican myths concerning the origin of maize, which was a sacred plant because it was the mainstay of humans. In the *Chilam Balam de Chumayel* there is an account that narrates the birth of maize in the beginning of time, and it is called metaphorically the "stone of grace."[77]

Female Gods

From the classic period the epigraphers mention references to ancestral female gods in the texts—principally from Palenque, such as the First Mother, who appears in the cosmogonic text and who was born one year after the First Father.

There have been no stone or stucco sculptures identified from the classical period that we could positively identify as mother gods, but they do appear among the clay figurines in various sites. One of the more important sites is Jaina, an island situated off the coast of Campeche. There we see female figures with sacred attributes such

---

[76] See Freidel and Schele 1993.
[77] *Chilam Balam of Chumayel*, 97.

as the bicephalous serpent on their backs and their hands in a ritual position over their chest. The presence of the bicephalous serpent, symbol of the supreme being, presents the god mother as his feminine aspect. Perhaps he is related to the moon, as is the mother goddess in the postclassical codices.

The postclassical representations of the female gods in the codices, as well as references from the written sources, describe the existence of a great mother god related to the moon, medicine, births, and the labors ascribed to this sex such as weaving. We know of various names of goddesses from the colonial texts, but that of Ixchel stands out. She has been associated with the female deities represented in the codices (fig. 31).

The texts do not mention Ixchel as a lunar goddess, but it can be inferred, because the name can be translated to mean "She of White Face." In addition, the mother gods are usually associated with the Moon because it is considered an energy that propitiates fertility not only of earth but also of the animals and humans. The moon regulates the cyclic rhythm of life, the tides, and the terrestrial waters, in order to fertilize the earth. Therefore, in the Mayan fertility rites, it is the Moon from whom one requests sexual energy and procreative ability. It is also evident that Ixchel, who is given various other names in the texts, was the lunar goddess and as such, she was venerated in such aquatic environments as Cozumel Island and the cave of Bolonchén. Water and fertility are always associated in religious thought.

There are two goddesses mentioned in the codices, one young and the other old, to whom the letters I and O were respectively assigned.[78] Noemí Cruz believes that the young goddess I is the new Moon, while the old goddess O represents the full moon. As such they represent two aspects of the same deity, whose principal name was Ixchel. The lunar goddess takes on various meanings, such as the young goddess, representing medicine and birth; and the old goddess, representing the earth, vegetation, and weaving.[79] In short, Ixchel appears to symbolize the moon and the earth, elements that most ancient cultures associated with the feminine.

---

[78] Thompson interprets goddess I to be Ixchel, the lunar goddess, and goddess O to be Ixchebel Yax, the companion of the god Itzamná (1970, 206-9).

[79] Cruz 1995, 14.

This interpretation is corroborated by the images from the classical period where we see the goddess represented as a young woman seated over a waxing moon and holding a rabbit, whose outline can be seen when the moon is full.[80]

The *Popol Vuh* mentions what appears to be a mother goddess, or the feminine aspect of the dual creator deity father-mother. The deity is known by distinct names such as Hunahpú Vuch, "*Zarigüeya* or *Tlacuache* (opossum) Hunter," and the goddess of the dawn, who forms a couple with Hunahpú Utiú, "Coyote Hunter," the masculine night god. They also call her Zaqui-Nimá Tziís, "Great-White-Badger," the old mother goddess who is the companion of Nim Ac, "Great-Forest-Boar."

Another mythological female in the *Popol Vuh* is Ixquic, the mother of the gods Hunahpú and Ixbalanqué (the Sun and the Moon). She is the daughter of the god of death associated with the initiatory death rite and rebirth in the underworld, an ordeal that the gods underwent before transforming into Sun and Moon.

There are many more deities and aspects of the principal gods represented in the arts of the classical period. But here we have limited ourselves to discussing those deities of the major cosmic environments and those related to fertility, which was one the fundamental concerns of the classical Maya.

Rites

General Characteristics

As is the case among many ancient and modern religions, the ceremony in Mayan religion essentially sought to unite with the sacred forces to acquire happiness, power, material goods, relief from evil, forgiveness for faults, and, in a more profound sense, an assurance for the survival of nature and humanity.

The priests, who were believed to have been elected by the deities themselves in order to function as the intermediaries for humans, conducted the rituals. Their place in society was of prime importance, because to serve the gods was primary objective of the entire life of the community. The Maya were convinced that without the rit-

---

[80] Schele and Miller 1986, 55.

ual, the earth would become sterile, the rains would cease, the live beings would not procreate, and the Sun would stop moving and die. Consequently, the cosmos would perish. Therefore, as stipulated in the cosmogonic myths, to sustain and venerate the gods was the fundamental mission of humans on earth.

The rites were complex public events dedicated to calendric periods; ceremonies of access to power for the rulers; fertility, social, curative, and initiation events; as well the life-cycle: pregnancy, birth, infancy, puberty, marriage, and death.

Rites were celebrated in the distinct ceremonial centers and villages. But some sites were especially sacred and were the destinations of pilgrimages from many points in the Maya territory. For example, Landa writes the following:

> They held Cuzamil and the sink-hole of Chichenizá in such high veneration as were the pilgrimages to Jerusalem and Rome, and as such they went to visit and offer gifts, principally to Cuzamil, as we do in the holy places, and those who could not travel, always sent their offerings.[81]

Common to all rites were diverse purification or preparatory ceremonies, so that the site as well as the participants would be in the condition to come into contact with the sacred. These ceremonies included sexual abstinence, sleep and food deprivation, baths, and bleedings.

The preparations of purification were followed by the principal rites. These were diverse as well, but all of them included prayer, fumigation (generally using copal resin), dances, chants, processions, dramatic presentations of the myths and histories of the illustrious forefathers who were deified, consumption of sacred food and drink and, as a central event—sacrifices.

Sacrifice

Sacrifice meant "to make holy" and included gifts that were offered to the gods. The offerings were many and varied. Because the gods were invisible and impalpable to humans, the offerings made to sustain them were subtle, such as flower aromas, incense, and the flavors of food and drink. But most important, sacrifices offered the

---

[81] Landa 1966, 48.

vital energy, or the spirit, present in the blood of animals and human beings. The fundamental gifts therefore consisted of those that implied the shedding of blood and the death of a victim, actions that permitted the liberation of the vital energy. As such, the majority of the rites involved the bloody self-sacrifice and ritual death of both animals and humans.

Human Sacrifice

Human sacrifice had the goal not only of communicating with the gods in gratitude for their benevolence but also of propitiating them. To do so there were diverse types of ritual death, among which we should mention heart extraction and decapitation. The heart is believed to be the seat of the vital energy. It was offered so that the gods would eat of it the moment that it abandoned the physical organ. We see examples of this practice depicted in markers 11 (fig. 37) and 14 of Piedras Negras and on page 3 of the *Dresden Codex*. Decapitation and killing with arrows were related to the fertilization of the fields, because the head was associated with the ear of corn and shooting arrows was interpreted as a sexual act.[82]

Bloody sacrifice in the Mesoamerican world is fundamentally explained by the concept of the gods and the significance of blood, especially that of humans. The cosmogonic myths explain that human blood is sacred for the Maya because it originates from the gods. It contains the spirit (vital energy) of the deities, which the latter gave humans when they created them. Therefore, there is an essential consanguinity between humans and the sacred: blood is the vital cosmic energy that comes from the gods and must be returned to them through the sacrifice. Blood itself is life; therefore, bloody sacrifice represents the surrender of life to the gods so that they might continue their existence and sustain the life of the cosmos. Without blood the gods would perish and the world would come to an end.

In an opposite sense, sacrifice also signified the feeding of humans with the essence of the divine. In many sacrifices, the human victim himself transformed into a god, was dressed and venerated as such, and after being sacrificed, was consumed by the faithful. This com-

---

[82] Nájera 1987.

munion with the god, besides making sacred the human, reestablished the unifying ties between the members of the community. In
a number of other rites, the incarnated deity was killed before the
temple on the summit of the pyramid and hurled down the stairs
onto the plaza, where he was quartered and consumed by the faithful. This act represented the descent of the god from the sacred
ambit of the sky (symbolized by the pyramid) to the earth of humans,
where he physically became one of them.

The particular significance of human blood as the only substance
of divine origin, and the distinguished position of humans in nature
because of their consciousness, allowed them to recognize and venerate the gods, thus making it logical and imperative that humans be
sacrificed. However, at the time of the Spanish conquest, the sacrifice
of human beings was being replaced by that of dogs,[83] which were the
closest to humans, the truest and the most docile animals. This pattern also occurred among other peoples who substituted domesti-
cated animals, such as the goat, for human victims. It also leaves us
to suppose that if human sacrifice had not disappeared as the result of
the violent imposition of another religion, it would have disappeared
through the spiritual evolution of that religion which created it.

Self-sacrifice

With the same basic idea of having to feed the gods with blood, the
Maya also practiced self-sacrifice, which consisted in the individual
offering his own blood without reaching the point of death.

Blood was extracted using cutting implements made from animal
bones, ropes of thorns, or other cutting objects. Generally the blood
was poured onto paper or into vases and subsequently offered to the
images of the gods. Various pieces of artwork found, for example, on
some lintels in Yaxchilán and on the friezes in Bonampak, show this
rite as having been practiced since the classical period.

Self-sacrifice also formed an essential part of ascetic rites that, on
the one hand, were rites of entrance or preparation for religious ceremonies and, on the other, were part of the initiation rites and habit-
ual practice of the priests and shamans. Many believed that ascetic

---

[83] Landa 1966, 65.

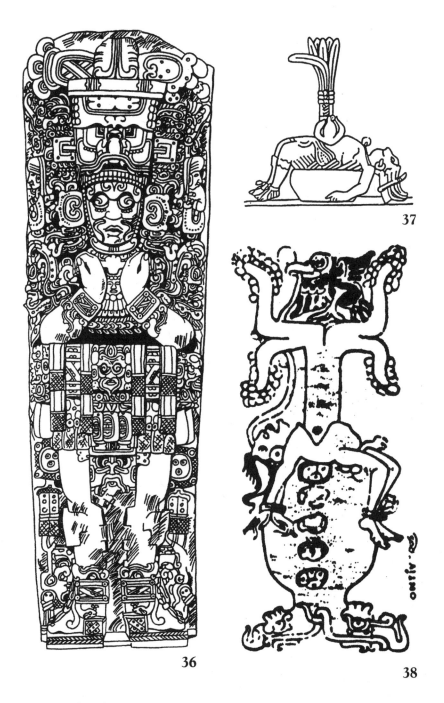

36

37

38

Fig. 36. Stela 1 from Copán.

Fig. 37. Scene of human sacrifice on marker 11 of Piedras Negras.

Fig. 38. Scene of human sacrifice. *Dresden Codex*, p. 3.

rites conferred supernatural powers that permitted a more direct tie with the divine.[84]

In addition to blood, semen was another sacred fluid believed to possess vital energy. It was offered by ascetics to the divine through monastic practices. The offerings of blood and semen were accompanied by sleep deprivation, fasting, sexual abstinence, purification baths or abstention from bathing, prayers, dances and rhythmic chants, and the ingestion or use of psychoactive substances such as tobacco, fungi, and hallucinogenic plants, as well as inebriating drinks.

The Concept of Humanity
and Sanctifying of the Ruler

In the Maya universe, impregnated by the sacred that originated motion, life, and death, one finds humanity forming a completely harmonic relationship with nature. According to the myths, humans are integrated into the universe because they contain, in their being, substances of plants, animals, and the divine. But they are distinguished from everything else because they are conscious beings who can understand and manage cosmic space-time through ritual action. These concepts are expressed in cosmogonic myths and archaeological remains since the classical period—for example, the extraordinary burial in the Templo de las Inscripciones in Palenque, where the skeleton of the ruler, Pacal, holds a jade sphere in one hand and a die in the other. Both are fundamental cosmogonic symbols representing sky and earth, time and space. This shows that the individual was aware of his universe and lived in harmony with it.

For being responsible for the existence of the cosmos, the human being functions as an *axis mundi*. The human is represented as such in many works of pre-Hispanic art, among which are stela 25 from Izapa (mentioned earlier; fig. 3), and on the tombstone of Pacal (fig. 7). In the latter, the ruler is placed in the center, between the sky and the underworld, over the surface of the earth and at the base of the cross—the axis of the universe, which is one of the images of the supreme god Itzamná.

The men represented in the classical works are generally rulers called *Halach unicoob,* "Venerated men," by the Yucatec Maya. Even though in some pictorial works and sculptures there are also commoners, these always appear in relation to the rulers and often in an act of submission, as we see in the Templo de las Pinturas in Bonampak.

The principal symbol representing the ruler is the dragon, who, as a celestial power (creative and organizing), bestows on the ruler the necessary powers to govern over the others; and as a terrestrial power, when consumed, the dragon transforms the ruler into a supernatural being. The ruler, represented on many stelae, lintels, and tombstones, especially in the central area, is depicted with a celestial dragon upon his chest in the form of a bicephalous serpent, which functions as a ceremonial staff; he carries it in his hand as a septum or cane mannequin and also on his headdress, along with other adornments such as belts, chains, and even sandals. In this respect, the dragon symbolizes the omnipotence of the ruler, whose face also has dragon features to demonstrate his assimilation to this supreme deity (fig. 36).[85]

The rulers also carry septums on which the celestial deity symbolizes the *axis mundi*, as those, for example, that are represented on lintels 2 (fig. 10) and 5 in Yaxchilán. It is another way to express that the *Halach uinic* has in his hands the power bestowed upon him by the celestial deity, which extends to the four paths of the cosmos.

Initiatory Rites and Shamanic Practices of the Rulers

The divine quality of the rulers was not inherited. Rather it was acquired through strict initiation rituals, surely to gain access to the throne, as well as through continual ascetic practices while they were men of importance. In other words, the Mayan rulers of the classical period, just as many Mayan *curanderos* and diviners of today, were shamans.

Many sculpted works, among which are various lintels in Yaxchilán, depict the monarchs emerging from the jaws of large serpents. The figure carries the instruments of self-sacrifice, which is one of the principal shamanic rites, or he receives them from a woman. In other cases this woman presents him with the sacred pouch con-

---

[84] De la Garza 1990.
[85] De la Garza 1984.

taining the shamanic paraphernalia[86] which also symbolized the supreme power. The ruler also emerges from the jaws of the terrestrial monster, as in zoomorph P in Quiriguá, and in so doing joins the Sun, whose image we often see emerging from the jaws of the dragon as well. The ruler is the Sun of the human world.

Having analyzed the iconography from the frieze of the "Casa de los Cuatro Reyes" (House of the Four Kings) in Balamkú, Claude Baudez wrote the following:

> Besides illustrating in detail the opposing and complementary aspects of the underworld, it shows that the dynastic cycle is equivalent to the solar cycle. In this concept, access to the throne is illustrated by the king emerging from the jaws of the terrestrial monster, as the sun rises from the mouth of the Earth; the death of the king is seen as a setting of the Sun, when it falls into the mouth of the terrestrial monster—as king Pacal of Palenque, where it is represented on the lid of his sarcophagus.[87]

The concept of the Sun rising from the jaws of the terrestrial monster also alludes to the initiation of the gods, which is comparable to that of the rulers, because the Sun comes from the underworld—that is, he is resurrected each morning. We will remember that in the *Popol Vuh* the individuals who changed into the Sun and the Moon first underwent a death initiation and rebirth in the underworld before ascending to the sky.

These images of the classical rulers are, without doubt, expressions of certain initiation rites depicted in the written sources[88] that persist today among the Maya and various other Mesoamerican peoples. The initiatory rites require that, after a long apprenticeship, the initiate goes to a dark and distant place (in the forest or mountains) and sits close to an ant hill from where will emerge an enormous boa constrictor (symbol of fanged powers), who swallows him, minces him within his jaws, and later defecates him. This is how the shaman appears, a sanctified man who has acquired, through the serpent, supernatural capacities which allow him to exert power over other

---

[86] According to the colonial texts, this pouch was the principal symbol of power. It contained the instruments for self-sacrifice, sacred stones, hallucinogenic and curative plants and fungi as well as other shamanic objects.

[87] Baudez 1996, 40.

[88] De la Garza 1984.

men. Here the role of the serpent is that of "Master of Initiation." Once sanctified, the shaman can practice through ecstatic trance and use the sacred plants (hallucinogenic and medicinal) to practice div- inations and healing.

In the Templo de la Cruz in Palenque, besides the solar and maize cycles, there is also shown an initiatory cycle of the rulers. Schele and Freidel say that the three sanctuaries symbolize the gateway to the underworld and associate them with the journey to the region of the underworld made by the twins mentioned in the *Popol Vuh*.[89] But in addition, the stucco reliefs that decorate the northern and eastern friezes of the Templo de la Cruz (drawn by Alfred Maudslay), of which today there remain only a few fragments, represent a frontal view of the dragon with open jaws (fig. 39). It is therefore a question of a monstrous temple whose main façade probably also contained the face of the dragon, with the mouth as a doorway. Thus, it is a temple for initiations, which confirms the existence of the initiation rites of the rulers represented there.

The transfiguration of those who possess power, the ancient *Halach uinicoob*, "True Men," and the actual shamans is linked to the serpent or terrestrial dragon because it is a fanged animal of the underworld and the incarnation of death. Initiation therefore implies dying and being reborn sanctified. In addition, the serpent is the ani- mal that undergoes transformation only to be reborn as himself. By abandoning his old skin he undergoes a cycle of renewal, as does the vegetation, to become eventually immortal. The serpent bestows sacredness on humans, because they are linked to the vital and divine cosmic energy, the great mother earth, the water, the phallus, and knowledge. Therefore, one who associates with the serpent acquires his qualities. One who is swallowed by the serpent dies, only to return to life transfigured into one who is capable of ascending to the mys- teries of the cosmos, to the secrets of life, death, and the future.[90]

The Ball Game as a Rite of Rulers[91]

One of the most common and important pre-Hispanic rites was the ball game. Ball courts can be seen in ceremonial places of all classi-

---

[89] Schele and Freidel 1990, 239.
[90] De la Garza 1984.
[91] De la Garza and Izquierdo 1992.

cal Mayan cities. The symbolic significance of the game is revealed by the reliefs found in the courts, particularly in the markers. They are often associated with the cosmogony, as demonstrated by the comparison of these reliefs with the myth of origin contained in the *Popol Vuh*.

The religious significance of the ball game forms part of one of the fundamental concepts of Mesoameican thought: the battle of opposites that makes possible the existence of the cosmos. This is expressed in various myths that refer to the struggle between luminous and celestial beings and the beings from the dark and the underworld—a battle that takes place on the ball court.

The game of the men and the sacred war symbolized the recreation of the struggle of the gods. During the classical period, the game may have had the ritual function of propitiating the movement of heavenly bodies through sympathetic magic, which is the equivalent of propitiating the existence of the universe. The ball game always appears tied to the fertility of the earth. The classical reliefs appear to represent both the game of the gods and the ritual game of the men, who in the classical epoch were represented by the rulers themselves.

An example of the ball game between the gods is seen on the reliefs that decorate the ball court markers in Copán—three works of the sixth century found in structure IIb (fig. 40). An analysis of the distinct elements of these disks reveals that the action takes place in the night sky, when the Sun is in the underworld, and this is where the initiatory episode of the appearance of the Sun and Moon in the *Popol Vuh*, where the ball game between the twin heroes and the gods of the underworld, is a central event.[92]

The markers in Copán demonstrate that, already in the classical period, the ball game constituted a mythical explanation of the origin and movement of the heavenly bodies and the oppositions in nature among the lowland Maya. This belief continued until the period when the *Popol Vuh* was written.

Because of its sacred significance, the ball game took on the character of an initiation rite which entailed the transcendence from a profane life to a sacred life and the acquisition of supernatural powers that permitted the direct communication with the deities. In the

---

[92] See the detailed analysis of these works in de la Garza and Izquierdo 1992.

same fashion that the astral gods in the *Popol Vuh* achieved their apotheosis through the ball game, the rulers of the classical period appear to have achieved part of their initiation as shamans through the rite of the ball game.

Various artworks from the classic period, such as the reliefs on the doorways of temple 33 in Yaxchilán, the marker of Cancuén, and the tombstones housed in the Museum of the American Indian in New York (fig. 41), all depict the ruler-priests playing the ball game. They are presented in luxurious headdress, diverse representations of god K (the deity of the rulers) and sometimes of the supreme god Itzamná. The personages are represented as either passive or actively playing, but always equipped with the implements of the game. Their names appear in the associated hieroglyphic inscriptions: Bird-jaguar in Yax-chilán, Claw of Jaguar in Seibal, and so on. The indigenous colonial texts corroborate that the game was indeed played by the rulers.[93]

The rites of sacrifice by decapitation or by the cutting of the throat carried a sense of fertility and were associated with the ball game. The extraordinary reliefs of the ball game in Chichén Itzá, for example, represent a rite of decapitation of a warrior-player. From the victim's kneeling body emerge six serpents and a plant (symbolizing blood and life) that demonstrate the profound ties between humans and plants. This concept is expressed also in the cosmogonic myths. The head is associated with the game because of the formal (spherical) relationship that exists between it, the ball, and the heavenly bodies; stars were believed to be the heads of decapitated gods that are also identified with the ball. At the same time, the movement of the ball in the court imitated the movement of the heavenly bodies in the sky.

Not one source suggests, as is sometimes asserted, that the players were sacrificed. The sacrifice by decapitation in the ball court or in association with the court might have been that of a prisoner of war or of a slave.

The reliefs and texts associated with the ball game, together with the location of the courts in the ceremonial centers, reveal that the game symbolized the cosmic struggle between opposites—a struggle essential in Mesoamerican thought—and that it was an initiatory rite practiced by the ruling shamans as part of their sanctification

---

[93] *Testament of the Xpantzay.*

process. They also demonstrate that the goal was to propitiate, through sympathetic magic, the movement of the stars, which produced temporality, fertility in nature, and the life of the cosmos in general.

The Priesthood

According to the written sources, the priests no longer ruled during the postclassical period. But they did create a complex priesthood structure that controlled all ritual activity. It was headed by the supreme priest Ahau Can, "Lord Serpent," or Ah Kin, "He of the Sun." He was the rulers' counselor and administered the cult in its entirety. He appointed priests by first "examining them in [the fields of] science and ceremonies"; he wrote the codices and taught the sciences that were, according to Landa:

> . . . the counting of the years, months and days, the feasts and ceremonies, the administration of the sacraments, the days and fatal times; their ways of divination, remedies for the ill, the ancient events, to read and write with their letters and characters in which they wrote with figures that represented scriptures.[94]

Landa also reveals the names and specialties of other Yucatec Mayan priests, such as the *chilames,* or prophets; the *ah menes,* or sorcerers, healers, and diviners; the *nacomes,* or those that sacrificed; and the *chaces,* or ancient ones, who assisted during the rites.[95] Of these priests, the *ah men* and the *chilam* were shamans.

The indigenous texts say that there were shamans in all Mayan communities. They are known by many names, but in the Quiché colonial texts they are called *nahualli*–a Náhuatl term designating a type of shaman. They describe them as prodigious men who govern the communities, just as we observe in classical art. Because of their supernatural powers obtained through ecstatic trance or the externalization of the spirit, the shamans interpreted and transmitted the messages of the gods to their people, practiced divinations to locate lost persons or things, and cured diseases, especially those caused by spirits. They magically controlled the natural elements and practiced sorcery, that is, causing harm through black magic. Distinguished in

---

[94] Landa 1966, 15.
[95] Ibid., 49.

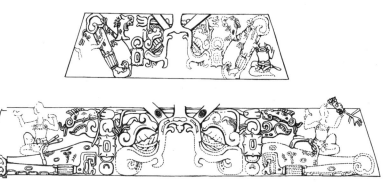

39

40

41

Fig. 39. Stucco reliefs in the Templo de la Cruz.

Fig. 40. Reliefs decorating the ball court markers in Copán.

Fig. 41. Depictions of ruler-priests playing the ball game.

the practice of divination employed by the healers is the interpretation of dreams and hallucinations, either those of the shaman or of a patient.

The *chilames* of the Yucatec Maya were priests who specialized in making prophecies. Their foundation was the concept of cyclic time, according to which natural as well as human events would repeat upon the return of the gods during a specified time. History, which is equated with the trajectory of human life, is also governed among the Maya by the laws of cosmic temporality. Therefore, if time is a cyclic movement, then human events recur, as do the cycles of nature. This is very clear in the prophetic texts of the Mayan colonial books, from which we can deduce that the historic classical texts are governed by the same basic concept as the historic trajectory. It is therefore necessary to document past human events in order to understand what will occur in the future, when the sacred influences return after a determined period of time, and, if these influences are malevolent, to be able to change them with benevolent charges effected through the ritual.

Prophecy was therefore a principal activity of Mayan priests. Landa says that during the feast of month *Uo* the priests met, took out their codices, invoked and presented offerings to Kinich Ahau Itzamná, "who they say was the first priest," purified the wood covers of the codices with virgin water "for its worldlyfication," made prognostications for the year, and recommended appropriate countermeasures for evil influences.[96] Many of these prophecies, besides those of the *katunes*, or twenty-year periods, have been preserved in the *Libros de Chilam Balam*.[97]

Based on a calendar ritual of 260 days, called Tzolkín among the Yucatec Maya, which is still in use today in Mayan communities, the priests made the horoscopes for the children because their lives were determined by the influences of the prevailing gods of each day. In addition, the Tzolkín was consulted for whatever action that should be taken. If the horoscopes and the prognostications were negative, they could avoid the evil influences through rituals. This implied that all life depended on the prognostications made by the priests.

---

[96] Ibid., 92.
[97] Barrera and Rendón 1969.

Common Rites

Thanks to the *Relación de las cosas de Yucatán*, written by Friar Diego de Landa, we have complete details of the principal official rites practiced in the postclassical period that were tied to time periods, most of all, the months (eighteen to twenty days) of the solar calendar called *Haab* by the Yucatec Maya and those of the New Year.

During the feasts of the months, homage was paid to one or more gods, and rites were celebrated by the men dedicated to a specific activity. For example, in the month Yax, they honored Chaac, the god of water, who was one and four, presenting him as the god of the cornfields; the representations of the gods and their censers were renewed; and the memory of the rite[98] was inscribed on the temple wall.

Among other things, the description of these feasts revealed that, with respect to the women, only the elderly could participate in organizing special dances for each occasion; that diverse sacrifices were offered, which included those of animals and men; and that there were distinct types of preparatory rites for the feast, such as fasting and sexual abstinence, and many other symbolic acts that enriched the celebration.

The more important ceremonies were those of the New Year, which were celebrated during the five "additional" days at the end of the year, called *Uayeb* and considered to bring bad fortune. The years were determined by the sign of the day in the ritual calendar on which they began, which could only be four in the gears of the two calendars. As such, the day O *Pop*, first of the year, coincided with the epoch of the Spanish conquest, with the days *Kan, Muluc, Ix,* and *Cauac* also giving their names to years.

The principal deities in these ceremonies were the Bacabe gods, who braced the skies from the four cosmic paths, and each of the years was associated with a particular path. As is the case for the other gods, each Bacab had various names. In addition, during the four feasts they venerated a distinct god such as Itzamná, Bolon Dz'acab, or Kinich Ahau, with various special rites. Pages 25 to 28 of the *Dresden Codex* depict the ceremonies of the New Year presided over by gods K, G, D, and A. The Bacabe appear in the form of opossums.

---

[98] Landa 1966, 73-103.

Fertility Rites

Fertility is life, potential, and the realization of life. Life was the good par excellence for the ancient Maya, because the fertility of nature and humans was believed to be a sacred energy and therefore a primary concern. Thus, the most important manifestations and symbols of the sacred were those that propitiated fertility and maintained life. But fertility includes death, in a harmony of contradictions, and thus the Maya symbols for fertility as the potential for life in the universe included the force of death.

Accordingly, fertility rights were essential to the Mayan cult. Since the classical period, the shedding of blood was fundamental to these rites, because blood, represented by the serpent, vital symbol par excellence, infuses vital energy into the earth. Likewise, the human sacrifice and self-sacrifice were a central part of the offerings dedicated to the gods of life.

The decapitation had an essential sense of fertility. This signification is manifested in various classical works, among which stands out the tombstone from the Templo de la Cruz Foliada in Palenque (fig. 9), where the ears of corn are represented as human heads. The head is associated with the cut corn and, as we said earlier, it is also formally associated with the stars and the ball used in the rite of the ball game.

In the fertility ceremonies there is an essential symbol, the serpent, who is associated with the female deities and the phallus—expressing one of the dualities of his religious symbolism. The goddesses of the codices, who carry a coiled serpent on their heads, often appear pouring water, which surely alludes to the rites of fertility that, according to the written sources, were practiced by women.

The codices mention additional fertility rites related to maize. On page 34b of the *Madrid Codex* we see god E with a crow perched on his head, in front of a vase that rests on a coiled serpent and contains the sign *Kan*, maize, and the leaves from that plant. On the other side is the god of death participating in the ceremony. On page 37a, a deity is carrying out a rite of planting corn in front of a dog that howls while beating a drum that is part of the leg of the deity.

One of the principal self-sacrifices to propitiate fertility involved the penis, because the blood from this part of the body was considered of greater fertilizing power. Landa refers to a rite involving various men, which consisted in completely perforating the penises of various men and then passing a single thread through one perforation to the other in order to unite the individuals:

> Other times they made a dirty and painful sacrifice. Those who participated met in the temple and, lining up side by side, they made two askew holes in the virile member. Once completed, they passed a long thread and were thereby interconnected.[99]

In this rite the string symbolizes union, the vital noose. Participants, joined together in the offering of their blood to the deities, were sanctified in the act of bonding of themselves to the gods.

There are many sculptures of the phallic cult among the Maya since the classical period.[100] In addition, there are various figures of gods in the codices shown to be partaking in the self-sacrifice of the penis.

Rites of the Life Cycle[101]

Infancy. The life of an individual needed to be protected and sanctified from the moment of conception. The rites of the distinct phases of life also functioned to integrate individuals into the community by giving them the functions that corresponded to the various stages of their lives.

From the time that a child is conceived, offerings and prayers are made for the success of his birth and to attenuate "the imbalance produced by the proximate arrival of a new being, new to society, who will erupt from within the crust of the earth."[102] Birth was surrounded with rites in order that it proceed without difficulty. It was put into the care of Ixchel, as we said earlier, and attended to by a professional midwife, who conducted diverse rites to assure that harm would not befall the child or the mother. When the infant was born, it was purified in a nearby river; bird sacrifices were offered to thank the gods who sent the infant to earth; and a meal was prepared. The umbilical cord was cut over a corncob that was later

---

[99] Ibid., 49.

[100] Templo del Falus in Uxmal and in Chichén Itzá.

[101] Nájera 1966, 224-32.

[102] Sotelo and Valverde 1992.

planted, alluding to the concept that humans were made from a dough of maize.

There are references to several birthing ceremonies in the codices. For example, on page 93c of the *Madrid Codex*, we see midwives purifying children with water.

After four or five days two small boards were bound to the head of the infant to deform its skull, not only for aesthetic purposes but also for magic/religious reasons; perhaps with the goal that the infant acquire mental powers that would identify him with the jaguar.[103] Later they would produce its horoscope based on the day of its birth and give it a name.

Another rite was conducted at three years of age, which signified a change into a new phase; perhaps associated with child sexuality. A white bead was placed on the head of a boy, and for the girls they placed a red shell over the pubis. Both sexes were expected to keep these protection objects until puberty.

Upon reaching the age of thirteen they celebrated the *caputzihil* or anointing, a community rite celebrated by all adolescents of this age. The rite had the goal of integrating the young into the adult world. The central part of this ceremony consisted in the blessing and anointing of the children with virgin water by a priest who, in the same act, would remove the white bead from the boys while instructing the mothers to remove the red shell from the girls.[104] The celebration was also called *emku*, "descent of god," which symbolized that the young had been successfully integrated into adult life. They could now marry and would take on the ritual obligations in accord with their sex and status.

Marriage. Marriage was determined between the parents of the couple. The father of the groom elected the bride and provided the funds with which to buy the ceremonial dress. Before the ceremony, the couple would confess their faults and an elderly man would conduct a rite which consisted in tying together the extreme ends of their coats while reminding them to comply with their obligations as a couple and to the gods. They received gifts and purified the house in which they would live with *copal*. The newlyweds were then

---

[103] Sotelo and Valverde 1992.
[104] Landa 1996, 44–47.

blessed, prayers were recited, and two elderly men conducted the couple into their new house, where they were enclosed.

Beliefs concerning the afterlife and the funerary ritual. Death ends the terrestrial life cycle, but it also opens that of a different and eternal life in other places. The Maya believed in life after death, which implies the belief that the human being is a dual being, composed of a visible body and an invisible and intangible energy similar to that of the gods. Thanks to the survival of these beliefs among the present Maya as well as diverse data in the sources that coincide with these, we know that the spirit was also divided into two parts. One part rational, conscious, and immortal, inhabiting the human heart, and the other impulsive, thoughtless, and mortal, residing in a forest animal. This *alter-ego* animal, named *tona*, lives in a sacred mountain, protected and fed by the gods and the spirits of the forefathers, and shares the destiny of humans. When the body perishes, its zoomorph *alter ego* and the spirit that resides within it also die.

The spiritual portion that inhabits the human body may leave involuntarily during life, dreaming, orgasm, or by accident. It may also leave voluntarily during ecstatic trance, which only the shamans experience. This part of the spirit detaches permanently upon the death of the body and goes to live eternally in one of three sites according to the type of death: (1) Xibalbá or Mitnal, situated on the lowest level of the underworld; (2) the sky, where it accompanies the Sun on its journey; or (3) in the Paradise of the Cedar, a terrestrial place of natural pleasures in whose center stands a great cedar.

These beliefs required complex funerary ceremonies designed to protect and help the immortal spirit on its journey to its place of destiny. This is why, in the burials, vases that contained water and food have been found, as well as sacred objects intended to defend the spirit, and skeletons of dogs, whose spirits guided and accompanied the dead. This Mayan belief was shared also by many other ancient cultures.

There were various techniques for burying the cadaver: inhumation (primary and secondary), cremation, and perhaps aerial exposure and abandonment.[105]

The dead were buried in places related to their social position and

---

[105] Ruz 1968.

activity. For example, while the rulers were buried under the temples, the peasants were buried in the fields. The skeletons of the inhumed dead are often accompanied by other human or animal remains such as canines and felines. There are also many types of burials ranging from the simple hole in the ground to large funerary chambers containing vaults. Some are covered with a large pyramid that functioned as a funerary monument, like that of Pacal in Palenque and that of the Templo del Búho (Temple of the Owl) in Dzibanché, of the early classical period.[106] We also find burials under temples and houses, caves, rock crevasses, abandoned granaries, and vases or coffins buried in springs.

In Uaxactún and other sites, there are skeletons of children accompanied by adult phalanges probably belonging to the mother, a custom that expresses that in one way, she had accompanied her child.[107] Infant burials are usually in the fetal position within vases, which obviously symbolize the maternal womb and are undoubtedly associated with the concept of rebirth.

Numerous burials have been found exhibiting secondary burials; the burying of bones and other parts of the body which had previously received a distinct treatment such as ingestion, exposure, or even inhumation. They are generally group burials and are surely those of the sacrificed.[108]

According to the colonial texts, before being buried, the cadaver was bound and in its mouth was placed ground maize and a bead of jade or other similar stone. The maize alludes to the substance from which humans were formed. The stone, which was given to the dying individual, was what the spirit would incarnate into. That is why the stones were carefully guarded and offered sacrifices. As such, the stone, because of its strength and enduring qualities, symbolized the immortal spirit called *ol* by the Yucatec Maya, which survives the destruction of the body.[109]

The tombs also contained such diverse objects as tools, weapons, ceramics, shell ornaments, obsidian, stones, bone, jade and other semiprecious stones, copper bells, musical instruments, figurines of deities, complete skeletons and parts of animals, and other objects

---

[106] Campaña 1995.

[107] Ruz 1968, 115.

[108] Ruz 1968.

[109] De la Garza 1978.

symbolizing the sacred energies to protect the spirit. They included things that were used in life such as tools of the trade of the individual, codices and other ritual objects (in the case of priests), as well as their paraphernalia (if they were shamans).

These practices corroborate the belief that the spirit would lead a life similar to its terrestrial life and that it would conserve its identity during the journey to the place determined by its death. We prefer not to consider these as "offerings," because they do not signify homage to the dead. Rather, they were gifts from the living to help the spirit for a period following its corporal death.

Because the Maya believed that animals, plants, minerals, and even those objects made by humans had a spirit, it is clear that it was this "invisible" aspect of the objects that would be used by the spirit of the dead. Therefore in the tombs, in addition to the stone in the mouth, there were vases that had been intentionally broken or "killed."

The objects of greatest significance in the tombs, besides the stone in the mouth, were inverted vases, turtle shells, or a slab of stone protecting the head of the cadaver; stingray spines placed over the pubis, and the bones, teeth, and claws of felines. The object placed over the head is for the protection of the immortal spirit. It was believed to leave the body through the fontanel. Perhaps this was done so that the spirit would not be stolen or destroyed when it began its journey to the beyond. We know that the stingray spines were used during self-sacrifice. Perhaps placing them over the cadaver alluded to the offering that man made of himself to the deities after death; that is to say, that in the beyond he would be able to continue sustaining and venerating the deities. The jaguar symbolizes, among other things, the Sun in its journey through the underworld. Therefore, the parts of the body placed in the tomb might allude to an association of the one who descends to the underworld with the Sun during his nocturnal journey. But we also know that the jaguar was the *alter-ego* animal of the rulers and priests, and that shamans practiced self-sacrifice utilizing the spines of the stingray. Therefore, perhaps the Maya burials that contained remains of these animals were those of shamans.

Red cinnabar powder was commonly used. It was applied to the body during the primary burial (with the disappearance of the flesh, the powder would adhere to the bones, as in the tomb of Pacal), or applied it over the bones during the secondary burials. The red color symbolized birth and its association with the east, the place where the Sun rises, and thus, the origin of life. The use of the red powder on the dead indicates a rite of sympathetic magic to propitiate life in the beyond—the immortality.

With respect to cremation, Landa says that it was reserved for the upper class. Some parts of the body such as the bones and hair were preserved. They were placed together with the ashes of the dead in large urns, which were deposited underneath the temples or homes. There are references suggesting that the ashes were mixed with water or *atole* (a drink made from maize flour, water, milk, and sugar) and ingested by members of the immediate family. In Yucatan, the ashes of the lords were emptied into hollow statues of wood or clay. A portion of the scalp was then used to seal the statue. These statues were then placed next to the representations of the gods.[110] They say that once dead, the Cocom lords were decapitated. Their heads were boiled in order to remove the flesh, after which facial features would be molded over the skull. These heads were kept in the temples and houses where the individual was honored.[111]

These references from the written sources are supported by several archaeological discoveries. From the sacred spring of Chichén Itzá a skull was retrieved whose crown had been perforated, the orbits were sealed with wooden plugs, and there were remnants of stucco that had been painted over the face. In the sacred sink-hole small wooden figurines where found that were molded with *copal* and oil-cloth, with a hole in their posterior side. This appears to corroborate the custom of pouring ashes into wooden statues.

The archaeological data also mention the veneration of dead deified men, but only those who were important men in life. This is corroborated by the stelae of Copán, for example, that represent rulers under which were chambers containing offerings.

Sacred Spaces

The sacred spaces, or places where the gods were manifested, could be special places in those environments not inhabited by humans

---

[110] Landa 1966, 139.

[111] Ibid., 139–40.

such as forests, springs, and mountains. But they are also the ceremonial centers, constructed in places that demonstrated certain
exceptional characteristics that distinguished them as the residence
of divine beings. The ceremonial centers that are in the heart of the
Mayan cities were made in the image of the cosmos. The cosmogony
and the cosmology were the models for the constructions, as occurs
in all ancient cities of religious peoples. Federico González writes:

> Every city is founded in the center of the universe; the construction
> was not possible except through the absolution of the profane space
> and time and the instauration of a sacred space and time. The city is
> always an *imago mundi*, an image of the world.[112]

Furthermore, Mayan cities were constructed using astronomical
orientations[113] which impregnated these spaces with the sacred energies that emanated from the celestial beings during their trajectories.
As such, the plazas, temples and pyramids, ball courts, arches and
paved roads, patios, and other buildings symbolize the primordial
spaces of the origin of time, the three great levels of the universe, and
the routes of the stars and planets.

The plazas were the space where the people could participate in
official religious ceremonies. The temples atop the pyramids, the
sancta sanctorum, were reserved for the priests. Only they could go
there to conduct the diverse ceremonies such as human sacrifices.
Accordingly, the plazas symbolized the terrestrial level, while the
pyramids and temples they supported represented the sacred mountains and the celestial level respectively.

But the temples located on top of their pyramid bases could represent the ultimate stratum of the sky as well as the terrestrial level,
from which one descends into the underworld. And the pyramids
that support them symbolize the celestial and underworld strata, as
seen in the Templo de la Cruz and the Templo de las Inscripciones
in Palenque—cosmological images of the sky and the underworld
respectively as we indicated above.

As an image of the celestial level from the postclassical period we
could mention the pyramid of El Castillo (the Castle), located in
Chichén Itzá. During the spring equinox, the profiles of the pyramid

---

[112] González 1989, ch. 4.
[113] Aveni 1980.

project a shadow over the support beam, producing the rhombus design representing the back of a serpent *Crotalus durissus durissus,* which, covered with feathers, represents the supreme celestial god. The head of the serpent finalizes the beam over the plaza. This hierophanic shadow symbolizes the descent of the celestial dragon to the human world (represented by the plaza). In the doorway of the temple are columns in the form of feathered serpents, and the four sides of the pyramid represent the four regions of the sky. The stairs located on the four sides of the pyramid, as described by Landa[114] total 364, which when added to the base of the temple, would represent the 365 days of the year. Thus, the temple also symbolizes time as determined by the solar cycle.

Another celestial pyramid is El Castillo of Tulum, whose temple has a frieze with three niches and large masks in the corners. In the center niche there is an anthropomorphic deity in descent, that is to say, with his head pointing downward. It appears to symbolize the Sun penetrating the west, for he already has the tail and wings of the eagle—one of the solar animals par excellence. The masks in the corners represent the god Itzamná in his anthropomorphic state, for he has a toothless mouth, small rounded nose, and an eye with an adornment on the lower part, very similar to that which god D has in the codices—identified as Itzamná. Over his forehead are feathers that corroborate his character as a celestial deity.

As a postclassical example of an image of the underworld, the place to which the spirits of the dead descend, we can mention El Osario of Chichén Itzá. It has a pyramidal base with four staircases on its sides, whose beams end below with great serpent heads. In the upper part is an entrance to a deep sink-hole that was covered with large rocks, in which they found up to seven tombs with human skeletons and numerous offerings. As is the case for the Templo de las Inscripciones of Palenque, access to the enclosure of the dead was gained from the top of the pyramid, symbolizing the descent of the spirits of the dead from the terrestrial level to the ultimate stratum of the underworld.

On the other hand, there are temples that are representations of the underworld. They have on their sides the head of the great ser-

---

[114] They say that each set of stairs had 91 steps (Landa 1966, 113).

pent, through which the rulers passed to end their initiatory rites, having experienced death in the stomach of the serpent followed by rebirth. These are the temple-monsters (or "zoomorphic façade") that we consider fundamental in the styles of Río Bec, Chenes, and Puuc on the Yucatan Peninsula. But they are also represented in classical sites in the central area, such as in Copán and Palenque (fig. 39). The complete façade of the temple-monster is an enormous central mask whose mouth forms the entrance. It is flanked by rows of teeth and has spiraled eyes over the embrasure. There are ears on the sides and other decorative elements such as serpents, huts, and repeated motifs.

The temple-monster appears to represent the divine site into which only those who had been sanctified through initiation could enter. Among the Maya and other groups, these individuals, having been swallowed by a serpent, acquired supernatural powers. Therefore, the interior of the temple symbolizes the entrails of the great serpent Master of Initiation, where some men are converted into shamans.

As we mentioned earlier, the ball courts represent the sky and ritually mimic the movement of the stars and planets. The stucco roads on earth mirror the astral paths. These, which we find in many cities on the Yucatan Peninsula are called *sacbeoob*, "artificial roads made by hand," and "white roads."[115]

Several interpretations have been offered with respect to their meaning, but they undoubtedly had symbolic and religious purposes, which is confirmed by various sacred (ancient and modern) myths about the *sacbeoob*.

In various cities of the Puuc region, such as Sayil, Labná and Kabah, we find an internal road system that joins the different groups of buildings on a north–south axis.[116] In addition, on the outskirts of some cities are monumental arches that constituted the beginning or end of a *sacbé* that joined two cities. For example, to the north of Kabah there is a great isolated arch constructed on an independent platform (structure 1B1), from which begins a great *sacbé* that ends at a similar arch in the city of Uxmal.

This great road appears to have had a fundamentally symbolic and

---

[115] De la Garza 1993.

[116] Pollock 1980, 140. Other great *sacbeoob* worthy of mentioning are those that united the city of Cobá with Yaxuná (20 km. to the southeast of Chichén Itzá), and Ixil with Kucican.

ritual meaning, that is, a "religious" link between the two cities. The road could have been used for religious pilgrimages, such as those made between other Mayan cities, because to travel on foot or even to transport goods did not require a work of the magnitude of the *sacbé*. The roads were so well and carefully constructed because the sacred journey had to be made on a sacred road that was a terrestrial mirror of the great "white road" of the sky—the milky way—which is also a representation of the celestial dragon.

The universal symbolism of the arch, as representing the passing from a profane to a sacred state, or as a threshold that permits access to a sacred space as the bridge or tie of the terrestrial level with the celestial (like the rain bow), helps us to understand these peculiar Mayan constructions, which marked the beginning and end of the sacred roads. Therefore the function of the arches that began and ended a *sacbé* seems to have been to mark the limit of the sacred space that constituted the ceremonial center, and passing through the arch must have been an important access rite.

In this fashion the Mayan cities, which are integrated in a dynamic and symbolic fashion to the surrounding landscape, which also has sacred elements, are places of encounter between humans and gods. Both landscape and city "are the manifestation of liberated internal forces that unfold in ways to reveal the qualitative and quantitative order of the invisible worlds that lay behind them."[117]

The religious concept of the cosmos grounded the entire lives of the Maya. All of the exceptional works that were left by them tell us of a great culture that has as its axis the link between humans and the sacred. They tell us so in their own words directed to the supreme deity:

> Oh you, Beauty of Day! You, Hurricane; You Heart of the Sky and Earth! You, the giver of riches and the giver of daughters and sons! Send upon this place your glory and riches; give us life and growth to my sons and subjects; that they may multiply and grow, those that will feed and maintain you; those that invoke you on the roads, in the fields, at the riverbanks, on the cliffs, under the trees, under the vines. . . .

> That good be the existence of those that give you the sustenance and the food into your mouth, in your presence, to you, Heart of the Sky,

---

[117] Ortega Chávez 1992, 8.

Heart of the Earth . . . Vault of the sky, surface of the earth, the four corners, the four cardinal points. That there be only peace and quiet before your mouth, in your presence, Oh God![118]

References

Adams, Richard E. W. 1986. "Río Azul." *National Geographic Magazine* 169, no. 4 (April).

Aveni, Antony. 1980. *Skywatchers of Ancient Mexico*. Austin: University of Texas Press.

Barrera Vásquez, Alfredo, et al. 1980. *Diccionario Maya Cordemex*. México: Ediciones Cordemex, Mérida, Yuc.

Barrera Vázquez, Alfredo, and Silvia Rendon. 1969. *El libro de los libros de Chilam Balam*. Mexico: Fondo de Cultura Económica.

Baudez, Claude-François. 1996. "La casa de los cuatro reyes de Balamkú." *Arqueología Mexicana* 3, no. 18 (March–April).

Campaña V., Luz Evelia. 1995. "La tumba del Templo Búho, Dzibanché." *Arqueología Mexicana* 3, no. 14 (July–August).

Carlson, John B. 1976. "Astronomical Investigations and Site Orientation Influences at Palenque." In *Segunda Mesa Redonda de Palenque*. Pebble Beach, Calif.: Pre-Columbian Art Research, The Robert Louis Stevenson School.

Champeaux, Gérard de, and Dom Sébastien Sterckx. 1989. *Introducción a los símbolos*. Madrid: Ediciones Encuentro.

Códices mayas. 1985. Facsimile edition. Introduction and Bibliography by Thomas A. Lee Jr. México: San Cristóbal Las Casas, Chiapas, Fundación Arqueológica Nuevo Mundo A.C.; Brigham Young University; Universidad Autónoma de Chiapas.

Coggins, Clemency. 1988. "The Manikin Scepter: Emblem of Lineage." In *Estudios de Cultura Maya*, 123–57. Mexico: UNAM, Centro de Estudios Mayas.

Cohodas, Marvin. 1974, 1976. "The Iconography of the panels of the Sun, Cross and Foliated Cross at Palenque." Part 2, "First Roundtable from Palenque." Part 3, "Second Roundtable from Palenque." Pebble Beach, Calif.: Pre-Columbian Art Research, The Robert Louis Stevenson School.

Cruz Cortes, Noemí. 1995. "Ixchel, diosa madre entre los mayas yucatecos." Thesis for a Licenciatura in History. Mexico: Universidad Nacional Autónoma de México, Facultad de Filosofía y Letras. Ms.

---

[118] *Popol Vuh*, 94–95.

Diccionario Maya Cordemex. See Barrera Vásquez et al. 1980.

Förstemann, Ernst. 1902. *Commentary on the Madrid Maya Manuscript (Codex Tro-Cortesianus)*. Dazing: L. Saunier.

Freidel, David, Linda Schele, and Joy Parker. 1993. *Maya Cosmos: Three Thousand Years on the Shaman's Path.* New York: William Morrow and Company.

Garza, Mercedes de la. 1975. *La conciencia histórica de los antiguos mayas.* Mexico: Universidad Nacional Autónoma de México, Centro de Estudios Maya.

———. 1978. *El hombre en el pensamiento religioso náhuatl y maya.* México: Universidad Nacional Autónoma de México, Centro de Estudios Mayas.

———. 1980. *Literatura maya: Compilación y Prólogo.* Biblioteca Ayacucho 57. Venezuela. Barcelona: Edit. Galaxis. Including "Cantares de Dzitbalché"; "Memorial de Sololá: Anales de los cakchiqueles"; "Testamento de los Xpantzay"; "Título de los señores de Totonicapán"; "Popol Vuh."

———. 1984. *El universo sagrado de la serpiente entre los mayas.* Mexico: Universidad Nacional Autónoma de México, Centro de Estudios Mayas.

———. 1987. "Los mayas: Antiguas y nuevas palabras sobre el origen." In *Mitos cosmogónicos del México indígena.* Mexico: Instituto Nacional de Antropología e Historia. Mexico.

———. 1990. *Sueño y alucinación en el mundo náhuatl y maya.* Mexico: Universidad Nacional Autónoma de México, Centro de Estudios Mayas.

———. 1992. *Palenque.* Mexico: Ed. Miguel Angel Porrúa/Gobierno del Estado de Chiapas.

———. 1993. "*Sacbeoob*, caminos sagrados de los mayas." *Revista Universidad de México* 48 (December).

———. In press. "Espacio-tiempo en la antigüedad maya y náhuatl." *México-India, similitudes y contactos a través de la historia.* Mexico: Fondo de Cultura Económica.

Garza Mercedes de la, and Ana Luisa Izquierdo. 1992. "El juego de los dioses y el juego de los hombres: Simbolismo y crácter ritual del juego de pelota entre los mayas." In *El juego de pelota en Mesoamérica, raíces y supervivencias.* Mexico: Siglo Veintiuno Editores.

González, Federico. 1989. *Los símbolos precolombinos.* Barcelona: Obelisco.

Guénon, René. 1969. *Símbolos fundamentales de la ciencia sagrada.* Buenos Aires: Eudeba.

Hartung, Horst. 1987. "Entre concepto y evolución: Apuntes sobre lo creativo en la arquitectura maya precolombina." In *Cuadernos de arquitectura mesoamericana* 9 January 1987. Mexico: Universidad Nacional Autónoma de México, Facultad de Arquitectura, División de Estudios de Posgrado.

Holland, William R. 1978. *Medicina maya en los Altos de Chiapas.* Mexico: Instituto Nacional Indigenista.

Landa, Fray Diego de. 1966. *Relación de las cosas de Yucatán.* Mexico: Editorial Porrúa.

León-Portilla, Miguel. 1995. *Tiempo y realidad en el pensamiento maya.* 2nd ed. Mexico: UNAM.

Libro de Chilam Balam de Chumayel. 1985. Translated by Antonio Médiz Bolio. Mexico: Secretaría de Educación Pública (Serie "Cien de México").

Lizana, Fray Bernardo de. 1983. *Historia de Yucatán: Devocionario de Nuestra Señora de Izamal y Conquista espiritual.* Mexico: Imprenta del Museo Nacional.

López Cogolludo, Diego. 1971. *Los tres siglos de dominación española en Yucatán, o sea, Historia de esta provincia.* 2 vols. Viena: Akademische Druck- und Verlagsanstalt.

Miller, Mary, and Karl Taube. 1993. *The Gods and Symbols of Ancient Mexico and the Maya: An Illustrated Dictionary of Mesoamerican Religion.* London: Thames & Hudson.

Nájera, Martha Ilia. 1987. *El don de la sangre en el equilibrio cósmico.* Mexico: Universidad Nacional Autónoma de México, Centro de Estudios Mayas.

———. 1996. "Los rituales." In *Los mayas: Su tiempo antiguo.* Mexico: Universidad Nacional Autónoma de México, Centro de Estudios Mayas.

Nalda, Enrique, and Javier López. 1995. "Investigaciones arqueológicas en el sur de Quintana Roo." *Arqueología Mexicana* (July- August).

Ortega Chavez, Germán. 1992. "Teoría de las ciudades mesoamericanas." *Cuadernos de arquitectura mesoamericana.* No. 16. Mexico: Universidad Nacional Autónoma de México.

Pollock, H. E. D. 1980. *The Puuc: An Architectural Survey of the Hill Country of Yucatán and Northern Campeche, México.* Memoirs of the Peabody Museum 19. Cambridge, Mass.: Peabody Museum of Archaeology and Ethnology, Harvard University.

Reents-Budet, Dorie. 1994. *Painting the Maya Universe: Royal Ceramics of the Classic Period.* London: Duke University Press.

Romero, E. Ma. Eugenia, and Juan H. Riqué Flores. 1995. "Explorando un nuevo sitio: *Chacchoben,* Quintana Roo." *Arqueología Mexicana* 3, no. 15 (September–October).

Ruz Lhuillier, Alberto. 1968. *Costumbres funerarias de los antiguos mayas.* Mexico: Universidad Nacional Autónoma de México, Facultad de Filosofía y Letras.

Schele, Linda, and Mary Ellen Miller. 1986. *The Blood of Kings: Dynasty and Ritual in Maya Art.* New York: George Braziller.

Schele, Linda, and David Freidel. 1990. *A Forest of Kings: The Untold Story of the Ancient Maya.* New York: Quill William Morrow.

Schellhas, Paul. 1904. *Representation of Deities of the Maya Manuscripts.* Papers of the Peabody Museum of American Archaeology and Ethnology. Cambridge, Mass.: Harvard Unversity.

Sosa, John. 1984. *Astronomía sin telescopios: Conceptos mayas del orden astronómico.* Estudios de Cultura Maya 15. México: UNAM, Centro de Estudios Maya.

Sotelo, Laura, and Carmen Valverde. 1992. *Los señores de Yaxchilán, un ejemplo de felinización de los gobernantes mayas.* Estudios de Cultura Maya 19. Mexico: Universidad Nacional Autónoma de México, Centro de Estudios Mayas.

Sotelo Santos, Laura Elena. 1997. "Los dioses antropomorfos en el Códice Madrid." Doctoral Thesis in Mesoamerican Studies. Ms.

Taube, Karl Andreas. 1992. *The Major Gods of Ancient Yucatan.* Studies in Pre-Columbian Art & Archaeology 32. Washington, D.C.: Dumbarton Oaks Research, Library and Collection.

Thompson, J. Eric S. 1960. *Maya Hieroglyphic Writing: An Introduction.* 2nd ed. Norman: University of Oklahoma Press.

———. 1962. *A Catalog of Maya Hieroglyphs.* The Civilization of the American Indian Series. Norman: University of Oklahoma Press.

———. 1970. *Maya History and Religion.* Norman: University of Oklahoma Press.

———. 1972. *A Commentary of the Dresden Codex: A Maya Hieroglyphic Book.* Memoirs, American Philosophical Society 93. Norman: University of Oklahoma Press.

Villa Rojas, Alfonso. 1994. "Los conceptos de espacio y tiempo entre los grupos mayances contemporáneos." In *Tiempo y realidad en el pensamiento maya,* Appendix I, by Miguel León-Portilla. 2nd ed. Mexico: UNAM.

Part Two
South America

5

The World and Its End: Cosmologies and Eschatologies of South American Indians

Lawrence E. Sullivan

> Meaning is bound up with the end. If there were no end, that is, if
> life in our world continued forever, there would be no meaning in it.
> Meaning lies beyond the confines of this limited world and the dis-
> covery of meaning presupposes an end here.
>
> –NICHOLAS BERDYAEV, *The Destiny of Man*

Dramatic images and practices of South American religious life are
associated with the imminent end of the world. Eschatological movements have swept across the continent ever since the first contact
with Europeans, reevaluating the relationship between sacred reality
and historical existence. Native contact with Christian millennialism
has fanned speculation. From the Andes to the Amazon, prophets of
doom have mobilized local populations in reaction to Christian
ideas, either by providing alternative scenarios or, as is more often
the case, by absorbing elements of Christian apocalypticism into
indigenous frameworks of meaning. Either way, the prophets com-
pose spectacular criticisms of Christianity and of the political regimes
derived from Europe, but also of their own traditional practices and
beliefs.

It is unlikely that the South American genius for eschatology arose
only in response to Christianity. The ethnohistorical and archaeological record as well as the scant written evidence from other native
civilizations (the Aztec and Maya empires of Mesoamerica, for
instance) indicate that eschatology was an important dimension of
native thought before contact with Christians. Christian and Euro-

pean imagery figures in native eschatologies because native peoples were interested in these concepts, which have formed an imposing part of South American history for five hundred years.

Eschatological leaders have scrutinized the historical circumstances that befell their communities like diviners in search of revelatory signs. History is the thread that the religious imagination weaves into eschatological fabric. Clothed in their peculiar readings of significant historical signs, some native prophets raised their communities in revolt against colonial authorities. Others led them on new spiritual quests, dance pilgrimages that meandered across the continent at its widest point. Whether arising in the forested homelands of traditional village communities or among indigenous miners or cotton-pickers, these visions of the end often opened new spiritual horizons and political possibilities.

This essay peers into several points on the continent of South America. In each case the eschatology glimpsed is comprehensive, encompassing religious practice, but also social structure, aesthetic expression, political policy, and ecological renewal of the cosmos. Even when manifest as the revitalization of a past tradition, religious eschatology programs powerful changes. Change is its focus: change that destroys the world as it is known; change that shapes the unknown world of the future. What remains constant across all these cases of eschatological upheaval are the shrewd analyses of present predicament and past preconditions as well as the prophetic eye fixed on sacred forces whose renewed manifestation ushers in the radically different future already foreshadowed in the religious imagination. The divining mirror of the religious imagination, embodied in eschatological prophets and made visible in their dramatic performances or pronouncements, displays a vision of history for all to reflect on and flashes forth images and insights that mobilize populations. While reviewing the rousing imagery of particular cases, the essay draws questions and lessons from the local contexts in order to help foster the development of a general religious anthropology.

Juan Santos Atahualpa

Late May rains fell from heaven to renew life and close the dry season of 1742. That was the moment when a thirty-year-old Campa native first made his dramatic appearance in Quisopango in the Gran

Pajonal area of eastern Peru. Juan Santos Atahualpa had trained with Jesuits in Cuzco, the capital of the former Inca empire. For most of the next two decades this self-declared messiah and Son of God would remain an undefeated military revolutionary. His maternal language was Campa. In Cuzco he learned Latin, Spanish, and Inca fluently. Though still young, Juan Santos was a man of wide and worldly experience, having traveled to Europe with a Jesuit companion. It seems that he also visited Africa and had contact with the British.

For his appearance with the first rains Juan Santos prepared himself carefully in the traditional Campa manner. He trimmed his hair in the customary short haircut and donned a *cushma*, the red-colored native dress. However, he claimed descent from the great Inca emperors Atahualpa and Huayna Capac. In fact, he announced that he was the reincarnation of the Inca emperor Apu Inca, and he invited tribes beyond the Campa to participate in his movement. What is more, he declared that he was the Son of God, come to free his followers from slavery and from work on the plantations and in the bakeries of the colonial overlords. All Indians, mestizos, and African slaves, not just the Campa, were his "children." He would lead them into a new kingdom, over which he would rule as the promised eschatological messiah. There his followers would find tools and the riches hoarded by the Spaniards. God himself had granted him the right to undertake this liberative mission at this propitious moment.

The divinized hero Kesha was central to the religious life of Juan Santos's community. Kesha lived during the age when the first world was formed. By floating on the trunk of a palm tree, he survived the flood that destroyed the earlier world. Kesha tossed seeds from the palm tree into the floodwaters. Eventually those seeds absorbed the waters and dried up the deluge. Thus Kesha made his way into the new world, bringing with him the possibility of renewed cosmic life.

It is easy to understand the devotion that Juan Santos developed for Kesha. Kesha gave hope to those living in chaos and destruction; he served as a model for those living in a world that was fast coming to an end. Juan Santos ordered that ritual dances be performed in Kesha's honor. Religious dance was the primary means of hastening the end of the world. Along with dance, Juan Santos encouraged drinking *masato*, the traditional manioc beer, and chewing coca which he described as the "herb of God." He prescribed a diet rich in beef and lamb but allowed no pork. Taking Kesha as their model

and Juan Santos as their leader, the Campa and their neighbors
would survive the end of the world and arrive at the new kingdom.

For all his revitalization of traditional elements, Juan Santos
sought to establish his religious life within the framework of the
Roman Catholic Church. He planned to train native clergy within
the ambit of the Catholic priesthood and, after becoming emperor of
Peru, to ask the pope to send the bishop of Cuzco to ordain his
Indian priests. Nonetheless, his uprising against the church and
crown was the most significant Campa rebellion of the eighteenth
century. Support for Juan Santos was immediate and widespread.
From the entire east-central forest area of Peru came support from
Indians of many tribal backgrounds: not only Campa but also Amuesha, Piro, Simirinche, Conibo, Shipibo, and Mochobo. He destroyed
some twenty-seven Franciscan missions east of Tarma, Peru, in his
opening campaign of 1742. By 1752 he had completely reclaimed all
of the traditional territory of the Piro, Amuesha, and Campa, exter-
minating the resistance of each and every Spanish installation in the
zone, both secular and ecclesial. His successful military ventures
guaranteed Indian autonomy and isolation in the area for the balance
of the century.

Some historians believe that Juan Santos died around 1755, others think he was killed by one of his own men in 1776. In fact, little can be certain about his death, since many Campa today contend
that he never died at all but disappeared in a cloud. Nonetheless, his
tomb lay under a destroyed Christian chapel on the Cerro de la Sal,
where it was the object of Campa devotion for more than 150 years.
Each year a new *cushma* was set over the tomb in the hopes that Juan
Santos would come back to wear it.

Juan Santos exemplifies the strength of traditional eschatological
visions as well as the creative ability to recast ancient redemptive
images, both native and Christian, into new shapes. Like many
South American messiahs, he rejected the colonial reading of reality,
delivered a biting attack on Christian culture, and sought to end the
world in which Indians, mestizos, and black slaves suffered. His followers knew that they were not alone, that they were reliving the
experience of heroes like Kesha and the successful Inca leaders of the
past. Moreover, their personal and communal renewal was shared by
cosmic life itself. To Juan Santos, the Campa and Christian cultures
offered competing and incommensurate visions of time. Typical of

many a millennial prophet, Juan Santos reimagined them both. Through terminal images of violence and destruction he refashioned them into a new, critical history that mobilized his followers into action—the efficacious actions of ritual diet, dance, and military rebellion. Ironically, by embodying sacred beings, Juan Santos acted as a human being should when facing the end of time: with hope, style, and deliberateness. He demonstrated to his followers that one understands the meaning of history when one grasps the final and catastrophic nature of the human situation.

Tata Dioses of the Chaco

The military success of South American eschatological prophets seems usually to have been short-lived or more often the exception than the rule. Instead, millennial movements were frequently suppressed by force. Among the Toba and Mocovi peoples of the Argentine Chaco, for instance, a series of millenarian mass movements exploded between the years 1905 and 1933. (There continued to arise movements of native revitalization in the 1940s centered on Pentecostal beliefs and practices.) Born in disasters provoked by natural or political calamity, they ended in violent defeat at the hands of policing authorities. The Toba and Mocovi had been nomadic hunters and gatherers squeezed into the eastern section of Chaco Province and the northeastern part of the Santa Fe Province. Their resistance to encroachment was strengthened during the nineteenth century when they took to riding horses. However, the Argentine army prevailed in a string of military advances (such as the one at the battle of Napalpi in 1870) and made way for European settlers. By 1905 the majority of Toba and Mocovi, living on reservations, were exploited as underpaid laborers on farms belonging to European settlers. In these circumstances *tata dioses* ("lord gods") arose, predicting that a disastrous apocalypse would end the world, destroying white settlers and obliterating any traces of European culture. The prophets announced that whites were growing pigs' tails, to match their pig-colored skin. It was time for the Mocovi to rise. Empowered by God and led by prophets, they would be invulnerable to bullets, which would turn to water when contacting their bodies. Armed only with spears, arrows, and spoons the Mocovi attacked white settlements to reappropriate their fields and destroy mission stations. They were cut down by machine-gun and rifle fire. After repelling initial attacks, settlers undertook punitive raids against the Mocovi.

In 1924 there was a religious uprising in Napalpí that spread throughout the province. It was the habit of native workers to move from the seasonal employment picking cotton around Napalpí to harvesting sugar near Salta and Jujuy. In 1924, the governor of Chaco Province issued an ordinance forbidding seasonal workers to migrate to the sugar mills. Wages for picking cotton were already insufficient income when not supplemented by sugar work. But when the pay for picking cotton fell by 30 percent and a 15 percent tax was set on the reduced value of the picked cotton, the native leadership organized a general strike. The labor movement was religious in outlook and led by three prophets: Machado Gómez, Dionisio Dios Gómez, and Pedro Maidana. Responding to the calls of Dios ("God") Gómez, Tobas and Mocovis assembled in large numbers in Pampa Aguara north of Napalpí.

Each day in the Pampa Aguara, God Gómez spoke directly with dead ancestors and with God himself. These supernaturals spoke back to the entire assembly through the mouth of God Gómez. They proclaimed their immediate return to earth and the complete and final destruction of white people and their culture. The property of the foreign settlers would return to native hands. Soon the indigenous people would possess power, liberty, and happiness. God and the ancestors dictated behavioral restrictions that were to be followed strictly. Those who observed the commands faithfully would live to see the passing of the current age and the arrival of the new one. No enemy would harm them. Those who ignored God's commands would suffer and die at the hands of the true believers. In the center of the camp, the prophets' followers constructed a temple and a large square for public meetings, rituals, and soccer games. On July 19, 1924, the assembly was attacked by 150 armed police. During the onslaught, the Tobas and Mocovis danced intensely, believing themselves to be invulnerable. Fifty of them were killed in the action, including the prophet Maidana and God Gómez. No police were injured.

Nine years later, in 1933, another powerful Toba prophet appeared during a crippling drought. His name was Evaristo Asencio, but he became known as Natochí. He announced that he was the son of God and the lord of thunder. Promising that the world would end if his followers would renounce the religion of whites and stop all normal activities, Natochí explained that ancient supernatural beings had returned as small batons which Natochí sold to his disciples. The batons were, in fact, part of the traditional ceremonial paraphernalia of Toba shamans. These batons served as "admission tickets" to the spectacles of ritual dance and song that constituted effective signs of the new age. The spectacles were dedicated to the deities of certain mountains, *wanika* and *salcheró*, as well as the morning star. After settlers' livestock were expropriated by the millennialists, police descended upon them. Natochí himself was said not to have been captured, however, but rather to have flown to heaven, whence he would return to earth at a future time to fulfill his plan.

At about the same time a Toba sleeping prophet named Tapenaik dreamed of planes landing near a mountain on a landing strip set up by his disciples. The planes came from Buenos Aires carrying cargo for indigenous people. The cargo was distributed in a ritual manner in a place built especially for ceremonies. In response to his dream, Tapenaik's followers ceased their daily labors and assembled on a hill during the day to sing and dance ecstatically. At night they dreamed dreams filled with the goods that were soon to arrive. In some nocturnal visions the Virgin Mary appeared as well as a new supernatural presence who declared himself to be Evangelio (Gospel). Tapenaik handed them shamanic batons and advised them to rid themselves of the pollutions caused by foreign food and clothing. The atmosphere was one of unending festival. Tapenaik and the fellow leaders of his movement were eventually arrested and deported from the region.

Using as illustrations the cases of Juan Santos and the *tata dioses* of the Chaco we can draw up a preliminary list of traits common to many of the eschatological movements that have appeared in South America over the past five hundred years. These include the return of primordial gods or supernaturals in full power and their incarnation in human form (the prophet) or material form (shamanic batons); the imminent end of the world through cataclysmic destruction; the restriction and ritualization of behavior (through dance, diet, vigil); the reinstatement of paradise; the cessation of normal labors; wondrous abundance; the extermination of all that has caused pollution and degradation; the prominence of heavenly powers (stars, thunder, ascension on high); transformation of the body (physical invulnerability of the faithful, bestial degeneration of the wicked); divestiture of foreign clothes, food, goods; ceaseless dance and festivity; prophets; economic and political displacement; Christian imagery; guidance through visions and dreams.

Eschatological movements place on center stage the ambivalent nature of religious life—indeed, of all human existence when viewed religiously. In the eschatological moment ambivalence is strongly marked. The contentment and invulnerability of paradise are ushered in only through the historical destruction that brings on the end of the world. Prophets locate themselves in the cross hairs of ambiguities, weighing the attraction toward European values and products against the rejection of every trace of European culture. Prophets develop a new critical posture that saves and rejects various realities by revealing their sacred origin or final destiny. Desirable items such as weapons, education, religion, and money are recontextualized. Their links to destructive, secular processes of production are severed, and their relationship to sacred sources of creativity is reestablished. Thus, in the eschatological view ritual dance compels the passing of time; trade goods and foods come from the sky. In other words, prophets assert that the value of desired goods stems from their sacrality and from their association with processes of production instituted by the gods or sacred heroes. The remaining objects without clear ties to sacred reality are unworthy and should be rejected before entering the new age.

A Mother's Embrace in the Land Without Evil

Let us turn to cases that feature the traits and ambivalences just mentioned but involve no military uprising or response. Though they mobilize for change in ways that can draw the attention of authorities and forces of order, eschatological movements are not inherently militaristic. For centuries, for instance, various Guaraní-speaking groups maintained visions of an imminent end to earthly existence, an ending to be brought on by their dance-pilgrimages toward the Land Without Evil (*Ywy Mará Ey*). The first such mass migration on record was led by dancing heroes and messianic prophets in 1515. Some spectacular movements among the Tupinamba in the 1540s saw whole populations on the march across the entire breadth of the continent at its widest point.

The Land Without Evil was a place where living human beings

could go. It was not a land of the dead or a postmortem home for the divine soul element in every human being. Rather, it was a place where the living would escape the coming destruction of the earth. Prophets instructed them to lighten their bodies by fasting and ecstatic dancing. Thus they would ascend to the zenith of the sky along the path taken by primordial heroes during the flood that destroyed one of the first worlds. Such feats had been accomplished in the past as described in myth. Kuarahy, for instance, had shaken his rattle-gourd and danced without cease until his father, the creator god Nanderú Guazú brought him to heaven. Following his example, dance has been a constant feature of Guaraní eschatological movements for four centuries. If one could only dance long enough, with the proper preparation, the ceremonial house itself would rise into the sky. Failure to do so was often attributed to bodily weakness brought on by disease imported by Europeans.

Another inspiring mythic model for Guaraní-speakers was Chary Piré, a "grandmother" living at the time of the universal deluge that destroyed the mythical world. As the floodwaters rose. Chary Piré stamped out a dance beat with her rhythm stick and sang a powerful chant without stopping. Her actions provoked the magical growth of a palm tree that bridged heaven and earth. Taking her son with her, Chary Piré took refuge in the top of the tree.

The Avá-Chiripá, like many other Guaraní-speakers, picture two visions about the end of the world. One is desired; the other dreaded. The fearful end is brought on by the increasing weight of imperfections (*tekó-achy*), which weigh down human souls so that they no longer can fly to the spheres where they are periodically revitalized. Contact with Europeans increased deadly weight. People more often ate foods not given by the gods and behaved in violation of the instructions given by cultural heroes. The cumulative weight of such imperfections would squeeze the light from the world. The pressing bulk of imperfections would force the sun to disappear and the earth would perish.

A second vision of the end coexisted with the first abysmal one. In the second view the Avá-Chiripá foresaw a final paradise to which powerful shamans led their followers. The shamans possessed techniques for cultivating wisdom and lightness. These shamans had flames rising from their chests and they defied gravity, flying magically across the great sea to reach the Land Without Evil. (Once upon a time pilgrims had been able to migrate to this land in cedar

canoes but now they must fly there under the guidance of the ecstatic leaders.) The shamans would lead dancing disciples on the same
magical flight path toward an immortal paradise of plenty. In the
course of the journey, the bodies of the devotees would be transformed into immortal substances.

Though messianic migrations increased in number after the Conquest (or at least the written accounts of such movements increased,
of course), many of the scholars investigating these matters concur
that dramatic eschatological beliefs and practices were already present before European contact. The motives for Guaraní eschatological
missions are rooted deep in their own accounts of primeval creation.
Before the creator, Nanderuvusú, modeled the surface of the earth,
he set in place the struts that undergird it. He first laid down a
wooden beam running east to west. On top of that he set a second
beam running north to south. When the earth of that first world
exhausted itself, the culture hero Nanderykey (the creator's son, who
lives in the zenith) grasped the far eastern end of the first crossbeam
and slowly pulled it eastward. The unsupported earth began to collapse, beginning in the west. Fire crept out from under the western
end of the earth and, spreading eastward, began to consume the
world. At the height of this calamity, the hero Guyraypotý appeared
and began to seek the sea to the east. He danced his way, arriving
finally at the great dam that holds back the eternal waters. The
moment he arrived, the dam burst and the waters spilled across the
world, extinguishing the cosmic fire. Guyraypotý intoned the solemn
funeral dirge that shamans now sing to accompany the deceased soul
to heaven. While he sang, the dance-house that Guyraypotý had built
in response to the final destruction floated above the floodwaters
and rose into heaven with all the faithful dancers inside. From the
soil revitalized by the flood the creator Nanderuvusú modeled a new
earth on top of the one heated by the fire. In the new world one
could experience *aguydje*, the fulfillment of all capacities for happiness and health. *Aguydje* was the goal of being human, the very point
of human existence. A mystical longing for the Land Without Evil
that preexists this world seems a long-standing element of indigenous
Guaraní religion, and it ties in with indigenous theories about the
imminent destruction of the world.

After completing his creative tasks at the beginning of time, Nanderuvusú left earth and moved into the eternal darkness far above
the zenith, where his son Nanderykey still dwells. This is the dark-

ness that waits to seep into the world and blot out all life at the end of time. There, in the obscurity of total night, the creator rests in his hammock, emitting beams of primal light from his chest. He keeps as pets the monsters who can destroy the earth: the bat who will devour the sun and the blue jaguar who will swallow up humankind, as well as the huge serpent who guards the threshold of the creator's dark house. These monsters are agents of the coming eschaton and are said to have inhabited the chaos and darkness that preexisted creation. When they spring into action, they will swallow the sun; night itself will be exterminated by total darkness. That is when Guaraní-speakers such as the Apapocuvá hope to cross over to where their mythical mother Nandé Cy has preceded them.

In the chaos of the first primordium, Nandé Cy, the mother of all, was devoured by a ravenous beast but was miraculously restored to life in a new world without evil. The real threat of extinction, evident in the dwindling numbers and lost lifeways of Guaraní tradition, compel the Apapocuvá to seek that new world urgently. There, mother Nandé Cy will welcome them with open arms and will greet them with tears that flow freely down on them, the traditional weeping embrace that commemorates, without a word being said, all the suffering and death that have occurred since their last meeting. She will explain to them that life on earth is now extinct and tell them that they should never return there. Instead they will live eternally with her. She nourishes them with *kaguyjy*, a corn pudding sweetened and fermented with her own saliva.

Impelled by such visions, Guaraní prophets led their disciples toward the sea, with song and dance, to escape doom. Over the centuries, most were exterminated by disease and warfare. The Guaraní were 1.5 million strong in 1530; by 1730 they had wasted to 150,000, according to Pierre Clastres's calculations. There can be no doubt that their plight—the devastating social and cultural disintegration—influenced their visions of the end of the world. And the successive failure of their eschatological attempts also took its toll on the understanding of the eschaton. Egon Schaden noted the transformation of myths and practices among the Nhandeva, Mbyá, and Kaiová groups of Guaraní-speakers from the nineteenth century to the twentieth. Increasingly they retold their myths so that the desire for eternal life without evil became a death-wish. Watching their social units unravel, spiritual leaders grew increasingly ignorant of their own tradition and helpless in the face of the new conditions. The Guaraní groups used Christian imagery to explain the postponement of the eschaton. Many Guaraní groups concluded that no path was open to them. The earth was bloated and old; the cosmos depleted and sterile. The tribe no longer multiplied. They believed that on their path to paradise the weight of imperfection (*tekó-achy*) had overpowered them, smothering them. No longer ritual agents of their own destiny, they were being returned to their mother Nandé Cy's arms not through the ecstasy of religious dance but through the torment of being devoured in a cosmic consumption.

Beginning around 1870, the Apapocuvá prophet Nimbiarapony, for instance, led his large Guaraní group along the route that runs the length of the Rio Tieté. Against all odds, the dancers arrived at the sea. Before long, however, Nimbiarapony saw the impossibility of reaching the Land Without Evil by flying over the immense sea from the eastern seaboard. Ecstatic powers were no longer what they once were in the days of the model shamans; despondence, despair, poor diet, and disease had weakened the bodies of his contemporaries. He decided to take direction from an alternate mythical tradition which located paradise at the center of the world rather than on its eastern edge. Following his lead, his community pilgrimaged inland until the point where only two dancers survived. Impelled even farther by the urgency of the situation, Nimbiarapony returned to Iguatemí in Mato Grosso and gathered a new following. The pilgrims trekked across Ivinhema and the state of Paraná seeking the center of the universe, directed by messages received during ecstasy provoked by prolonged dancing and fasting. Nimbiarapony died on the march in 1905, thirty-five years after setting out on his mystical journeys through the world.

The Guaraní eschatologies, taken together with cases examined earlier among the Toba, Mocovi, and Campa, help us better understand the proximity of paradise and apocalypse. Both paradise and apocalypse are visions of the same reality, the final condition of the cosmos. The religious preoccupation with terminal imagery and significant boundary never cease, as is evident in the celebrations of liturgical calendars, commemorative ceremonies, and rites of passage. However, eschatological hope and despair are the most comprehensive and summary expressions of the religious preoccupation with termination. One could say that in paradise and apocalypse religious life realizes its own end and accomplishes its integrity, bringing about the sense of entirety required to assess the meaning of symbolic existence itself. We can see from the case examples that religious actors catch hold of the meaning of life in this world by grasping it on either end at the same time: creation and final destruction. Eschatological vision unites the catastrophes that occurred during creation with the final destruction that ends it. The reappearance of primordial figures inspires terror as well as hope (and the full range of emotions in between them). The inevitability of the world's end does not eliminate uncertainty about its meaning and consequences. Rather, eschatological vision provides religious ambivalence a focus and allows communities to reflect on the terminal nature of existence and one's relationship to it. Moreover, eschatology submits the ambivalence of human experience to summary judgment. Paradise and apocalypse are alternate solutions to the same historical predicament of terminal existence. The one condition lies latent in the other. Paradise for the saved involves the apocalyptic extermination of those who are not. Conversely, the ordeals of apocalypse purify all those who enter paradise (while reducing the rest to terms of utter insignificance). The intimate relationship of heaven and hell is manifest in the fact that these contrasting evaluations of existence in time are equally imminent; that is, they press themselves forward, especially in instances of crisis and ultimacy, as equally available terminal conclusions to draw about significant life at any moment.

The Dance of the Pleiades

In the 1560s, an eschatological movement swept through the central Peruvian highlands, especially in Huamanga. The movement was known as Taki Onqoy, meaning "the dance of the Pleiades" (also perhaps the "disease of the Pleiades"), and the term came to refer to a religious group, its beliefs and its ritual practices. It was a mass movement of large proportions. By the time it ended a decade later, the Spanish inquisitor Cristóbal de Albornoz penalized some eight thousand leaders with fines, corporal punishment, and exile. A close look at some of the movement's characteristics clarifies some transformations provoked by eschatological movements in South America.

The heart of the Taki Onqoy spirituality was a rite of possession. The supernatural beings associated with *huacas* in the Andes seized native devotees. *Huaca* is a Quechua term for a shrine in the form of a sacred rock, hill, or water source generally fixed to the landscape.

Their fixity lends creation an order. In the 1560s, however, the powers of the *huacas* set themselves free and went on the loose, the way they were before creation began. The fact that they bolted from their fixed spots was a sure sign that the order of creation was giving way to chaos. The *huacas* penetrated and possessed the bodies of native peoples and forced them to dance frenetically without cease. The frenzied movements of the dance consisted of shakes and trembles beyond the dancer's control and amounted to a purificatory ordeal that prepared the devotee to become a spokesperson for the native divinity associated with a specific *huaca*. In fact, the dance movements combined elements of the ritual dances performed at both the seedtime and the harvest. Thus, the dance of the possessed fused opposite moments of time (within the agricultural cycle and, by analogy, the cycle of cosmic time) into one mad movement. The Taki Onqoy dance choreographed—literally, graphed in the form of danced movements—the lines of eschatological force pressing in on the world to destroy and transform it. Dancers renounced Christianity and spoke as messengers for the native gods. In 1564, they announced that the Andean gods were joining together to afflict the Spanish representatives of Christ with deadly diseases of local origin. Through dance, moreover, the local gods would bring this sad world to an end.

The messengers announced that a new age would soon dawn, free from colonial rule. To usher it in, a cleansing flood would sweep away the pathological residues of the current world. When the floodwaters receded, they would leave a new paradise of abundance, inhabited by a renewed people. The ocean would be thereafter fixed firmly at the outer limits of the new world. Native people could pass through the calamity if they returned to worship of the local deities manifest in the *huacas*. Through their spokespeople, the *huacas* made it known that they were ravenously hungry. They no longer received adequate food offerings and libations of corn beer. Native populations responded to this call with offerings of animals, clothing, beer, and other goods. The possessed dancers proclaimed their messages in sermons given at the *huacas*. The word spread through every social group and class of Andean peoples, explaining in clear terms, consonant with Andean schemas of creation and history, the reasons for the misfortune, sickness, and disaster devastating the local peoples.

Andean cosmologies of the day held that four epochs (*mita*) had preexisted the imperial Inca age. Each *mita* had its own sun and its own form of humanity. Each endured for one thousand years, at the end of which time there was a universal disaster (*pachacuti*) that brought the age to an end. In the *pachacuti*, the disaster that reigns between epochs, the world was spaded over and turned upside down, the way a field is turned over to end one agricultural cycle and prepare for the next. According to this reckoning, the year 1565 marked the end of the era begun in 565 with the Inca empire, an end signaled by the appearance of the Taki Onqoy. The possessed dancers were like diviners who could read the pathological signs of the times, symptoms of the confusion that was destroying the cosmos. The word from the dancers was clear: to save oneself from impending disaster one must renounce the Christian God, disassociate oneself from Spaniards, swear off European habits and imports, and recant Spanish names, foods, and clothing. One must never visit a church or other colonial space, should not sing hymns or use the Spanish language, and should not observe feasts of the Christian calendar. Those who performed the forbidden activities would suffer dire physical consequences, for example, walking with one's head on the ground and feet in the air or becoming an animal of one sort or another. Those who underwent Christian baptism, for example, would become llamas or *vicuñas* and die of disease. The *huacas* were rising up against those who had defiled them. They invited all native peoples to side with them in the war they were waging against the biblical God of the Spaniards. The Spaniards would be annihilated and their cities destroyed, when the ocean would sweep inland to drown them all and obliterate any trace of them and their God.

For all its criticism of European custom and religion, it would be an error to suppose that the Taki Onqoy led followers back toward an unchanged past. Together with an obvious religious conservatism that upheld traditional practice, there was also a spirit of cunning change. In fact, the movement integrated elements of Spanish influence. For example, the tutelary spirits invoked during the preaching of Juan Chocne, a leader of the Taki Onqoy, were Catholic saints: Santa Maria and Santa Maria-Magdalena. Women devotees, who represented more than half of those mobilized in the Taki Onqoy, were frequently seized by the spirits of Catholic saints who preached messages of repentance rather than rage.

Instead of retreating into a past that was closed, the Taki Onqoy called for the re-creation of ancient realities, announcing the transformation of past powers and their reappearance in new forms. In the place of the strictly localized gods associated with *huacas* fixed in geographic space (springs, lakes, outcroppings of stone), the possessing deities became interiorized and took on the mobile form of incarnate human beings walking the landscape. The discourse of voluntary, individual faith in the *huacas* was introduced. No longer were the ascriptions of culture a sufficient basis for religious practice. Now one had to join the cause of the Taki Onqoy through a process of conversion. This was something new, and it emphasized an act of will. The conversion experience followed on the heels of several days of abstaining from sex, salt, and colored maize. Now cultural rites were set within the framework of personal choice, an arbitrary act of human will, just as the *huacas* chose arbitrarily the possessed devotees in whom they incarnated themselves. By transcending the association of *huacas* with specific localities, the Taki Onqoy also introduced a major innovation: the notion of a pan-Andean solidarity, transcending affiliation to any specific local group. Not only was the God of biblical Christianity devalued; the major deities of the Inca pantheon played no leading role in the forces marshaled by the Andean gods.

Like so many eschatological movements in South America, the Taki Onqoy placed dance at the center of the eschatological stage. Their *taki* (song, dance, ritualized labor) accompanied the last cycle of the Pleiades, whose movement was timed to appear in concert with the final harvest, the terminal afflictions of human beings, and the last round of cosmic time. Eschatological dance crazes emphasize the connection between dance and the passage of time that undergirds all liturgical calendars. In addition, the eschatological dance movements highlight how dance lies at the foundations of morality, serving as the model of upright and graceful action. Dance lays open to judgment the preconditions of culture. It renders visible the otherwise unnoticed currents of emotion, color, sound, and stylized movement that form the hidden matrix of culturally significant action. Thus, by embodying cultural values in highly charged ways, eschatological dance exposes them to critical reevaluation. Dance not only keeps pace with rhythms of multiple times but prioritizes diverse temporal experiences. Through new critical experiences dance helps a community figure out, literally, its evaluation of existence in time. Especially in periods of crisis, when different kinds of time fuse, there surfaces a moral imperative to dance, that is, to create moral order and put it on view by acting gracefully and critically. The prophetic emphasis on eschatological dance demonstrates the conviction that the end of the world, when properly realized, is a ritual achievement.

Conclusions

Speculation about the end of the world and the end of human history is part of the euphemizing impulse of the religious imagination and may be found in association with every religious tradition. Gilbert Durand described the creative religious imagination as an *intellectus sanctus*, a hallowing intellect that rearranges the world for the better. Nowhere is this more evident than in South American eschatological movements that envision change in the social and physical universe; eschatological prophets project magnet-images of paradise meant to pull humankind toward a different, better future. Nearly all of these movements, however hopeful they may be, also inevitably pass through the chaos of fire, darkness, flood, noise, moral disorder, or some other deconstructive experience of inherent formlessness. In various ways South American myths promised an ending from the very beginning. Eschatological leaders invoke these mythical accounts of origins to announce that the end-time, long promised but long deferred, is now imminent. They show how historical circumstance will be forced to conform to mythical pattern.

Awareness of imminent total change provokes a summary judgment, a reevaluation of every aspect of existence: food, dress, and language; dance, labor, and song. All these elements of symbolic life are reoriented toward sacred powers about to appear more fully than ever before. Whatever cannot be marked by the sign of those sacred realities appearing at the end of time becomes unremarkable and invites its own destruction. Thus the Conquest and its aftermath risk elimination, whereas disciples of native messiahs, marked by their uniform, diet, and gestures, will become invincible and find salvation from the end.

With self-reflective irony, eschatological movements reveal how the religious imagination constantly reaches beyond its own grasp: tired of the customary symbolic props it has produced, it provokes new revelations, whose appearance will surpass its own ambivalent expressions. With giddy and sometimes morbid fascination, such as in the case of so many Guaraní communities, the religious imagination evident in eschatological movements yearns to leave behind what is already apparent, already known, and pass over toward what is as yet unmanifest and unclear. Limits and boundaries, experienced in the very process of surpassing them, clarify the purpose of space and time as well as the existences unfolding in them. That is why symbolic existence, in all its expressions, is drawn toward termination. The end of imaginable being becomes the ultimate expression of human destiny.

Those destined for salvation assemble together. Display is the purpose of the final gathering of the saved. They muster to show off their uprightness. Their diet, dance, and fashion demonstrate the dazzling presences who simultaneously destroy the cosmos and free the saved. Other kinds of fusion also mark the final moment: the heavens merge with earth when the sky falls; mountains are leveled and valleys are filled when the earth quakes; the cardinal points become indistinguishable from the center when the fires or waters held at bay on the edges of the earth (as oceans or solstitial fires) now sweep across the land; night blends with day; seedtime with harvest; the beginning with the end.

The ordeals suffered by those living through the end of the world win for them a heroic destiny. The end of the world proves to be a test, an initiatory experience leading to a new kind of existence. Humans who survive the end-time are transformed by the experience and live like supernatural beings, immortals, and primordial ancestors. They are freed from the rounds of exhaustion, the constraints of body weight, and the cycles of daily labor. Instead they find themselves transformed, with a boundless capacity for ritual dancing, feasting, and well-being. We began this essay by suggesting that South American eschatological movements reevaluated the relationship between sacred realities and historical existence. In their strongest form, found amply throughout the continent over the past four hundred years and represented in such cases as Juan Santos, the Tata Dioses of Chaco and the Taki Onqoy, South American eschatologies embody a time when human existence and sacred reality became fully fused and consubstantial. Naturally enough, then, this coexistence brings about the end of the world as we know it.

Suggested Reading

For a fuller examination of South American eschatologies along the lines suggested in this article, see Lawrence E. Sullivan, *Icanchu's Drum: An Orientation to Meaning in South American Religions* (New York: Macmillan, 1988). For overviews of South American eschatologies see Egon Schaden, "Le Messianisme en Amérique du sud," in *Histoire des religions*, edited by Henri-Charles Puech, 3:1051–1109 (Paris: Gallimard, 1976); Alicia M. Barabás, "Movimientos étnicos religiosos y seculares en América Latina," *América Indígena* 46 (1986): 495–529; Robin M. Wright and Jonathan D. Hill, "History, Ritual, and Myth: Nineteenth Century Millenarian Movements in the Northwest Amazon," *Ethnohistory* 33 (1986): 31–54.

On Campa cosmology, see Stefano Varese, *La Sal de los cerros: Notas etnográficas e históricas sobre los Campa de la selva de Peru* (Lima: Universidad Peruana de Ciencias y Tecnologia, 1968); and Gerald Weiss, *The World of a Forest Tribe in South America*, Anthropological Papers of the American Museum of Natural History, vol. 52, part 5 (New York: American Museum of Natural History, 1975).

Regarding the impact of Christian missions, especially Seventh Day Adventism, on Campa eschatology, see Ramón Aranda de los Rios, *Marankiari: Una comunidad de la selva* (Lima, 1978). On Juan Santos Atahualpa, see Alfred Métraux, "A Quechua Messiah in Eastern Peru," *American Anthropologist* 44 (1942): 721–25; Egon Schaden, "Le Messianisme en Amérique du Sud," in *Histoire des religions*, edited by Puech, 3:1071ff.; John Rowe, "El Movimiento nacional inca," in *Juan Santos: El Invencible (Manuscritos del año 1742 al año 1755)*, edited by Francisco A. Loayza (Lima, 1942).

Regarding Toba and Mocovi eschatological movements, see Leopoldo J. Bartolomé, "Movimientos milenaristas de los aborígenes chaqueños entre 1905 y 1933," *Suplemento Antropológico* [Asunción, Paraguay] 7 (1972): 107–20; and Elmer Miller, "The Argentine Toba Evangelical Religious Service," *Ethnology* [Pittsburgh] 10 (1971): 149–59.

On the eschatological beliefs and practices of various Guaraní-speaking groups see Miguel Bartolomé, "Shamanism among the Avá Chiripá," in *Spirits, Shamans, and Stars : Perspectives from South America*, edited by David L. Browman and Ronald A. Schwarz (The

Hague: Mouton, 1979); Hélène Clastres, *La Terre sans mal: Le Prophétisme Tupi-Guaraní* (Paris: Editions du Seuil, 1976); Alfred Métraux, "Migrations historiques des Tupí-Guaranis," *Journal de la Société des Americanistes* n.s. 19 (1927): 1–45; idem, "The Guarani," *Handbook of South American Indians* 3:69–94; idem, "Religion and Shamanism," *Handbook of South American Indians* 5:559–99; idem, "Les Messies de l'Amérique du Sud," *Archives de sociologie des religions* 4 (1957): 108–12; idem, "The Tupinambá," *Handbook of South American Indians* 3:95–133; Egon Schaden, *Aspectos fundamentais da cultura guarani,* Faculty of Philosophy, Sciences, and Literature Bulletin No. 188 (São Paulo: Universidade de São Paulo, 1954); idem, *Aculturação indigena: Esaio sôbre fatôres e tendências da mudança cultural de tribus indias em confacto como mundo dos broncos* (São Paulo, 1965); idem, "Der Paradiesmythos im Leben der Guaraní–Indianer" *Staden-Jahrbuch* 3 (1955): 151–62; Wolfgang H. Lindig, "Wanderungen der Tupi-Guarani und Eschatologie der Apapocuva-Guarani," in Wilhelm E. Mühlmann, *Chiliasmus und Nativismus: Studien zur Psychologie, Soziologie und historischen Kasuistik der Umsturzbewegungen* (Berlin, 1961); Jürgen Riester, *Die Pauserna-Guarasug'wä: Monographie eines Tupí Guaraní-Volkes in Ostbolivien* (St. Augustin bei Bonn, 1972). Regarding the connection between Guarani messianism and accounts of creation, see especially Curt Nimuendajú, "Die Sagen von der Erschaffund und Vernichtung der Welt als Grundlagen der Religionen der Apapocuvá-Guaraní," *Zeitschrift für Ethnologie* 46 (1914): 284–403, also available in Spanish under the title *Mitos de creación* with valuable retranscriptions of the Guaraní texts and commentary by Juan Francisco Recalde.

Early chronicles and sources describing the Taki Onqoy include Cristóbal de Molina (de Cuzco), *Relación de las fábulas y ritos de los incas* [1575] (Lima, 1916), 96–101; and Cristóbal de Albornoz, "Instrucción para descubrir todas las Guacas del Pirú y sus camayos y hacindas," edited by Pierre Duviols in the *Journal de la Société des Americanistes* 56 (1967): 17–39. See also Luis Millones, ed., *Las Informaciones de Cristóbal de Albornoz: Documentos para el estudio del Taki Onqoy* (Cuernavaca, 1971). For interpretation of the Taki Onqoy movement, see Reiner Tom Zuidema, "Observaciones sobre el Taki Onqoy," *Historia y cultura* [Lima] 1 (1965); Nathan Wachtel, *La Vision des vaincus* (Paris, 1971); idem, "Rebeliones y milenarismo," in *Ideología mesiánica del mundo andino,* edited by Juan Ossio (Lima: Ignacio Prado Pastor, 1973); Franklin Pease, *El Dios creador andino*

(Lima: Mosca Azul Editores, 1973), 69–81; Steve J. Stern, *Peru's Indian Peoples and the Challenge of Spanish Conquest: Huamanga to 1640* (Madison, Wis.: University of Wisconsin Press, 1982); Pierre Duviols, *La Destrucción de las religiones andinas* (Mexico City, 1977), 133–45; Luis Millones, "Un Movimiento nativista del sigio XVI: El Taki Ongoy," *Revista Peruana de Cultura* 3 (1964): 134–40; idem, "Nuevos aspectos del Taki Ongoy," in *Ideología mesiánica*, edited by Ossio, 95–102.

6

Contemporary Indigenous
Religious Life in Peru

Juan M. Ossio

In Peru two kinds of indigenous populations can be distinguished. On the one hand, there are the descendants of the pre-Hispanic high cultures, who can be considered as peasants because of their capacity to produce surplus from agricultural and pastoral activities and because of their interrelationship with urban settlements. On the other hand, there are those acknowledged as tribal because their production, based on hunting, gathering, and horticulture, inhibits major accumulation of goods and consequently any strong stratification. The first kind inhabit mostly the inter-Andean valleys (although there are some few on the northern Peruvian coast who have lost almost completely their native dialects). They distribute their productive activities in different ecological levels and are organized in seven ethnic groups divided over two linguistic families that exist from the pre-Hispanic period: Quechua and Aymará. The people that live in the Amazon tropical forest are divided over a much wider number of ethnic groups. According to the official ethnolinguistic map of Peru (1994) they add up to sixty-five groups distributed over fourteen linguistic families.

Although there are no official statistics about the size of these indigenous populations, by using different indicators such as language, residence, social networks, productive orientation, and others, it is possible to estimate that the number of Peruvian Indians is close to ten million. If this is so, they represent near 45 percent of the whole Peruvian population.

While it is true that the most isolated populations are those close to the traditions of their pre-Hispanic ancestors, it is no less true that living in a communal organization with an endogamous pattern of marriage alliances favors the maintenance of those traditions even among those who participate more intensely in the national society. Even peasant communities living a few kilometers from the capital of Peru still celebrate rituals and transmit myths that are similar to those described in the sixteenth- and seventeenth-century chronicles. This is even more true in Bolivia, where on some occasions the president of the Republic has to participate in rituals of this kind.

The most pervasive pre-Hispanic influence in the conceptualization of the spiritual and social world among the contemporary Andean populations is the combined use of dualistic and triadic classificatory patterns. As noticed by Lévi-Strauss among the Bororo, these patterns reflect two kinds of dualisms: one diametric and another concentric, which correspond to symmetrical and asymmetrical or hierarchical principles of organization.

One contemporary myth recorded by the Peruvian anthropologist Salvador Palomino in Sarhua tells that the moieties in which they are organized originated to facilitate the transportation of the extremely heavy Angola bell by means of competition. Previously Sarhuinos were undifferentiated. This made the burden of carrying it heavier and slow. Thus, the myth says, they decided to split into two halves that, by competing, could accomplish the task more rapidly.

In correspondence with this myth we notice that whenever the Andean communities are organized within such a dual pattern or in nonlocalized social groups that adopt a symbolic classification derived from this pattern, then this organization is mostly associated with communal tasks.

Competition is one of the most important aspects behind the dualistic organization of the social order. The diametric kind of dualism is emphasized for its egalitarian character. It allows for dynamism as well as the image of social unity. This last is clear from the fact that any bounded realm, such as a community, a wider localized realm, a nonlocalized social group, units of time, and even the human body, a textile or other cultural expression, frequently appear divided into two complementary parts.

An important paradigm of this unitarian image conveyed by complementary opposites is the human couple. Clear evidence of this can be seen in the tradition about the origin of the moieties in the ancient city of Cuzco as recorded by the Inca Garcilaso de la Vega. According to this seventeenth-century chronicler, it was believed that

each of the two parts in which the city of Cuzco was divided originated from the couple of founders: Hanan Cusco from Manco Capac
and Hurin Cusco from his wife Mama Ocllo.

In Quechua any pair of equal things, such as the hands, the feet,
the eyes or a human couple, is known as *yanantin*. From it follows
that one of the words used for marriage is *yananchacuy* and that in
order to be a full social being an individual must have an institu-
tionalized partner. Indeed, to the idea of order conveyed by complementary opposites is added the idea of fertility whenever those
opposites are the sexes. Hence the unity of male and female becomes
the paradigm not only of order but of life itself. This is why in
Andean society aesthetics, as expressed in music, cooking, textiles,
and so on, is so closely associated with this paradigm.

Together with this symmetrical connotation, *yanantin* also hides
another meaning that is more asymmetric. Thus, for instance, *yana-
cona* refers to a kind of servant. As mentioned before, this double
connotation of the root *yana* is for me the expression of the coexistence of egalitarian and hierarchical values condensed in the form of
a diametric and a concentric kind of dualism.

If this second value associated with dualism had not existed, the
expansion of Inca society and the reproduction of Andean society
until now would be very difficult to explain. In the Inca past, the
main expression of concentric dualism came from the opposition of
the Inca king and the rest of the population, or of the city of Cuzco
and its periphery. At the communal level, today the opposition takes
the forms of the main village and the rural periphery, and of the
plaza and its surrounding area, and so on.

Given the asymmetrical relationship between the center and the
periphery, these can be mediated by a number of stages of different
hierarchical value. It is my impression that, in spatial terms, concentric dualism influences its conceptualization as vertical and in the
shape of a circle. In temporal terms, it is associated with a cyclical
division of time where a limited number of ages may appear as having different hierarchical values.

The combination of a vertical with a circular image of space seems
to result in a view of the world as a gourd that floats upon the waters
of a sea. This is the way in which the world inhabited by living beings
is conceived in many contemporary Andean communities. It also
explains why the sea is intimately associated with foreignness and,
beyond it or near its shores, with the realm of the dead or of the devil.

In terms of verticality, space is conceived of as a succession of ecological levels in which three levels are the most important ones: the valley, the *puna*, and the region in between the two. The first is generally associated with female values and socialization. The *puna*, on the other hand, is also called *orqo*, which is a term loaded with strong masculine and nonsocialized connotations. The last connotation is also acknowledged as *sallqa*, and its inhabitants as *sallqa runa*, savage men. In contrast to the valley, where an image of permanence is associated with the cultivation of crops, in the *puna* an image of randomness and transhumance predominates, closely linked to pastoralism, the main economic activity of this ecological level.

The ecological floor that is in between these two shares characteristics of both. With the valley it shares agricultural potentialities, and with the *puna*, the practice of alternation and rotation common to pastoralist activities.

Related to this vertical image of space, the Andean people think of the cosmos as divided into three superimposed levels. The top level, equivalent to the sky, is called *Hanan Pacha*, or upper world. The middle one is equivalent to our inhabited world, *Cay Pacha*, or actual world. The level below is *Ucu Pacha*, or underground world.

In contrast to the Aztec, Maya, and some Amazonian cosmologies, neither the upper nor the lower world is represented in further clear-cut subdivisions, although some stars are conceived of as being on top of one another, as in the famous drawing of the altar of the Temple of the Sun (*Coricancha*) made by Pachacuti Yamqui. Alternatively, some sky divinities may be identified as heavenly mediators with the earth, such as the planet Venus (*Chaska*) or lightning (*Illapa*), and others as earthly mediators with heaven, such as the mountains (*Apus*, *Huamanis*, or *Jircas*).

Concentric dualism, while enhancing the image of hierarchical vertical stages, focuses on the representation of a sacred center with its metaphysical connotations. A paradigmatic expression of this representation was the figure of the Inca at the top of the political hierarchy and at the same time as the mediator between the complementary opposites of *Hanan* and *Hurin* Cusco.

As is the case in several other societies, concentric dualism influences diametric dualism by introducing a unitarian principle that mediates between the complementary opposites in the social order. A close resemblance can be seen in China's Taoism, where the Tao mediates between Ying and Yang.

Although the Andes are no longer physically ruled by an Inca, the mediating image of this sovereign still remains in mythology. The position he assumed can be replaced by other symbols in rituals. This is the case of rivers in some water festivals, of the beam that divides the two parts of a roof, or of the central line or "heart" that is in between the two sides of a textile. Contemporary political authorities, such as the highest one of *alcalde vara*, generally are also seen occupying this position. Together with this prerogative, they are commonly regarded as androgynous beings similar to Viracocha, as represented on the altar drawn by Pachacuti Yamqui (1993). Correspondingly, they are referred to as *taytamama*, which is equivalent to "fathermother."

This unifying principle that transcends or mediates between complementary opposites is still an important characteristic either in the field of art (as in the case of the stripe decorations in different kinds of textiles), or in politics (as can be seen in the organization of the *varayocs*, or "stick holders"), or in religion (as in the organization of the saints, mountains, or other divinities). They all are seen at the top of a hierarchy.

The position corresponding to the top of the hierarchy is associated in terms of space with an area that is thought to be the most encompassing one, according to different contexts. In relation to the hierarchy of local saints within a community, the saint called the "Patron" is generally regarded as the highest, because he represents the totality of the communal universe. As a consequence of his position, the sponsorship of his celebrations is commonly the most expensive one, to the point that only individuals who have reached the apex in accumulating wealth and social relationships can accomplish this duty. The same is true of those who fulfill the role of *Alcalde Vara*.

At a regional level, beyond the communal one, saints which occupy a top position tend to be associated with centers that are generally important in either religious, political, or economic terms. Apart from the magnificence of their celebrations, they frequently motivate pilgrimages coming together from a vast area. One example of these pilgrimages is the one to the sanctuary of the Lord of Qoylluriti, which takes place every year some days before Corpus Christi, coinciding sometimes with the June solstice. It is true that the divinity involved in this occasion derives from the Christian tradition—an image of Jesus Christ carved in a rock. However, because of its

location, its position in the year, and some of the ceremonies performed in this and some nearby localities, it becomes evident that
behind this is a cult rooted in the pre-Hispanic past which involves
the worship of the Sun and of Ausangate, the most revered mountain of the Department of Cuzco. Moreover, this example suggests
that the mountains are organized in hierarchical terms, that celestial
divinities continue to be regarded as the highest and the most widely
worshiped, and that Jesus Christ, like the Christian saints, has
become incorporated within the criteria of this hierarchical structure.

In the past, celestial divinities such as the Sun, the Moon, and the
planet Venus, or the Thunder were associated respectively with the
Inca, his wife the Coya, and the successor son. Their high hierarchical position had a universal projection all along the Andean realm.
Today, this pattern is preserved through some superimposed Christian images. This seems to be the case with the revered image of
Jesus Christ, who is associated with earthquakes in the two main
centers of Peru: Lima and Cuzco. Narrowly linked to him, the holy
cross occasions an agrarian celebration associated with harvest all
over the Andes. Another example is Santiago, associated with thunder since the first moments of the colonial period and, as this meteorological divinity, with the growth of animals linked to pastoral
activities.

Above these divinities a Supreme Being is acknowledged who generally is conceived of in similar terms to the Christian God. Hence,
he is thought of as the Creator of the world and, in general, of life.
In some communities of Cuzco and Puno he is known as Qollana
Amo, which means the First or the First Lord. More extended
throughout the Andes, however, is Taytanchis (Father). This term is
also frequently used to refer to Christ, as normally the Father and
the Son are not clearly distinguished. According to an oral tradition
recorded in the Colca Valley (Arequipa) by the Peruvian anthropologists, Ricardo Valderrama and Carmen Escalante, God is located in
the Above World. He is described as very old and without a woman.
Next to him sits a son who is identical to him. As the tradition says,
"the son is his father and his father is the son . . . and that is the reason why He is alone without a woman."

A clear derivation from Qollana Amo is Amito, a name given to
this Supreme God in some communities of Cajamarca in a context
of complementary oppositions, where he is contrasted with a being

who is associated with chaos and who behaves as a trickster. This last is the Shapi, who is represented as a kind of devil that upsets the order of the world.

Perhaps because of the fact that one of the most important attributes of this Supreme God is being a Creator, another name given to him in some communities of Cuzco is Roal or Ruwal, which clearly derives from *ruay,* "to make."

At the lower end of this vertical conception of the space, and opposite to the celestial realm, is the underworld. Here the most prominent divinity is Pachamama (Earth Mother) or Santa Tierra (Holy Earth). As in the case of the mountains, once more we meet a cult that directly derives from the pre-Hispanic period and is extended within the same area that corresponded to the expansion of the Inca empire.

Being thought of as female, Pachamama is mainly conceived of as a fertility goddess necessary to enhance the productive capacity of the land and of the animals. There are two moments in the year when she is particularly active: in February, just before carnival, and in August, when many Andean communities are about to start their agricultural cycle through the sowing of maize. In several parts this last time coincides with the ritual cleaning of the water canals, because it is believed that since the earth is active or "open," it is ready to be fertilized by water, which in its turn is conceived of as the "blood" or impregnating fluid of the spirit of the mountains.

As happens with earth mothers of other cultures too, under the influence of Christianity, this divinity has been associated with the worship of different kinds of virgins. Thus, she is presented with benevolent attributes. Many times an idea of maternity is emphasized which also coincides with the fact of being acknowledged as "mama," the *quechua* equivalent of "mother." In some other contexts, however, she may obtain a more negative image, as when referred to as *achiqué,* which is represented as a cannibalistic witch who devours little children. Perhaps because of this image, sometimes she is represented as a frog or a serpent. This last image and that of a black dog may also be linked to her in the role of companions. Other underground beings may also assume the form of a kind of dwarf or tiny being of the female sex who wears a red dress.

As in the case of the spirit of the mountains, ambiguity is a very important attribute of this goddess. On the one hand, she is in demand for her fertile powers. On the other, however, she is feared, because she may turn harmful to the point of causing illnesses by trapping the souls of her victims or producing emanations that affect the hearts of human beings. For this reason she must be approached extremely reverently and protected with a great variety of ritual gestures. Offerings to her may include up to thirty or forty different items, ranging from alpaca fetuses, minerals, incense, coca leaves, ground maize, several kinds of seeds, liquors, sweets, and so on, all of which are buried in particular spots of the ground from whose emanations the attendants are protected by smoking cigarettes or by using other magical procedures.

Indeed, there are many resemblances between the spirit of the mountains and Pachamama. Apart from their ambivalence and of being represented as having small size in some contexts, their residence in the inner world is thought of as a luxurious city or building decorated with gold and different kinds of jewels. However, the fact that these two are conceived of as having opposite sexes marks a very strong difference, since in relation to each other the spirit of the mountain assumes the role of the active part while Pachamama is of the passive one.

The union between mountains and the earth mother coincides with some versions about the origin of some mythical heroes and even human beings, who are said to have been procreated by the copulation of a sky god and an underworld goddess. In modern times, this is the case of the Andean hero Inkarrí, who is said to have been born from a savage woman impregnated by the Sun. In the past, the religious chronicler Antonio de la Calancha recorded a myth from the central coast that mentions that the first human being was born from a poor woman impregnated by the Sun's rays.

Indeed, all these versions are not very different from the extended Andean belief that the different ethnic groups in the world emerged from the underground through *pacarinas,* which could assume the form of caves, lakes, and so on. Since this lower realm is thought of as dark, these versions are not very distant from others that describe the first humans inhabiting a world of darkness before the emergence of the sun. Moreover, whenever the route of the civilizing heroes is described, it generally moves from southeast to northwest or from east to west.

Corresponding to these conceptions, history in the Andes is thought of as a process that unfolds from low to high according to the dual pattern in which the Andeans organize time, space, and, in general, their whole reality. Thus, the past, in opposition to the present and the future, is always represented as dark. A clear example of this can be seen in the names given to the two faces of a coca leaf in Ayacucho: the dark one is called *ñaupa*, which means ancient, while the clear face is *qepa*, which is a term that refers to the back as well as to the future. In divinatory contexts, the first one is regarded as positive and the second one as negative. This coincides with the fact that the east is always better regarded than the west, which is associated with death. In terms of the qualities of the inhabitants of these periods, however, those of the first are regarded as noncivilized, and even evil, and those of the second are regarded as civilized. Those first inhabitants are the "gentiles," or *soqas*, whose mummies can be seen in the ancient ruins. Of them it is said that they were so powerful that they even pretended to defy the Creator. As a consequence they were extinguished by a rain of fire or, according to other versions, by the rays of the sun or by smallpox. Today they are regarded as nocturnal devils that revive on Good Friday and, in general, represent the forces of evil. After their destruction, a second generation of human beings was created, which is the one existing today. But again this one is not free of destruction. Eventually it will also reach its end and be succeeded by a third generation, which will be free of all evil. When is this going to take place? Some said in the year 2000; some others, when a hummingbird delivers a carnation flower to the Glory, or even when the souls of Coropuna finish building a tower that constantly is in the process of collapsing.

Perhaps because both time and space are referred to with the term *pacha*, their organizations have many features in common. First, both can be seen according to a pattern of diametric dualism. Second, both can be subdivided into further divisions of different hierarchical value, presided over by a unifying principle, which is proper of concentric dualism. As described by Guamán Poma de Ayala, this is the case of the Inca at the center of the four representatives of the Suyos. His locality was Cuzco, regarded as the most sacred and civilized city. In terms of time, he was situated at the end of a series of five ages. His presence in the fifth age granted to this stage the condition of being the most civilized in a sequence where each of the previous ages marked an evolutionary transition from nature to culture.

Being conceived of as a divine king, the Inca was regarded as a principle of order whose central position in time and space gave him the possibility of transcending the contingencies of history and of

sustaining the universe. Always under the threat of recurrent cata-
clysms that could destroy the world, the Andeans entrusted the Inca
with the role of overcoming them and maintaining order. For this
reason they could not be defeated by death. As mummies, they were
made participants in the ceremonial events of the living. As a result
of the practice of royal incest, they could be thought of as one in
many. The living king was undifferentiated from his predecessors.
But when he was distinguished it was according to different structural models, which served to enhance the role he was assuming.
One frequent role was the association of the living king with his
father, the Sun, as well as with Thunder and his ancestors with Viracocha, as suggested by R. T. Zuidema. Another role was to identify
himself with Pachacuti Inca (also identified with Thunder) in the role
of restorer of order and to leave the maintenance of order to a future
Inca located in the last position within a dynasty of ten Incas, as suggested by the Indian chronicler Felipe Guamán Poma de Ayala.

The expectation of a permanent order provided by a divine king
was associated, in temporal terms, with a future age encapsulated
within a predetermined sequence of time. In spatial terms, this
future age was replaced by a Land Without Evil, known as *Paititi*,
located at a southeastern point inside the jungle. These two ingredients became the basis of a messianic ideology that expanded extensively in the Andes after the Conquest. These temporal and spatial
premises permitted the wide acceptance of Joaquim de Fiore's theory
of the three ages, the idea of the return of the Inca or the belief that
the Inca remains alive in that Land Without Evil, where only individuals who speak an uncontaminated quechua may arrive.

In this messianism and in the eschatology that accompanies it, the
aim is for the restoration of order in this world. The Christian idea
of salvation associated with a realm of reward and another of punishment was not rooted very deeply in Andean society. Heaven, or
the Glory, is a place mostly for souls of human beings who never had
the chance of committing incest. In other words, it is conceived of as
a place where only the souls of baptized children go, or eventually of
all human beings after the last judgment. There the duty of those
children is to take care of the gardens of God. While the little boys
have to clean the fields, the little girls are the ones in charge of water-
ing the plants. Unbaptized children, although not having the chance
of committing incest, are nevertheless considered dangerous for not
having been socialized by this sacrament, which is mostly conceived

of as a rite of passage. If not properly buried outside the socialized space of a cemetery or below the crosses that protect the agricultural fields of the communities, they can bring hail, frost, and other kinds of calamities. Their destiny is a dark place known as *Tutayaucuman* (*Tuta* = night, *ucu* = underground) where they spend their time suckling the stones or the (badajo) of a bell.

Adults, on the other hand, if they have not been incestuous or selfish, all follow an ascending route to a common destiny which ends in the last judgment. For many Andean communities, this destiny is the volcano Coropuna located toward the southwest in Arequipa. A widespread belief, confirmed by some people who say they have returned from the dead, is that once a person dies, one of his souls starts an ascending pilgrimage toward this mountain. On their way the souls have to cross a river, frequently known as Jordan, which can be crossed only with the help of a black dog. White dogs are not appropriate, as they have same color as the *mistis*, or white people, who are unhelpful and who do not want to get dirty in the unclean waters of that river. Their pilgrimage ends on the top of Coropuna, which is guarded by St. Francis, and there they have to build a tower, which falls down whenever they are about to finish. The day they finish it will be the last judgment.

Incestuous or selfish people in turn become *Condenados*. They remain with the living, frightening them because of their cannibalistic tendencies. It is said that they feed themselves with living people and that after eating three of them they may obtain salvation.

Corresponding to this belief, the main aim of the funeral ceremonies associated with adults is to radically separate the deceased from the living. This is because the possession of sexual potency entails the possibility of committing incest. A confirmation of this is the moment when a child begins to be buried as an adult. As has been reported by several anthropologists, this change takes place as soon as this potency is developed.

Accordingly, the funeral rituals of those who have developed their sexual capacity are of more concern to those who remain alive than to the soul of the deceased. Separation is therefore the means to attain this safety. This is suggested by the extended practice of washing the clothes of the deceased either after the burial or five, eight, or ten days later. It is also suggested by the use of some devices, such as pouring flour on the ground looking for prints that suggest the departure of the soul, and, finally, by the aggressive whipping of the corpse, requesting its integration into the world of the dead.

All this suggests that the Christian notions of sin and salvation in the afterlife have not taken root very deeply in Andean society. Wrongs are repaid in this life, not in the afterlife. Offenses are punished with illnesses, a bad harvest, the death of a beloved child, witchcraft, and so on. They are considered to have a supernatural origin. Correspondingly, to overcome them people resort to magical practices, which generally fall in the domain of different ritual experts. In many cases these can be regarded as shamans.

In contemporary Peru there are a variety of ritual specialists. Some can be considered shamans. Entering into a trance by means of hallucinogenic substances figures prominently in their ritual techniques for communicating with the spirits. As is the case with shamans from other cultures, this communication supposes a symbolic ascendant journey attained not only by the use of hallucinogenics but also by the rhythmical beat of a drum and by the chanting of songs. This is particularly the case of shamans in the northern departments of Peru and of tribal groups in the Amazonian jungle. In the first case, the hallucinogenic substance derives from a plant called San Pedro (*Trichocereus pachanoi*); in the second, from the bark of a tree known as Ayahuasca (*Banisteriopsis caapi*). But apart from distinguishing them by the use of these plants, other more essential differences mark them as derivations from two different cultural areas.

To understand these differences one must bear in mind that the northern coast has long been associated with highly differentiated societies, based on economic activities, such as agriculture, that generated surplus. These societies developed complex political systems with a divine ruler and a hierarchical and very specialized bureaucracy. Social control was, and continues to be, a basic responsibility of the state more than of the ritual specialists. In this context, shamanism assumes a more specialized shape. As can be seen today in Las Huaringas (Department of Piura) or in Salas (Department of Lambayeque) or in Trujillo (Department of La Libertad), shamans serve as medical doctors who are hired by the patients for a given price. In contrast, Amazonian societies, which are politically stateless and less differentiated than those of the northern coast, depend basically on shamanism to keep social control. Within this context, shamanism, with its accusations of witchcraft practices—which are severely avenged—is entrusted not only with restoring the health of individuals but also with enforcing law and order.

For these reasons, shamanism in the Amazonian jungle is central to the interests of tribal groups, and from them it has expanded to the mestizo population in the cities located in this region. Its relevance is expressed also by the dominant position it occupies within their religious systems. As has been reported by investigators such as Chaumeil, about seventy of the eighty myths recorded among the Yaguas were closely related to shamanism.

Apart from these functional differences and from using *ayahuasca* as the main hallucinogenic plant, Amazonian shamanism contrasts with that of northern Peru in the ideas about the transmission of illnesses and in the methods of curing them. Witchcraft has a major role in disrupting the health of humans, and it is thought that shamans are capable of exercising this practice. Hence shamanism has an ambivalent nature: it cures but can also harm. Moreover, shamans may be victims of witchcraft by a more powerful shaman. Thus, they should always be alert and ready to increase their power, for which they have to seek several helpers in the spiritual world.

The helpers are frequently spirits associated with plants and animals which a shaman acquires by his own power. A contractual dimension seems to be behind this institution, which is confirmed by the fact that the role is not inherited. On the contrary, becoming a shaman supposes an act of free will and a period of apprenticeship with another shaman who may or may not be a relative. This characteristic gives the institution a certain competitive tone that stops only with the death of the medicine man.

Since illnesses are basically thought to originate from spiritual darts thrown by witches or from some actions derived from spiritual beings, the training of shamans supposes the ability to remove those darts and to restore some basic components of the human being that could have been taken by a spiritual being. This is the case with those who have become ill as a result of the theft of their soul by a spirit.

The removal of darts is a very dangerous task, as these can turn against the shaman in the same way as those thrown by an antagonist shaman. Apart from the chants, spells, and other techniques when sucking the darts or some pathogens, a shaman has to be protected by the spiritual helpers already mentioned. This supposes a great capacity for transcending ordinary reality in order to penetrate into the realm of the spirits. This realm is densely populated by a huge variety of supernatural beings with particular attributes, who demand a specific behavior toward them. As can be expected, a realm as complicated as this demands a long period of training to become familiar with it. In some cases this period may last for eighteen or twenty years.

Apart from *ayahuasca,* which enables one to enter the spiritual realm, tobacco is a plant that fulfills an important role in the removal of the darts. In contrast to the shamans of northern Peru, who emphasize its consumption as a beverage through the nose or the mouth, those of the Amazon forest, in addition to drinking it, also smoke it, but mainly when they are in the process of removing the illness from a patient. For this purpose they have developed different techniques and methods that range from rolling the leaves of the plant to using particular material artifacts such as pipes. Smoking within this cultural area goes along with the technique of sucking the illness. It implies the inhalation of large quantities, so much so that in some groups the inhalation is seen as a form of eating. This kind of inhalation, which is combined with the sucking of the patient's body, produces a reaction of vomiting saliva. It is in this vomit that shamans see if they have been able to remove the pathogenic projectiles thrown at the patient.

The cure through sucking seems to be another important difference between the practices of the Amazonian shamans and those of northern Peru. As suggested by Lawrence Sullivan, this is a practice "directly related to the shaman's expertise in ecstasy." It "cannot be understood in terms of a mechanical process for eliminating an inert substance. It is a cosmic drama, in which the shaman enlists the aid of all the ecstatic techniques and spiritual powers with which he is acquainted."

Although witchcraft in northern Peru also can be responsible for disturbing the health and normal life of individuals, the position of shamans in the north may be as ambiguous as in the Amazon, but it does not have the same meaning. Hardly any shaman of northern Peru mentions belief in spiritual darts, and sucking and vomiting saliva by smoking tobacco is not a common technique for expelling

---

[1] Sullivan 1988, 454, 455.

the source of harm. Indeed, the curing sessions are more concerned with purifying and raising (*levantar*) the patient by means of different instruments that are displayed on a table. These instruments consist of different kinds of swords and sticks, which are rubbed on the patients. Perfumes or liquors are blown from top to bottom over the patients and to the spirits located at the four cardinal points. A variety of images of Christian saints, some objects of pre-Hispanic origin, stones, crystals, shells, herbs, and even dry remains of some animals are added. Douglas Sharon, who studied a table organized by the shaman Eduardo Calderón, counted up to seventy-eight different elements, all distributed within three different fields: *ganadero* (cattle raiser), *medio* (middle), and *justiciero* (justice maker). Although it is difficult to tell how widespread this division is, since it has not been described for the *mesas* of other shamans, Sharon suggests that the first field, situated on the left hand, represents the shaman's own capacity for evil. The third field, associated with the righthand side, stands for the positive forces, while the middle field accomplishes the role of mediator or of equilibrator of the forces belonging to the two previous fields. Correspondingly, in the middle field are displayed objects that have to do with divine mediators such as the Sun and even with the shaman himself. Other objects deal with cattle raising and fertility. The left side deals with objects from pagan origin. That of justice maker is in the middle field. The right side deals with objects associated with Christian saints.

This organization of the table is dominated by the recurrent Andean representation of order, in which complementary opposites are mediated by a unifying principle. As I had the opportunity to verify among the shamans of Las Huaringas, in the northern part of Peru, a great deal of importance is given to the distinction between the objects derived from the pre-Hispanic past and those of the Christian tradition. Apart from keeping each in its respective place within the table, shamans dedicate special rooms to each kind of object without intermingling them. Those of Christian origin are stored in what resembles a small chapel, and those derived from the pre-Hispanic past are in another room, together with the rocking chair that the shaman uses in the night sessions. In addition to these rooms, there is another, where the medicine herbs are stored.

This emphasis on dualism in the shamanic practices is closely linked to an old Andean concept of health as a state of equilibrium between opposite forces. The sixteenth- and seventeenth-century

Indian chronicler Guamán Poma de Ayala mentions that the Peruvian Indians believed that illnesses originated either from hot or cold substances. This belief is not exclusive to the Andes, but the importance attached to dualism among the local cultures of this area allowed this foreign idea to be adopted easily. Today this concept is widespread. Therefore, the importance granted to dualism by the shamans of northern Peru in the process of curing patients is not an exception to this process of adoption. The fusion between objects derived from the Christian tradition and from the pre-Hispanic past situates the syncretic process of *mestizaje* inside an Andean structural matrix which is extended to the representation of the whole cosmos. It is in this framework, which enhances the mediating role of the shamans and its identification with the middle field, that the integration with the cosmos is obtained.

Within this context, trance is a means of identifying and expelling the evil forces that may be acting against a patient. It also gives the opportunity of traveling toward some magical places that increase the power of the ritual expert, and of communicating with the spirit of the medicine herbs and with the objects that are on the ritual table, which accomplish the duty of restoring health to the patient. Additionally, it allows the shaman to visit the environment of the patient's family, to become acquainted with his social position and activities, and thus to forecast his future.

In the southern highlands of Huancavelica, Ayacucho, Apurímac, Cuzco, Puno, and Bolivia, the use of hallucinogenics disappears. Instead, coca leaves figure prominently in the curing sessions of the ritual specialists. One detail in common with the northern area is the use of "ritual tables" that combine pagan and Christian objects. However, in the south most of the ingredients are offerings to the gods, which later are consumed by fire, while in the north the majority are used as talismans, which the shamans keep as precious objects. Another similarity is that in both areas shamans have to pass a long period of training. Nonetheless, in the south the spirit of mountains (Apu) is the main source of power of these religious men, and this power may increase according to the importance of the mountain with which the shaman is linked. From these facts emerges a kind of hierarchical priesthood, which corresponds to the hierarchy of the mountains, as well as with the amount with which he is linked. Thus Altomisayoqs, if they are capable enough, can ascend all the way up the hierarchy of power throughout their life.

As in the previous cases, this office is not acquired by inheritance. The general idea is that one is selected by an Apu when one is struck by lightning in a lonely place away from the sight of any human being. It is said that the first strike kills the person, that the second destroys his body, shattering it into small parts, and that the third one reunites all these parts and resurrects him.[2]

Given the absence of hallucinogenics among these ritual specialists, there is no evidence of spiritual journeys or of any of the ecstatic symptoms that accompany the cases of shamanism already mentioned. However, if it is true that the spirit of the ritual officer does not transcend his body to the gods with whom he is associated, the spirit of a mountain or of the mother earth can show up in a session. In Ayacucho informants tell that the mountain spirit comes in the shape of a condor, waving its wings, while in Cuzco it is said that after being invoked at midnight in plain darkness, the mountain spirit falls heavily upon the roof of a house as a shapeless object. His voice is masculine and authoritative, and he answers the questions that are raised to him by the patients. In addition he has the capacity of summoning other spiritual beings to help him answer the questions. One of these can be the mother earth, or Pachamama, whose voice is feminine and thin. In all these sessions the ritual table, bearing a variety of offerings from animal, vegetable, and mineral groups, presides over the whole act.

This description has been concerned with ritual specialists whose role is to attend the anomalies that individuals suffer. In addition to them there are other specialists, both in the Amazon and in the Andes, that since long ago have been concerned with restoring the health of society. These are the leaders of some religious movements which can be regarded as messianic.

Messianism in this part of South America has a long history that can be traced back to the pre-Hispanic period. However, during the colonial period these movements were better documented and more frequent. Indeed, the most outstanding peculiarity of this religious phenomenon in this part of the world is its continuous existence from the first colonial movement known as Taki Onqoy until today with the expansion of the Incarrí myth and the emergence of new movements such as that of the Israelites of the New Covenant.

---

[2] Casaverde 1970, 212.

To finish this description of the religious life of the contemporary Indians I shall make a brief commentary about this last movement, whose leader is a Quechua-speaking Indian born in 1918 in the community of Huarhua located in the Provincia de la Unión (Department of Ayacucho). His name is Ezequiel Ataucusi Gamonal, and he is considered by his followers to be a reincarnation of the Holy Ghost, the new Christ, the Son of Man, Father Israel, and even a new Inca.

Although this movement is derived from adventism, and consequently their rituals and doctrine are based on a reinterpretation of the Old and New Testaments, behind its discourse is a set of ingredients that underlie Andean messianism. Among these is an eschatology based on a division of history into a fixed number of ages, each ending in a cataclysm. Accordingly, it is stated that the third of these cosmic destructions would take place in the year 2000, putting an end to this world. Only those converted to the leader's movement would be saved.

Combined with this eschatology, narrowly linked to the Andean concept of time, is the search for the Land Without Evil. As in the myth of Paititi, once again salvation will be attained in the jungle. Paititi is located in a particular point in the forest of the Department of Junín, where the Israelites will wait for the end of the world, in order to be transferred to a promised land that always lies toward the east. For this reason many of them are now migrating to this area, where they are developing new colonies. Indeed, this part of Peru is very significant for this movement, because here the leader received the Ten Commandments from God and started his preaching, and it is here that they have organized a number of colonies that have become one of the most important financial sources of the movement.

From this description it can be deduced that, as with time, the conceptualization of space also suggests a connection between the doctrine of the movement and Andean ideology. This is even more evident from their representation of the world divided according to the diametric dual pattern so characteristic of Andean society. Hence, the world is represented as split into two parts: one represents the east, associated with Africa, Europe, and Asia, and the other the west, associated with the two Americas. Within this framework the messianic role of Ezequiel in the west is made equivalent to that of Moses in the east, and his connection with the Incas is enhanced by comparing Machu Picchu with Mount Sinai. As stated in a song, "Moses received the Law of God in Sinaí, / In Peru Israel-Israel has received it; / In Horeb Moses received the Law of God, / In Palomar Israel-Israel has received it. . . . Moses was born in the east-East, / Israel-Israel was born in the west-Western; / Moses made the ancient pact with Jehova, / the new pact with Jehova has been established by Israel. . . . Machu Picchu is the mountain of the Inca, / in Palestine is the mount of Sinaí. . . ."

In addition to these Andean overtones, it is possible to add the presence of a nativistic ideology similar to that behind the Taki Onqoy movement of the sixteenth century. Once more the idea of this movement is to return to ancient religious practices that had been abandoned for mistaken reasons. This does not mean that they are recommending a return to the cult of the ancient Andean divinities or *Huacas*, but something similar: to go back to the roots of Christianity in order to free the world from the wrong interpretations of the Bible initiated with Constantine. This explains why they call themselves Israelites. It is not because they have been born in Israel but because they identify themselves with God's chosen people and with the authentic ritual practices and modes of life before the reforms introduced by Constantine. This is taken so far that they even dress like the biblical Israelites described in the Old Testament. On the other hand, they have developed a calendar exclusive to them, where the year starts in April, which is the month of Ezequiel's birthday, Saturdays replace Sundays as the Lord's day, and the rest of the festivities correspond to those of the Hebrew calendar. Moreover, starting with the organization of the priesthood and sacrifices, baptism, circumcision, and marriage are all modeled according to the descriptions contained in the Bible.

Finally, the indigenous background of this movement is also evident in the way some biblical notions are interpreted. A kind of magical reading of its pages departs from the idea that everything has been forecast in them. It becomes a source of general legitimation and also one of prediction. In order to accomplish this it is enough to open the Bible randomly to find the answers to the questions that are raised. In cases of doubt about certain paragraphs, the final word is in the prophet Ezequiel because he is considered to be the most authentic interpreter of the Sacred Scriptures.

In a more secular context, this kind of background also becomes explicit in the organization of the Israelite colonies and in their political project for Peru. In both cases the model derives from what they consider to have been the organization of the Inca empire. This matches the old messianic myth of a return to the time of the Incas.

A quick glance at the social composition of the Israelites reveals that the majority of them are migrants from highland provinces, where Quechua is the dominant language. From the life histories of several of them, it appears that their social position is similar to that of the leader. Like him, they are mostly of Quechua origin and marginal within their own localities. They are the poorest of the poor, although they are still very much acquainted with different indigenous traditions. Many of them possess knowledge about Inkarrí and other mythical beings.

Among the different nondenominational Christian groups that exist in Peru, the Israelites are the ones who have expanded most rapidly and the ones who have more adherents. They are distributed all over Peru and even outside, in Bolivia, where there is a large group, in Ecuador, Colombia, and even the United States. Their number is estimated to be more than one hundred thousand, and most are concentrated in the Department of Lima. This growth coincides with the peak of the Peruvian crisis, making evident the extent to which the religiosity described in this article can be used by a changing Indian society to face the transformations that are taking place in this country.

References

Calancha, Fray Antonio de. 1974. *Coronica Moralizada.* Lima: Ignacio Prado Pastor.

Casaverde, Juvenal. 1970. "El mundo sobrenatural en una comunidad." In *Allpanchis*, no. 2. Cuzco: Instituto de Pastoral Andina, Cuzco.

Chaumeil, Pierre. 1979. "Chamanismo Yagua." *Amazonía Peruana* [Lima] 2, no. 4.

Garcilaso de la Vega, Inca. 1960. *Los Comentarios Reales de los Incas.* Biblioteca de Autores Españoles. Madrid.

Guamán Poma de Ayala, Felipe. 1968. *El Primer Nueva Corónica y Buen Gobierno.* Paris: Institut d'Ethnologie.

Instituto Indigenista Peruano. 1994. *Mapa Etnolingüístico Oficial del Perú.* Lima: Ministerio de Agricultura.

Santa Cruz Pachacuti, Juan. 1963. *Relación de Antigüedades deste Reyno del Piru*. Cuzco: Instituto Francés de Estudios Andino e Instituto Bartolomé de las Casas.

Sharon, Douglas. 1980. *El Chamán de los Cuatro Vientos*. México: Siglo XXI.

Sullivan, Lawrence. 1988. *Icanchu's Drum*. New York: Macmillan.

Zuidema, R. T. 1989. "Mito e Historia en el Antiguo Perú." In R. T. Zuidema, *Reyes y Guerreros*. Lima: Fomciencias.

7

The Baniwa

Robin M. Wright

The Arawak-speaking Baniwa live on the frontier borders of Brazil, Venezuela, and Colombia. The majority live on the Brazilian side, a total of approximately 3,750 people distributed in over a hundred communities along the Içana River and its tributaries, the upper Rio Negro and the Xié and Uaupés Rivers. In Venezuela and Colombia, where they are known as Curripaco and Wakuenai, their population is approximately two thousand, living in communities along the Guainia and its tributaries, and the upper Içana.

Horticulture and fishing are their principal subsistence activities, although a long history of contact has involved them in various forms of production for markets and extractive labor. They are organized in approximately a half-dozen, localized, exogamous, patrilineal phratries, each consisting of four or five siblings ranked according to a mythic model of agnatic siblings.

Traditional religious life was largely based on the mythology and rituals of the first ancestors represented by sacred flutes and trumpets, *Kuwai*; on the importance of shamans and chant specialists; and on a variety of complex dance festivals, *pudali*, coordinated with seasonal calendars. In the latter half of the nineteenth century, Baniwa prophets created a new form of belief called the "Religion of the Cross," which attracted large numbers of followers in millenarian movements of resistance to colonial domination. Since the 1950s, Protestant evangelical and Catholic missionaries have promoted the conversion of the Baniwa, adding a further dimension of complexity to their religious situation.

221

Cosmogony

The spiritual bases of the Baniwa millenarian tradition can be understood only through an examination of the themes and concerns predominant in their myths. Here we summarize the principal myths, which consist of four major cycles:

1. The myth of Yaperikuli, the creator and transformer, and the origin of the universe, which tells how the universe was saved from total destruction.

2. The myths of the Animal and Thunder spirits, enemies of Yaperikuli, who constantly threaten the universe with chaos, Yaperikuli's struggles against them, and the eventual destruction of the primordial world.

3. The myth of Kuwai, the child of Yaperikuli and Amaru, the first woman. Kuwai is an extraordinary being whose entire body produces music, through which the universe is opened up/revealed during rituals of initiation, but Kuwai also leaves fatal sickness and misfortune for humanity.

4. Myths of the new order created by Yaperikuli, defined by the conditions and ways of living which sustain humanity, providing for its prosperity, growth, and well-being.

In this progression, one immediately perceives that the process of creation of order is one of salvation from destruction and of transcendence over the primordial forces which constantly threaten humanity with chaos. Historic millenarian movements, led by powerful shamans who most clearly incorporated the mythic model of savior represented by Yaperikuli, thus testify to the fact that cosmogony is far from being a closed history of a distant past; to the contrary, cosmogony is open to new episodes of creation, in which the conditions of order are constantly renewed.

The Bone God

The mythology of Yaperikuli consists of a complex corpus of more than twenty stories, beginning with the emergence of Yaperikuli in the primordial world and ending with his procuring of the first ancestors of Baniwa phratries and withdrawal from the world. More than any other figure of the Baniwa pantheon, Yaperikuli is responsible for the form and essence of the universe; one could thus consider him the supreme being of Baniwa religion.

The name Yaperikuli means "he-inside-of-bone," recalling his origin from inside the bone of a dismembered and devoured person, the victim of jaguars and other fierce and cannibalistic animals who roamed the world in the beginning of time. So great was their destruction that there were hardly any people left in the world. Then, the chief of the animals, called *Enúmhers*, took the bone of a devoured person and threw it into the river below. An old woman wept at the loss of her kin, so the chief ordered her to fetch the bone from the river. Inside the bone were three crayfish. The old woman took the bone back with her to the house, where the crayfish transformed into crickets. She gave them food and they began to sign and grow. Later she took them to a garden and again gave them food. They continued to transform, as they grew and sang, until they appeared in human form: they were the three brothers *Yaperikunai* (they-inside-the-bone) and already knew how to make everything. In spite of the old woman's constant warnings for them to remain quiet and to do nothing, they continued to transform things, as they ascended a tree to its top and later descended. Thus, they began to transform everything, to make everything that there is in the world, in the way that only they knew how to do.

Upon completing their work, they seek revenge against the animals who had killed their kin, thereby reestablishing order in the world. But the chief of the animals plots their destruction. He calls them to help him make a new garden, ordering them to stay in the center of the garden as he sets fire to its borders. As the fire burns toward the center, the chief cries, "You will burn!" To which they reply, "No, we will never burn." They climb inside a small hole in the trunk of an *ambaúba* tree (*Pourouma cecropiafolia* Mart.) and close off the opening. When the fire (described as a conflagration that burned the world) reaches the tree, suddenly it explodes three times as the three brothers fly out unharmed by the flames. They descend to the river to bathe and, as the weeping chief, thinking that they had died, meets them at the river, they affirm that they can never be burned for they are the "universe people."

From this summary of the myth, it is evident first of all that the

initial situation is one of chaos and destruction coinciding with the
near total annihilation of the first people. In various other Baniwa
myths one finds similarly catastrophic situations, but they serve as a
prelude to the creation of a new order—in this instance the re-creation
of the universe in which the forces of chaos are controlled. The bone
is the symbolic vehicle of the new being that recreates order in the
new world. In this sense, Yaperikuli—he-inside-the-bone—is the essence
of the Baniwa universe.

Second, spatial movement in the myth—from the river to the
house and from the house to the garden—represents a process of the
recovery of form, that is, a way that leads from an absolutely form-
less state (the river) to a place of human creation and domestication
(the house) to a place of the domestication of nature (the garden).
The house and garden are the places of culture where the heroes—
gradually emerging from the bone, changing and growing—assume
the power of transcendence, symbolized by their ascents and descents,
thus creating the all-important vertical axis of the new cosmos.

Finally, the chief of the animals seeks to destroy the brothers (i.e.,
the universe) a second time through a world conflagration which
threatens to consume all material existence and, like the voracious
appetites of the animals, to take the universe back to its initial state
of chaos. From this imminent catastrophe, however, spiritual existence emerges as eternal and indestructible—once again a central
theme in Baniwa mythology and millenarian movements: the miraculous escape from death, immortality which bursts forth from its
material enclosure.

The Animals and Thunder

The struggles of Yaperikuli and his brothers against the animals continue over a sequence of myths the result of which by no means represents a clear victory for the heroes. These myths may be seen to
contain a lengthy discourse on the themes of death and the demise
of the primordial world taken from several points of view. In one of
the myths, Yaperikuli seeks to kill the chief of the Thunders,[1]

---

[1] The Thunders (*Eenunai*) of the primordial world are "tribes" that inhabit the
trees and are the masters of poison. Today they are seen as the different species of

another form of the animal chief, by means of a great flood, total darkness, and a storm in which the animals are devoured by piranha, all except for one—the chief, who stays in the world as a constant reminder of the end of the primordials and that humans will likewise die by sorcery.

Different forms of death (cannibalistic feasts, poison), manners of dealing with death (vengeance or "return" deaths, tricking the assassin), and the permanent traces of death (evil omens, poisonous plants, a heap of bones, and the spirit of the recently deceased) comprise the central themes of this mythic discourse on the end of the primordial world and the new order created from the remains of the old. The new order contains elements of the old, since Yaperikuli never succeeded in totally eliminating the destructive energies represented by the Thunders: poison (*mahnene*) and sorcery are still today among the most persistent "causes" of human death in the world, despite the existence of norms to control them.

The catastrophic destruction of the world remains a very real possibility. When the world seems to be infested with insupportable evil, as this is represented in the myths (demons, ferocious animals, or an excess of poison), then conditions are sufficient for its destruction and subsequent regeneration. Cosmic history attests to this pattern: before Yaperikuli brought forth the first ancestors, he caused a great fire and flood to purify the world of demons, forest spirits, and spiders, whereupon he looked for the ancestors who emerged from the holes in the rapids of Hipana, the center of the Baniwa universe. Various forest spirits escaped, however, and, as with the animals, continue to persecute humanity with sickness.

Kuwai

The myth of Kuwai is the third of the major cycles of cosmic history. Infinitely rich in symbolism, this myth has a fundamental importance to Baniwa culture, in explaining at least four major questions on the nature of the world: how the order and ways of living of the

---

arboreal and ground-dwelling animals (sloths, monkeys, the tapir). The Chief of the Thunders assumes different forms and names in the myths, but his essence as enemy of Yaperikuli remains the same.

ancestors are reproduced for all future generations (*walimanai*, for those unborn); how children should be instructed on the nature of the world; how sicknesses and misfortune entered the world; and what the relations are among human beings, spirits, and animals that are the legacy of the primordial world.

The myth recounts the life of Kuwai, the child of Yaperikuli and Amaru, the first woman. Kuwai is an extraordinary being whose body consists of all the elements of the world and whose humming and singing represent powerful processes of natural reproduction. The birth of the hero sets in motion a rapid process of growth which opens the chaotic and miniature world of Yaperikuli to its real-life size, with forests and rivers inhabited by humans and containing the different species of forest animals, birds, and fish. Kuwai teaches humanity the first rituals of initiation; at the end of these rituals, when the initiation is complete, Yaperikuli kills Kuwai by pushing him into an enormous fire which burns the world, causing it to shrink back to its original size. From the ashes of the fire emerge the plant material with which Yaperikuli produces the first sacred flutes and trumpets, the "body of Kuwai" (i.e., its material form), with which human beings henceforth would initiate their children into ceremonies modeled after the first ritual taught by Kuwai. Amaru (the mother of Kuwai) and the women then steal the instruments from the men, which sets in motion a long pursuit. The world opens for a second time as the women play the instruments throughout the world (concretely, over a vast area of the northern Amazon region, which is remembered in detail in lengthy chants known as *kalidza-mai*, sung at the final stages of initiation rites today). Yaperikuli eventually recovers the instruments and, with them, brings forth the first ancestors of humanity.

It is evident that the myth of Kuwai marks a transition between the primordial world of Yaperikuli, the Animals and Thunders, and a more recent human past, directly connected to the experience of living people in rituals. The first world of Yaperikuli was doomed to demise and destruction; humanity today sees its vestiges as a given condition. By comparison, the world of Kuwai connects the distant world of the beginning to the new worlds constantly being re-created by humans. This explains why shamans say that Kuwai belongs both to "this world" (*hliekwapi*, of the present) and the "other world" (*apakwa hekwapi*, of the ancient past), and that he lives in the "center of the world" (Hipana rapids, which is connected by a spiritual umbilical cord to the "center of the sky" where Kuwai dwells). In their cures, shamans bring together the two worlds through their chants in order to recover the lost soul of an afflicted person. To the shamans, Kuwai is the "Owner of Sicknesses" (*idzamikaite iminali*), since his body consists of all sicknesses, whose manifest forms he left in the world during the great conflagration which marks his death and withdrawal from the world. It is the spirit of Kuwai that is most often invoked by the shamans during their curing sessions.

Shamans state that the spiritual body of Kuwai is covered with fur, like the black sloth *wamu*.[2] Kuwai entraps human souls by embracing (as the sloth does) and suffocating them unless some action is taken. But Kuwai also allows the shamans to recover and restore souls to their owners. The more serious ailments, then, are understood as a process of entrapment of the human, individual soul by Kuwai or by the chief of the animal souls (*awakaruna*); recovery involves the shaman's search for the lost soul, bargaining with the spirit-owner(s) who have entrapped them, and banishment of the animal spirits from the world of the living. This is why ritual fasting and abstaining from the eating of animal meat are forms of voluntary suffering to which individuals must submit if they wish to be cured or if they wish to become fully cultural beings through initiation.

The New Order

The world created by Yaperikuli was not entirely one of perilous dangers for, parallel to these struggles, Yaperikuli creates the conditions for the sustaining and constant renewal of life: the alternation of day and night and the temporal ordering of human activities, the growth and fertility of the earth for the planting of gardens, the production of tobacco for the sustenance of the soul, and the use of cooking fire. In all cases, Yaperikuli obtains these elements and conditions from

---

[2] Kuwai is also known by the name *Wamundana*, a word comprised of *wamu* (black sloth) and *·ndana* (shadow; dark, invisible interior). The notion is of a spiritualized animal, another aspect of Kuwai that is particularly dangerous for its associations with sickness, death, and catastrophes. *Wamu* is considered the "owner of poison," as Kuwai is, and is one of the forms assumed by the Chief of the Thunders, whom Yaperikuli failed to kill. Kuwai is his "shadow-soul."

their spirit-owners. In order to transfer/give them to all future humanity, a transformation occurs marked by powerful images of transition or passage (powerful sounds, darkness, fire), as sealed or hidden containers open up or burst apart, as if through a "wrinkle" of space and time from which the new order is awaited and created. The new order sustains the life of humanity, by defining a meaningful symbolic order of how people can live and prosper.

In a similar way, shamans obtained their powers (*malikai*)—as visionaries, mediators, and transformers—and the sacred powder (*dzato*) through which they receive visions. This powder is considered a highly potent and ambivalent substance: it is the means by which the shamans constantly renew the connections of humanity to the celestial world of the divinities. Yet, according to the myths, it is a source of fatal illness (madness, transformation into animals) if abused. The proper utilization of the substance, in short, is essential to sustaining the mediation between the two worlds.

The images of the first world confirm, on the one hand, its catastrophic and violent nature, death-dealing and chaotic, in which the creation of order suffers the constant threat of being dismantled. The very beginning of the cosmos is a state of dismemberment, of awesome and devastating events. Such a condition was never really eliminated from possibility; humanity is constantly reminded of its presence. On the other hand, the primordial world is the source of renovation, renewal, and change. *Spiritual creativity eternally transcends the destruction of matter.* This is the essence of the creator, Yaperikuli. Spiritual creativity is the source of abundance and happiness that sustain life and create meaningful existence for the future, for the "others who will be born" (*walimanai*). Such images inform and shape the religious life of the Baniwa and the powers of the religious specialists, masters in traversing the space and time that separate the world of the present from the beginning.

Cosmos and Self

The Baniwa universe consists essentially of four levels (see diagram on next page). From bottom to top: *Wapinakwa*, the place of our bones; *Hekwapi*, This World; *Apakwa Hekwapi*, the Other World; and *Apakwa Eenu*, the Other Sky. Most levels consist of flat disks; the centers of three of these are hollowed-out, open spaces, while the center of the highest level is closed and pointed. Cosmic unity is represented by the line, called the "universe way," running through the center and passages connecting the world of Yaperikuli to the lower part of This World, where the chief of the animals and forest spirits dwells.

Wapinakwa is closely associated with the bones and bodies of the dead. Strange, inverted beings inhabit the place who may appear in This World as treacherous, cannibalistic spirits. It is said that these

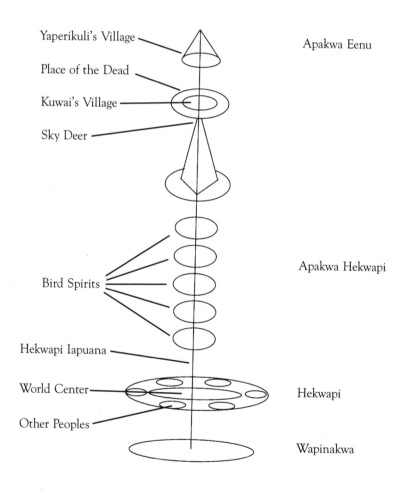

Fig. 1. The Baniwa Cosmos

beings will emerge at the "end of the world." *Hekwapi* consists of two planes: the "world center" and the house of animal souls and forest spirits (*iaradate*). The world center is the rapids called Hipana, where the earth began and the first ancestors emerged. It is the place of connection between the worlds above and below, where Kuwai was burned and his sacred flutes produced. On the horizontal level of This World, the periphery of the center is defined as the places of "other people"—affinal groups, enemy tribes, sorcerers and witches, and nonindigenous peoples. This World is often characterized as *Maatchikwe* (evil place), *Kaiwikwe* (pain place), in contrast to the Other Sky, which is notable as a source of spiritual remedies against the sicknesses and afflictions of This World.

Above This World, the Other World begins with five separate places of the bird spirits, helpers of the shaman in his search for lost souls, and owners of spiritual remedies. The top of the Other World and the beginning of the Other Sky is a complex place of transformation, where the souls of the dead are purified and changed into their eternal essence, and where the shamans must "die" in order to return to the world of the deities and first people. For the souls of the dead, the way continues to the periphery of Kuwai's place, where they remain eternally alienated from the living. For the shamans, the way leads to Kuwai's place in the center, which is said to contain all the kinds of lethal sicknesses that entrap human souls. It is there that the shamans must bargain with Kuwai to regain the souls of the sick.

Beyond Kuwai's village, another way leads to the place of Yaperikuli, the sky tip where the universe ends. It is said that this world is a "hidden place," a "place of happiness" (*kathimakwe*), of eternal light and unfailing remedies. It is the source of all knowledge (*ianheke*) that began and made the universe. In their apprenticeship, shamans must reach a point near this level, where they, like Yaperikuli, demonstrate their power to create, in their thought, all that exists in This World again.

From this description, it is easy to see how cosmology organizes the concerns of cosmogony in the creation of a vertical hierarchy of spiritual being and power. The highest level represents omniscience, as the hidden and eternal source of creation and happiness. The second level represents the soul both as the generative source of life and as the dark seat of pain and the soul's entrapment. This World is at once sacralized by its connection to the primordial world, bearing its sacred mark at the center, yet it is eternally flawed, constantly threatened by the chaos of pain from the periphery. Finally, the world below represents inverted being, which potentially may emerge at the end of time.

For the Baniwa, there is an intimate connection between the process of the formation of individuals into fully social and cultural human beings and the structure and processes of the cosmos. This connection is established at birth and is renewed throughout a person's life in rites of passage such as initiation and in curing rites. The socialization of individuals is conceptualized as a process of transforming raw, animal (biological) nature into a fully human and cultural dimension consisting of the vertical relations between mythic ancestors and human descendants. Giving birth, ritual fasting in initiation, and the eating of sacralized food—important activities in rites of passage—define the human qualities of individuals and connect them to a ritual hierarchy of ancestors, ritual specialists, elders, children, and grandchildren. They are the processual material through which the macrocosmic creation of a vertical structure of the cosmos, generations, and the stages of human development become imprinted onto the microcosmos of individual body space. Thus, fully social and cultural human beings are those who live according to the laws and principles established by the ancestors, who observe ritual relations and fasting and who have incorporated the vertical structure of the relations of power of the cosmos into their person.

Birth is conceptualized as a progressive separation from a spiritualized and alien nature, mediated by a protective enclosure (the natal house) that is gradually opened outward as the spiritual elements of the newborn become fixed, as the spirits of nature are metaphorically "cooked" and consumed, and as a vertical connection is made between the souls of the first ancestors and the newborn. Death is conceptualized as a progressive alienation of the person from the living; an absorption into an alien, spiritualized nature; a vertical descent and integration of the bodily remains into the inverted, predatory underworld; a vertical ascent and integration of the spiritual elements of the person into the ancestral soul; and a final enclosure of the deceased's soul into the eternally repetitive world of the dead.

Shamanic knowledge is essential to the process of human development, as it is to the life and well-being of the cosmos, for cosmogony shows that This World is intrinsically flawed by evil, misfortune, and death. Like a sick person, This World constantly needs to be healed, that is, restored to a state of integrated temporal and spatial order. The "death of This World," that is, when the world collapses into total darkness, is considered to be the equivalent of total consumption by death-dealing sickness. Cosmogony shows that salvation of the world from death follows a narrow escape from inside a closed container. The shaman's apprenticeship and constant journeys to the Other World during curing rites replicate this process of narrow escape, so that every time a shaman completes his apprenticeship and remakes the world, he saves it from death. The shamans thus have the most vital job of sustaining ordered life, of healing and preventing the death of the world.

Prophets in Historical Experience

The key to understanding the millenarian consciousness of the Baniwa lies in the multiple meanings attributed to the vertical and horizontal dimensions of the cosmos. The vertical dimension is associated with generational time, creation birth, resurrection, or reversible death. It is associated with ritual hierarchy and the transmission of culture from ancestors to descendants. The horizontal dimension, on the other hand, is associated with other peoples and places, with dangerous, death-dealing, alien powers that, in order to be controlled, have to be socialized, incorporated into the vertical structure of the cosmos. It is associated with ritual exchange relations, egalitarian relations, and the organization of society through warfare and alliance.

These dimensions coincide with two complementary aspects of the millenarian vision—utopian and catastrophic. Utopian, in the concrete sense, is temporal and spatial; that is, the vertical dimension is the ultimate source of creative power that transcends the chaos and destruction of time and matter. The world of Yaperikuli, *kathimakwe*, the place of happiness, signifies beauty and order, harmony. It stands in contrast with this world, *Maatchíkwe*, the place of evil, *Kaiwíkwe*, the place of pain, the world where people suffer and die. The horizontal dimension is marked by catastrophic images, when *all* is drastically reduced to one single survivor, a time of night and darkness, when multiplicity and magnitude are reduced to singularity and the miniature. Time and space are reduced from their complexity and differentiation to an undifferentiated, unique state. Such images inform the vision through which the Baniwa interpret not only the mythic past but also their history and local events.

It is through the vertical dimension that total catastrophe is averted and multiplicity regenerated. More specifically, it is through a return, a bringing back from the periphery to the center and the vertical source of life. Hence, oral narratives often describe a movement from the center to the periphery (horizontally down or away), where the subjects meet with death, and back up to a center, which, like a sanctuary, permits the regeneration of life and return to order. The return back to and up through the center is often a gradual process, passing through phases of metamorphosis or concrete changes until, fully integrated with the vertical, subjects assume their place as fully autonomous, cultural beings.

Shamans and chant specialists most clearly embody in their practice mastery over both dimensions. First, because the shamans undergo a process of metamorphosis which in the highest instance identifies their souls with the creative powers of the beginning. Their dream-souls may be in constant communication with Yaperikuli. These prophets are thus the living testimony of the omniscient and omnificent power of creation. They are the messengers of utopia. In "knowing everything," they are like Yaperikuli. Second, because the shamans and chant specialists utilize the vertical dimension to revert the potentially catastrophic destruction of the horizontal—sorcerers, false prophets, and enemies. Third, the chant specialists especially, through the music of their chants, socialize the alien and dangerous powers of the spirit world, in essence empowering the universe with the central symbols of growth and reproduction.

Baniwa history of contact with nonindigenous society has been characterized by periods of population dispersion and concentration. Oral narratives and evidence from the written sources indicate periods when the Baniwa were taken away from their territory to work for the whites, often becoming assimilated into ethnically mixed populations. Yet the Baniwa also describe a return to their home villages and territory, and a consolidation or renewal of their ties among themselves and with others of their kind. These periods of return have sometimes coincided with concentrations in large villages, in defined territories, and have been accompanied or followed by an explicit desire to remain autonomous from the whites. Prophetic or messianic figures have often been instrumental to these times of return and concentration and decisions for autonomy from the whites. It would further seem to be the case that prophets have appealed to the vertical, hierarchical dimension of the cosmos in order to reinforce their message. A brief review of the historical cases illustrates this point:

In the mid-nineteenth century, the prophet Venancio Kamiko warned of an imminent world conflagration, which recalled the fiery transformation of Kuwai at the moment of his ascent to the sky. Oral histories recount Kamiko's miraculous powers to produce things, to avert the death plotted for him by the whites, and to rise, rejuvenated, from the dead. Kamiko urged his followers to avoid the whites and to give their full allegiance to his new religion of the cross. The utopia that he promised was a world free of "sin" and debt to the white merchants and military.

At the beginning of this century, the prophet Anizetto was also considered to have creative powers to produce things, make gardens grow with the sign of the cross, and so on. Likewise, he was known as a miraculous healer and identified himself with Yaperikuli, or "Jesus Christo." He established a sort of sanctuary, where he and his followers sought to avoid contact with white rubber gatherers and military.

Nearly fifty years later, the prophet Kudui, a shaman of enormous prestige known for his miraculous cures and powers of prescience, emerged among the Baniwa. The utopia he promised was that "there would be no more sickness," which again may be understood as a sanctuary in the vertical sense (the place called *litalewapi riko Dzuli*, where there is no sickness, in the Other Sky). He spoke of a place of happiness, *kathimakwe*, or the "city of God." Like the others, he was identified with Yaperikuli, with whom his dream-soul communicated constantly, and Jesus Christo, "our salvation." He didn't so much preach autonomy from the whites as prophesy their "coming," for which the Indians should prepare by strict observance of the traditional laws of living.

When Sofia Muller, a North American evangelical missionary, began preaching among the Baniwa in the 1950s, her demonology, eschatology, and claims to divine origin produced a quickening of Baniwa messianic and millenarian expectations. Her attacks against the shamans and initiation rituals, however, collapsed in effect the vertical, hierarchical dimension of the cosmos, thereby ushering in the "end of the world" as the Baniwa understood it. This left the horizontal dimension, with all of its contradictions and difficulties, as the principal axis of orientation. Since the horizontal dimension had come to prevail, the Baniwa understood that they would "become whites, half-civilized." By the same token, converted Baniwa today understand that evangelism produced a moral reform among the faithful. Since vertical access to the primordial source of creative power had been severed, the most one could expect of a utopia would be that people would live a fully moral life within a temporal community of believers. Yet, without an eschatology that could offer a solution to the problem of sorcery and poison, the legacy of the horizontal dimension, evangelism foundered against the powers of the prophets, whose continuous access to the vertical dimension proved to be more effective than the evangelists' apocalyptic prophecies and assertions of greater authority. Today the Baniwa are divided among Evangelicals, Catholics, and the followers of the few prophets who remain.

Yet the Baniwa have for a long time lived with varying interpretations of both their own religion (variant myths of Yaperikuli and Kuwai, for example) and varying relationships to Christianity (from selective assimilation of the Christian saints into Baniwa mythology to a preference for the calendric rituals of the feast days of Catholic saints or the evangelical meetings). Such an exploration of alternatives to spirituality is also far from being a closed question: people convert and de-convert, return to the dance festivals in new contexts, giving them new meanings and interpretations. What is constant and continuous, however, are the quest and the expectation of a "place of happiness" as it was made in the beginning "for those unborn," or until "another end of the world."

References

Wright, Robin M. 1981. "History and Religion of the Baniwa Peoples of the Upper Rio Negro Valley." Ph.D. dissertation, Stanford University.
———. 1994. *For Those Unborn: Cosmos, Self and History in Baniwa Religion.* Departmento de Antropologia, Universidade Estadual de Campinas.

8

Inca Religion: Its Foundations in the Central Andean Context

R. Tom Zuidema

The study of Inca religion at the time when the Spaniards entered the capital of Cuzco, poses some rather unique problems. Before trying to define this religion, let me refer to the practical issues that color our approach.

The chroniclers writing on the peoples from southern Colombia to northern Argentina and Chile, transmit the impression that the Incas organized them in a recent empire with extraordinary political skill but without much of a tradition derived from earlier cultures and states. Still, the Incas worshiped the ruins of ancient cities in the mountains, such as Tiahuanaco, southeast of Cuzco (there, or on the nearby Island of Titicaca, the Creator would have brought forth the sun and the moon); Huari, northwest of Cuzco (its name refers to a complex concept of ancestry); and Chavin, in northern central Peru (which name means "the Center"). The statues found there were thought to have been of people living in a former age. Only recent archaeological explorations in the valley of Cuzco begin to confirm the immediate historical links of this city to the extensive ruins of Choque puquio and the earlier ruins of Piqui llacta—probably the largest city in the Huari empire after its capital—that ethnohistorical information had induced us to intuit.[1] The Cuzco urban tradition of religion, with its temples and rituals, probably had deep Huari roots and Huari culture, in turn, had its roots in the cultures of Nazca, on the nearby coast, Moche, on the north coast of Peru, and ultimately

---

[1] McEwan 1995.

Chavin. Little effort has been expended to define these roots, and less can be said about symbolic continuities of interest for the study of Andean religion in general.

The Andean area produced the only major civilization in the world not dependent on writing. We realize how important *quipus*, knotted cords, were for Inca administration, and recently much interest has been generated in their possible narrative content. The art of textiles was highly developed, and examples of complex designs are preserved from about a millennium B.C.E. on. Some Inca textiles show regular as well as irregular distributions of rectangular designs, and these, as signs, may have had symbolic significance in a wider context. Other textiles clearly also expressed a narrative intention. But even an understanding of some of their iconographies would not compare to the elaborate accounts found in Mesoamerican codices of calendars, deities, priests, and rituals, establishing connections between codices and chronicles and continuities with monuments of the classical Maya and preceding Olmec. Here, the unified calendrical systems allow us to suggest correlations between theological systems. In the Andes, however, few systematic studies have been accomplished searching for correspondences, correlations, and continuities. For instance, no profit can be made yet of realistic depictions of Moche deities in order to understand better Huari and Inca religions, or vice versa.

The situation sketched here influenced also Western approaches to religion in the Inca empire. Notwithstanding the genuine appreciation of many Spanish intellectuals in Peru for Andean culture, all-pervading were the official critique of local "idolatries" and the necessity of replacing them by the dogma of the Catholic Church. Even in Cuzco, the empire's example, no Spaniard had a more than passing, untechnical idea of what we now realize was a highly sophisticated calendar that organized state religion. While the descriptions of ritual details may be right, their significance and meanings became garbled and falsified. As far as calendars go, modern students are not instructed much better, and there is still hardly a way to compare ancient Andean rituals from one area to another.

In the first forty years after the Conquest, Spaniards still described Andean culture as they saw it, although they might interpret as "Inca" what, in fact, already was an indigenous reaction to colonial society. Later, they allowed themselves more and more to reinterpret second-hand information according to theories that little had to do with direct observation. Recently, much critical reading has evaluated this colonial literature for what it says in its own right.[2] The interest is in colonial opinions. Less emphasis has been placed on the question of how early and later sources can and should be used in reconstructing Andean culture itself. How do we place pieces of information in a supposedly Incaic context, if almost none are transmitted as explained in a pre-Hispanic way? Which elements of pre-Hispanic art and material culture can serve as a check on our conclusions comparable to the use of written sources in colonial literature?

Our information on Andean religion in Incaic times is scattered. Only some areas have been reported upon, with unequal quality and quantity. Each text shows its own strengths and weaknesses. Most chroniclers, while claiming to discuss Andean culture in the whole empire, take as their example the Cuzco situation. They concentrate on political organization, and almost no data exist on the social composition of constituent groups. Inca myths are either formulated according to Spanish monotheistic expectations or integrated as pseudo-historical events into an imperial history of conquest parallel to old-world histories. Perhaps our best descriptions of religion concern state rituals in Cuzco, although their astronomical and cosmological connections are replaced by a calendar of Spanish-type months. Nonetheless, the account of 328 sacred places, *huacas*, in the landscape of Cuzco, organized by forty-one directions, *ceques*, from the central temple of the Sun, *Coricancha*, the "golden enclosure," and used in the ritual calendar, apparently was recorded following the instructions of an Inca *quipu* expert. There is no reason so far to doubt the original order and most of the information. The *quipu* was not a register of all *huacas* in the valley, but an organized scheme of their political and ritual uses. The *ceque* system is perhaps our only Andean instrument approaching the utility of Mesoamerican codices for the study of pre-Hispanic religion. *Ceque* systems were said to be a common political feature in the southern central Andes. Reports to Spanish authorities keen to destroy *huacas* can reveal useful traces of *huaca* organizations, but they contain mostly disorganized lists. *Ceque*-like features are included in some descriptions, and

---

[2] Adorno 1986; MacCormack 1991; Duviols and Itier in Pachacuti Yamqui 1993.

I will mention these not so much for their own interest as to provide us with a systematic basis for the study of Andean religious systems and their religious thought in general.

Of regions outside Cuzco, most important is the "mythological history"[3] of the province of Huarochiri.[4] The reason that induced people, sometime around 1608, primarily from the village of San Damián de Checa, to record their myths and rituals was not only the immediate historical circumstances but also this province's strategic location on the road from Cuzco to Lima, the capital of the vice royalty, and even more so its position between Pachacamac, the most important coastal temple, and Pariacaca, the most sacred snowcapped mountains in central Peru. Only in Huarochiri were some major Andean myths recorded that were reminiscent of later recordings east of the Andes. We lack, however, much of the information on Andean learning that, to some extent, can be reconstructed in Cuzco.

The third important source on Andean religion is legal documents of the "extirpation of idolatries" in villages of the mountain province of Cajatambo, north of Huarochiri. They judge indigenous reactions to Spanish cultural and religious domination. Nonetheless, much material—especially in the accounts of Hernández Príncipe—is given without Spanish interpretation and can lead to questions of pre-Hispanic religion.[5]

Peoples living in the valley oases of the desert coast were decimated so rapidly that little was written on them. Only some early testimonies survive of the Pachacamac temple with myths on its god and some material from the north coast.[6] Finally, as important as the Titicaca region was in pre-Inca times, references to myths and rituals of peoples living there in the sixteenth century have to be extracted from an Aymara dictionary[7] and chronicles on the sanctuary of Copacabana, which first was Inca and then Catholic.[8]

In the following pages I will concentrate on those examples of Andean religious practices that explain best their systematic features as shared in one form or another. A first, perhaps most fundamental, feature deals with the claim that present-day society resulted

---

[5] Duviols 1986.
[6] Calancha 1974.
[7] Bertonio 1984.
[8] Ramos Gavilan 1988; Calancha 1974.

from the meeting of two peoples, one with old roots in the land and the other newcomers. The first people were recognized in Huarochiri as *Yunga,* from the time when a warm climate had reigned, as on the coast, and before later people, mostly conquerors from the province of Yauyos, had arrived. Each group had its own villages, *ayllus* (local divisions), *huacas,* myths, and rituals. In Cajatambo, the two groups were recognized as *Llacta,* farmers of established towns and villages, or Huari, named after their primordial underworld deities, and as *Llachua,* named for the sacrifice of llamas that they as herders practiced. The Llachua descended from an Eagle deity who had come from Titicaca, a faraway place and lake in the underworld where the dead returned.[9] The Llachua were not everywhere in a dominant position and could be looked down upon also as rustic newcomers. But in the towns of Choque Recuay and Allauca, inland from Cajatambo, they worshiped higher-ranked natural features as *huaca* and the Llacta lower-ranked ancestors as *mallqui,* and to these ranks corresponded also mythological distinctions like of male-female and land-water. In the valley of Lambayeque on the north coast, a similar distinction was applied between a dynasty whose mythical founder Ñampallec—the valley name derives from his—had come from across the sea with an idol of green stone and the local people that they governed.[10] The Pachacamac myth, with its report of movements along the coast, may have referred to a similar interpretation.[11] Cuzco's version of the distinction places it, however, in the most political context. I will come to it after reviewing the Huarochiri myths of three kinds of deities that here and elsewhere are found in the context of this first distinction.

Before humans cultivated the earth and were distinguished from animals, the god Coniraya, with the epithet of Viracocha, artificially impregnated Cahuillaca in a place near San Damián de Checa. She fled with her infant son down the river to Pachacamac and disappeared in the ocean, taking with her the first fishes. Coniraya pursued her but was stopped in Pachacamac. Along the way he defined the future ritual uses of animals and on his return to the mountains made possible the use of water in rivers and springs for future irri-

---

[9] Duviols 1973; Zuidema 1989, ch. 3.

[10] Zuidema 1990.

[11] Calancha 1974.

gation. The actual appropriation of those rights depended, however, on the later actions of the second god, born from five eagle eggs and identified as Thunder god with the Pariacaca mountains. In one myth, a man, helped by Pariacaca, obtained prescient knowledge from two foxes and wrested power from a lord who himself was identified in another source as a fox in the service of Pachacamac. The myth ends with a separation of men and animals and with a flood that swept tropical plants and Yunga people down to the coast. In another myth, a man switched worship from a primordial mountain deity to Pariacaca after the latter, fighting with rain, had defeated the first, fighting with fire. In both myths, we conclude, Pariacaca introduced atmospheric events, dry and wet seasons, agricultural technology, a calendar, and government. He was a god of changes, but while elsewhere the Thunder god normally is represented as a Twin god, here elements of duality are relegated to earlier times, and Pariacaca is represented by five brothers, next to whom five sister deities are mentioned.[12] Besides their names, not much is reported of the actions of the sisters, a fact that may be due to lack of Spanish interest. The brothers, their sisters, and a series of local gods said to be sons of Pariacaca introduce the themes of later myths that deal with actual political circumstances. One of these myths raises political interests to a truly cosmological level. It discusses the deal struck between the god Coniraya, departing from Pachacamac on the coast, and the last king in Cuzco, Huayna Capac. They meet in Titicaca and divide the spheres of interest of these two most sacred temples in the Inca empire. The myth ends with the disappearance of Huayna Capac. He probably reached his apotheosis in the Sun, his name still being used in this capacity around Cuzco.[13]

The last myth, and by implication all political myths, introduces us to a theme pervasive in Andean theogonies, in particular that of the Incas. With the exception of Pachacamac's myth and a minor one from Cajatambo, nowhere is the Sun given shape as an actor. In striking contrast, east of the Andes many stories are told of the joint exploits of the Sun and the Moon. Nonetheless, specific solar observations were at the basis of the Inca calendar, and the living king as "Son of the Sun" was given numerous ritual expressions. Even the

---

[12] Zuidema 1992.
[13] Urton 1981.

Moon as wife of the Sun was hardly personalized, nor was Venus considered a deity close to the Thunder. This kind of political and ritual reductionism of divinities can be illustrated best by way of the Inca example. Here, with the exception of Viracocha, the only recollection of divine actions was as filtered through the life histories of royal ancestors.

Central to the political organization of Cuzco were ten groups of Inca nobility, *panacas*, whose first royal ancestor had conquered the valley. They were ranked, five of Hanan (upper moiety) living north of the valley river, and five of Hurin (lower moiety) living south. Ten *ayllus* of commoners, whose ancestors had settled in the valley before the Incas, matched the *panacas*. However, not these but some *ayllus* outside this canonical list claimed that their ancestors had lived in the valley before the Flood. While in Huarochiri the worship of the great deities was distributed over groups of conquerors and conquered, in Cuzco it was the concern of the ranked *panacas*. Our descriptions of the three great festivities organized by the state (for planting around September, December solstice, and harvest around April-May), include various lists of sacrifices to the major deities and *huacas*. Thus we know that the first *panaca* of each moiety dedicated its sacrifices to the Sun, and the other four, in sequence, to the Moon, Thunder, Viracocha, and the Earth.[14] It is not the place here to identify each *panaca* and suggest how, in association with a common *ayllu*, it carried out the cult to its particular deity and ancestor as part of its civic duties. (The *panaca* membership of Inca nobles and their individual links to royal ancestors depended on considerations of, among others, mother's rank, fraternal succession, success in initiation and war, and choice. Inasmuch as the religious data contribute in their own way to our understanding of the *panaca* problem, I will not detail this any further.) The fourth *ayllu* will suffice as an example; moreover, to simplify the task, I will take the information of the Hanan *panaca* as valid for both. Then I will discuss the general interests of the other *panacas*. In this way I can cover the major aspects of Inca religion as represented by these gods: its institutional organization (the Sun), the dependence of people on outside forces (Viracocha), its handling of transitions in life and society (Thunder), and the fertility of the earth (Earth and Moon).

---

[14] Cobo 1956; Zuidema 1992.

The fourth *panaca* named its royal ancestor after the god to whom it sacrificed, Viracocha Inca. Its own name Sucsu, "sickly," also referred in general to old age. The high priest in the temple of the Sun was a descendant of Viracocha Inca as well as a close relative of the ruling king, but we have no way to judge how both statements were made compatible with each other. The best way to understand the priestly role of Sucsu *panaca* is in the context of our information on its associate *ayllu* of the Tarpuntay priests. First, we observe that while their name meant "planter," their role was defined as "priests of the Sun" and they were elected as "sons of the Thunder." Their ritual activities served the concerns of the other *panacas*. This we notice reviewing the major moments of their participation in the agricultural cycle.

When the month of the June solstice announced the coming of the first irrigation and plowing/planting in the fields (July-August), the Tarpuntay went on a long pilgrimage to visit the temple of the Sun called Villcanota "house of the Sun," situated at the continental divide southeast of Cuzco and halfway to Titicaca. During ten days they followed a straight route through the mountains, and on the ten days of their return, they followed the river, also called Villcanota, which, some thirty kilometers from Cuzco, passed through the most productive valley in southern Peru. At this time, the Tarpuntay functioned as priests of the Sun. Just after planting, their fasting accompanied and encouraged the sprouting of the maize seeds until, some two months later, the young plants had grown a finger high. They ate some cooked maize with (probably wild) herbs and drank the dreg of maize beer. Only now did the name Tarpuntay refer to their priestly activity. Their third major task took place around March, when the plants had flowered and set seed. The preceding rituals had been concerned with the end of heavy rains, sending off the ashes of sacrifices in the rivers of Cuzco and Villcanota to Mama-cocha "Mother Sea," where "maybe lived . . . the Creator,"[15] or "to the sea to Viracocha."[16] In the months to come concerns were with the defense of the standing crops against the inclemencies sent by the Thunder and with harvest considered as conquest. Now, in March, all priests, including the high priest, went to the sacred mountains

---

[15] Molina 1989, 116.
[16] Cobo 1956, 214.

around Cuzco that influenced the weather. Among other sacrifices they killed "black llamas that had not eaten" because "just as the hearts of these had fainted, so their adversaries would faint."[17] Hail and rain were compared to human enemies, and whereas previously the priests had induced growth by way of fasting, now their sacrifices encouraged the defense of the crops. The Tarpuntay priests were "sons of the Thunder," either because they were born in the fields during a thunderstorm, or their mothers affirmed to have conceived them from the thunder, or they were twins. While in March their intentions were as of young warriors, only when they were old did they take office and fulfill the destiny of their birth. We understand why the high priest and Viracocha Inca normally were represented as old men.

The coherence of our information on Viracocha Inca, Sucsu panaca and the Tarpuntay—with which we might compare information in Huarochiri on the old Yacana priest and his young Huacsa helpers, chosen among recently initiated men—allows us to approach the central issues of Inca religion. The priests influenced the desired outcomes indirectly, either by going out to Villcanota and to the mountains or by fasting for the growth of the standing crops outside town. Their rituals matched the interests (1) of the king, who as head of state watched the risings and settings of the Sun, his "father," at critical moments of the year for the benefit of all his subjects, (2) the interests of the young men who went to war in foreign countries after initiation and before marriage, and (3) of the married farmers, descendants of the original inhabitants of Cuzco. At all times the rituals of the priests involved water: either they went to the source of the Villcanota river before irrigation, or they drank the dreg of maize beer during growth or they fought against hail and rain. Before addressing the final question of the identity of the god Viracocha, let me review first these other interests.

We can approach the worship of the Sun best through our information on the temples in Cuzco, Titicaca, and Pachacamac. In Cuzco, the Inca made his observations of sunrise or sunset in different places, each for another purpose of administration and accompanied by other subjects. The only observation mentioned for Coricancha, the central "golden enclosure," was of the sunrise that a

---

[17] Polo 1981, 474-75.

month before the June solstice would announce the next agricultural year. The king was joined by the mummies of his ancestors. The temple also kept normally the golden image of the Sun, in daytime out in the courtyard and at night inside a room attended by two hundred *acllas*, "virgins of the Sun." At the three times of planting, December solstice, and harvest, a small garden of golden maize plants was set out in front of this room. However, for the observation of sunset during the June solstice itself, the king went out, with men of high nobility and *acllas* but without their wives, to a temple just north of Cuzco where they would shell maize of the last harvest. On the day of the December solstice sunrise the king concluded the initiation rituals of noble boys in a temple just south of Cuzco. But during the rituals of harvest in April he would observe sunset out in the valley of Cuzco and conclude this observation with ritually plowing a special field together with the queen and forty lords and ladies from the whole empire. An important element in temples of the Sun was the use of a basin called the *Ushnu* for making libations. In Cuzco, however, the major *Ushnu* was in the great plaza. After planting, when the earth was pregnant with the recently sprouted maize, the king made the most important public observation of the year, of sunset, and drank with the Sun, begging him to send rain with the increase of his heat. The king poured the maize beer offered to the Sun in the *Ushnu*. Nobody else was allowed to drink independently with the Sun and thus the king, seated on a small pyramid erected for the occasion, was joined by the ancestral mummies and all Cuzco people on the *Ushnu* side of the river Huatanay, while visitors observed from a distance on the other side.

The temple on the island of Titicaca, "Rock of the Cat" but called "Island of the Sun" by the Spaniards, probably inherited its ritual eminence in the highlands from Tiahuanaco times. Most sacred was the rock, surrounded by a temple wall.[18] Its northern concave side was said to be encased in gold, and its southern convex side to be covered with a beautiful curtain (a situation perhaps reminiscent of the Sun temple in Machu Picchu now known as the *Torreón*). While we might expect that the reflection of the solar rays on the golden front was intended for a special date, only a tradition about the institutional aspect of the cult is preserved. The island is located in front

---

[18] Cobo 1956.

of the former Inca town of Copacabana, with its own temple of the Sun and a house of *acllas*, located near the end of a peninsula. Pilgrims had to pass various gates here and on the island each time making confessions. But no visitor was allowed to pass the last gate on the island. The worship of the whole empire was represented by the envoys (*mitimaes*) from forty provinces, and they lived on the peninsula. Only their lord, from Sucsu *panaca*, was allowed to stay on the island.

The importance of temples of the Sun in all administrative centers is best demonstrated by the situation in Pachacamac. There were two principal temples, one for Pachacamac, "He who animates the world," the underworld god of earthquakes, and one for the Sun. To approach the pyramid of the first, pilgrims had to fast for a year, and only priests entered the dark inner precinct on top. The second temple was open and light and included a house of *acllas*. The Sun temple represents Inca conquest, and Pachacamac was a temple of the conquered—archaeology attests its importance in earlier times. But the power of the conquered was respected and Pachacamac was the greatest oracle in the Andes, where lords from the whole empire wished to be represented by their own temple and be buried there.

Sacrifices to the Thunder can be understood best by focusing on the religious interests related to war. I mentioned already the elaborate priestly rituals aimed at weakening the enemy. Inca armies were divided into three parts, each with its own captain. The names and titles recorded for some of these are suggestive of their symbolic meanings, but apart from this we know only the division to the right carried the image of the Sun. These are minor details, and more should be said of those who prepared for war—the noble youths in their initiation rituals, and the age-class of young initiated men who only after army service received a wife and land allowing them to enter the group of married men.

The chronicles contain elaborate descriptions of the initiation rituals carried out in *Capac raymi*, "the royal feast," before the December solstice. Boys competed outside town in races and received names of more or less esteemed animals according to their performance, qualifying them for government service. Inside town, on the plaza, their *huari* songs commemorated the ancestors. Their dances with old men in lieu of these ancestors suggest a particular connection between both groups. Two of our most imaginative accounts of

Inca beliefs (one a myth and the other a funeral ritual) illustrate these connections.

The myth, preserved in a late chronicle,[19] is a version of the story of the future king Pachacuti Inca as heroic defender of Cuzco, but here as a son, not called for succession, of the first, mythical Inca king, Manco Capac. In a month of torrential rains, a man with a trumpet and staff, dressed in red, came down on the waters of the Villcanota river to near Cuzco. Pachacuti begged him not to play the trumpet and thus warded off a flood. Agreeing to become "brothers," one "turned into stone" and one "was disinherited from his due"–the text is vague about what happened to whom. Nonetheless, it does make clear that the name Pachacuti refers to these two statements as well as to the fact that the Flood would have "turned around the country (*pacha*)" and time (also *pacha*). The myth ends claiming that the feast of *Capac raymi* with the initiation rituals was held because of these events; moreover, it boasts of the extravagant deeds of young, irresponsible men.

The theme of the man in red dress, or of a red animal riding the turbulent waters of a river after heavy rains, remained popular. In the myth the man acted like the god Viracocha. Its ambiguous use of two cooperating opponents calls to mind the old, weak priests of Tarpuntay *ayllu* and Sucsu *panaca*, who, nonetheless, help to fight against natural and human enemies. The myth may well have been the theme of one of the *huari* songs.

While Pachacuti Inca was the hero of young warriors, of special interest also is the description of his funeral rituals, called *Purucaya*, during four months leading to the coronation of his successor. Two things stand out in our information. First, the description is based not simply on traditional knowledge but on one of the few actual observations that Spaniards could make of Inca state rituals, in this case a royal funeral. The occasion was the death of Paullu Inca, the Spanish-installed puppet king, in May 1549. The day before his death, fully armed men had already mounted the walls of his house to defend it against whoever might want to take possession of their lord's wife and children and thus of the crown. They stayed until Paullu Inca was buried, but in Inca times they would have remained

---

[19] Murúa 1946.

until the chosen successor had ascended the throne.[20] Enemies were, however, not only competitors but also forces of nature. A year later, the Purucaya was coordinated with the Spanish "Anniversary" honoring the deceased. The original intent of the noncalendrical rite had been, however, to make it similar to the calendrical rituals beginning after initiation and December solstice and ending with harvest, when the former initiates were presented as young warriors to society, when foreign lords arrived to renew their allegiance to the king, and when a new king was presented to his subjects. The other thing to realize is that our chroniclers confess to having reconstructed the Purucaya rituals for Pachacuti Inca's death from what they witnessed at Paullu Inca's anniversary. This happened to coincide with harvest; the first major part of the celebration was, however, similar to the rituals in January, when, instead of foreign lords, the Cuzco nobility itself pledged allegiance to the king. We can now follow the description of the Purucaya.[21]

First, all the noble men and women went out, with blackened faces, to the mountains around Cuzco, where he (Pachacuti Inca) had planted and harvested. They called him there and in the streets of town and asked, now that he was with his father the Sun, to send them good crops and take away illnesses. Then four masked men came out on the plaza, two on one side and two on the other, in rich dresses with feathers, each held on a long rope by ten women, and these accompanied by a girl with a small sack of coca leaves and a boy dragging an *ayllu*, "boleadoras," over the ground. Each group of women was said to represent the "will of the (deceased) lord" that they could release or restrain with the rope. After this episode, two squadrons of soldiers came to battle each other in the plaza, the upper moiety defeating the lower moiety just as Pachacuti always had won in war, and two squadrons of women, dressed as men with feather crowns and shields and halberds, that went around the plaza dancing. "With those ceremonies their lord was going to heaven" (maybe, like Huayna Capac had done after his meeting with Coniraya Viracocha). The rituals ended as done in a minor way during and after harvest. Lords from the whole empire returned to Cuzco offer-

---

[20] Segovia 1968, 81.
[21] Betzanos 1987, pt. 1, chs. 31–32.

ing their services to the new king; mourning dresses were burned and thousands of llamas sacrificed, their meat being distributed to all the people in town.

Ritual battles such as that mentioned above were carried out according to the calendar by the recently initiated boys with the advent of the first new moon after the December solstice. During the next full moon, noble lords and ladies, attached to a long rope, danced through all the streets and at dawn spiraled in upon the king sitting on his throne in the plaza. After these rituals the ashes of sacrifice were sent to Viracocha in the ocean and the priests of Viracocha went off to sacrifice the black llamas in the mountains. We get the impression that the Purucaya rituals as well as the ritual sequence from December solstice to the harvest depicted a visit to Viracocha as a passage through death, from the time that crops began to ripen to the time of harvest.

We come now to the religious interests reflected in the sacrifices brought to the Earth and the Moon. These had an important feminine component, and we should look at some female customs in their own right and then the role that concepts with a female connotation received from an institutional, mostly male, point of view. When in 1622 Hernández Príncipe discovered the case of sacrifice of an *aclla*, "chosen virgin," he made the unique observation that, as men worshiped the Sun and women the Moon, they did not know much of each other's cult. And as male "extirpators of idolatries" would discover even less of female interests, he recovered her story only because she had been sacrificed to the Sun. Nonetheless, other priests did discover, for instance, how only women would honor and consult foxes or worship the pots in their houses while men worshiped the house. Coming to the institutional use of female concepts, we observe first that a distinction was made between the cultivated earth where people lived, called Camac Pacha ("He/She who animates the Earth"), and the uncultivated earth, called Pacha Mama ("Mother Earth"), a distinction that may have paralleled that between the god Pachacamac and the goddesses Pacha Mama and Mama Cocha, "Mother Sea." But although the term Pacha Mama gained much popularity in colonial times and later, few details are given of the Incaic goddess. Lesser female deities seem to have been of more interest and came to be included in the ancestral system.

The female component in Andean religious thought was more

prominent than is sometimes thought. This can be seen, for example, in the symbolic importance of the numbers 4 and 40 (or 41 and 42) in Andean political thought. In the village of Allauca near Cajatambo, its four *ayllus* were served by, respectively, 24 (8, 4, 8, 4) male and 42 (12, 16, 6, 8) female priests. Besides the regularity of the numbers, it is remarkable that the religious duties of the forty-two women were also specified.[22] Alliances between a single political center and a multiple outside (of 4 or 40 units) were established through marriages; myth and ritual underlined their importance. Let me give two examples from Cuzco.

Anahuarque was the name of a mountain on the southern border of the Cuzco valley—the only one to have risen with the waters of the Flood—and of the *ceque* leading to it. As ancestress of the pre-Incaic people, she was also worshiped by the noble boys going through initiation "because of her swiftness." At the time of planting, during the lunar "feast of the Queen," *Coya raymi*, women worshiped Anahuarque because of her fertility. Thus one queen, Mama Anahuarque, was said to have had 150 children (in fact, children of her husband in secondary wives). At the time of harvest, however, a very different kind of ancestress was worshiped. Mama Huaco, a sister of Manco Capac, the founder of the Inca dynasty, was the most fierce conqueror of the Cuzco valley. She planted the first maize there. The maize tended by the king in a special field was used to brew beer in honor of her mummy. In general, however, the best seeds were stored in a vessel dressed as a woman, Mama Sara, "Mother Maize," representing Mama Huaco, and used for planting in the year to come. Both months, of planting and harvest, had a female connotation, but a contrast was added between fertility and peace, on the one hand, and virility including sterility and conquest, on the other. Elaborate and authentic myths are also told of female actors in central Peru, and some of these, like Mama Capyama in San Damián and Mama Rayguana in Cajatambo, are still known today. While the characters of Mama Anahuarque and Mama Huaco had to be reconstructed from fragments, an advantage was the elaborate ritual context of their cults.

We might claim that the sacrifices to the Sun, Thunder, and Earth reflected the respective religious interests of the three classes in soci-

---

[22] Zuidema 1989, ch. 3.

ety of high nobility, low nobility, and farmers. Aspects of female fertility were considered in relation to the earth and its farmers. Feminine aspects were, however, not unidimensional and belonged to the interests of all classes. The *panaca* and *ayllu* of priests may have been distinguished from others, their members being elected for reasons other than only social rank. In this overview I had to forgo many important themes—for instance, the *capac hucha*, "royal obligation" (or "obligation to the king") with its use of child sacrifice, divination, and so on—that need to be analyzed in detail before a more general definition of Inca and Andean religions can be attempted. Thus I chose to concentrate on the *panaca* sacrifices as a heuristic device to classify some representative beliefs and practices. To end this essay, let me return briefly to the colonial interpretations of Viracocha and similar Andean gods.

The Spaniards saw in Viracocha a Creator and compared or contrasted him with the Christian God. Colonial myths claimed that once either St. Thomas or St. Bartholomew had come to Lake Titicaca to preach the gospel as Viracocha had done too. Questioning theological speculations does not lead to better knowledge of who this god was in pre-Hispanic times. Perhaps a way out of this dilemma is to focus more on the great pilgrimage to the temple of Villcanota, the "House where the Sun was born," with which I began this overview. The Inca cult on the island of Titicaca seems to have been an extension of the cult brought to Villcanota. In the imperial myth as recorded by the chroniclers, Viracocha, traveling from Titicaca to the Ecuadorian coast, passed by the Villcanota River and Cuzco. Before entering the valley of Cuzco he visited a temple, dating from Huari times, of which a detailed description of its cult is preserved.[23] Once King Viracocha Inca had a vision there of the eponymous god. Near the temple are located the mountain called Viracocha and the towns of Urcos and Huaro, which provided Cuzco with priests for the cult to Viracocha.[24] Fragmentary as these materials may be, they do seem to retain authentic elements that would allow analysis in an archaeological context. A critical method might be developed to study the problem of Viracocha in particular and of Inca and Andean religion in general.

---

[23] Molina 1989.
[24] Ibid.

References

Adorno, Rolena. 1986. *Guaman Poma: Writing and Resistance in Colonial Peru*. Austin: University of Texas Press.

Bertonio, Ludovico. 1984. *Vocabulario de la Lengua Aymara*. [1612]. Edited by Xavier Albo and Felix Layme. Cochabamba: CERES.

Betanzos, Juan de. 1987. *Suma y Narración de los Incas*. [1551]. Edited by María del Carmen Martín Rubio. Madrid: Atlas.

Calancha, Antonio de la. 1974. *Crónica Moralizada*. Edited by Ignacio Prado Pastor. Lima: Ignacio Prado Pastor.

Cobo, Bernabé. 1956. *Historia del Nuevo Mundo*. Biblioteca de Autores Españoles 92. Madrid: Atlas.

Duviols, Pierre. 1973. "Huari y llacuaz, agricultores y pastores: Un dualismo prehispánico de oposición y complementaridad." *Revista del Museo Nacional* [Lima] 39:153-91.

———. 1986. *Cultura Andina y Represión: Procesos y Visitas de Idolatrías y hechicerías. Cajatambo, siglo XVII.* Cusco: Centro de Estudios Rurales Andinos "Bartolomé de las Casas."

Lévi-Strauss, Claude. 1978. *Myth and Meaning*. New York: Schocken Books.

MacCormack, Sabine. 1991. *Religion in the Andes: Vision and Imagination in Early Colonial Peru*. Princeton, N.J.: Princeton University Press.

McEwan, G. F., A. Gibaja, and M. Chatfield. 1995. "Archaeology of the Chokepukio Site: An Investigation of the Origin of the Inca Civilization in the Valley of Cuzco, Peru: A Report on the 1994 Field Season." *TAWANTINSUYU: International Journal of Inka Studies* 1.

Molina, Cristóbal. 1989. *Fábulas y Mitos de los Incas*. Edited by Henrique Urbano, 1-136. Madrid.

Murúa, Martín de. 1946. *Historia del Orígen y Genealogía Real de los Reyes Incas del Peru*. [1590]. Edited by C. Bayle. Madrid: CSIC, Instituto Santo Toribio de Mogrovejo.

Pachacuti Yamqui Salcamaygua, Joan de Santa Cruz. 1993. *Relación de Antigüedades deste Reyno del Piru*. Edited by Pierre Duviols and Cesar Itier. Cusco: IFEA; Centro de Est. Reg. Andinos "Bartolomé de Las Casas."

Polo de Ondegardo, Juan. 1981. "Los errores y supersticiones de los Indios sacadas del Tratado y averiguacion que hizo el Licenciado Polo" [1585]. In *El Catecismo del III Concilio Provincial de Lima y sus Complementos Pastorales*. [1584-1585], edited by J. G. Durán, 457-78. Buenos Aires: Facultad de Teología de la Universidad Católica Argentina.

Ramos Gavilan, Alonso. 1988. *Historia del Santuario de Nuestra Señora de Copacabana*. Edited by Ignacio Prado Pastor. Lima: Ignacio Prado Pastor.

Salomon, Frank, and George L. Urioste. *The Huarochiro Manuscript. A Testament of Ancient and Colonial Andean Religion.* Austin: University of Texas Press.

Segovia, Bartolomé de. 1968. *Relación de muchas cosas acaescidas en el Peru.* [Here attributed to Cristóbal de Molina, el Almagrista]. Biblioteca de Autores Españoles 209. Crónicas Peruanas de Interés Indígena, ed. Francisco Esteve Barba, 56–96. Madrid: Atlas.

Taylor, Gerald. 1987. *Ritos y Tradiciones de Huarochiri: Manuscrito quechua de comienzos del siglo XVII.* Lima: IEP, Inst. Francés de Estudios Andinos.

Urton, Gary. 1981. *At the Crossroads of the Earth and the Sky: An Andean Cosmology.* Austin: University of Texas Press.

Zuidema, R. Tom. 1989. *Reyes y Guerreros: Ensayos de Cultura Andina.* Edited by Manuel Burga. Lima: Fomciencias.

———. 1990a. *Inca Civilization in Cuzco.* Austin: University of Texas Press.

———. 1990b. "Dynastic Structures in Andean Culture." In *The Northern Dynasties: Kingship and Statecraft in Chimor,* edited by Michael E. Moseley and Alana Cordy-Collins, 489–506. Washington, D.C.: Dumbarton Oaks Research Library and Collection.

———. 1992. "Inca Cosmos in Andean Context from the Perspective of the Capac raymi Camay quilla Feast Celebrating the December Solstice in Cuzco." In *Andean Cosmologies through Time: Persistence and Emergence,* edited by R. Dover and K. Seibold. Bloomington: Indiana University Press.

———. 1993. "De la Tarasca a Mama Huaco: La Historia de un Mito y Rito Cuzqueño." In *Religions des Andes et Langues Indigènes Equateur–Pérou–Bolivie avant et après la Conquête Espagnole.* Actes du Colloque III d'Etudes Andines, ed. Pierre Duviols. Aix-en-Provence: Publications de l'Université de Provence.

———. 1996. "Fête-Dieu et fête de l'Inca: Châtiment et sacrifice humain comme rites de communion." In *Le Corps de Dieu en Fête,* edited by Antoinette Molinié, 175–222. Paris: Cerf.

9

The Religion of the Chamacoco (Ishír) Indians

Edgardo Jorge Cordeu

The Chamacoco, or Ishír Indians, constitute a southern branch of the Zamucu language family, which is widely distributed in the Chaco Boreal.[1] Although the origins of the denominations "Xamacoco" and "Xamicoco" are unknown, they first appear recorded toward the end of the eighteenth century and may have been derived from Chamóc or Zamúc, another tribe belonging to the same family. The Chamacoco prefer the autodenomination Ishír, "person" (pl.: Ishíro), which identifies them as the "true" [people] or "*ejnábsa*" in contrast to the *ajnábsa*, "strangers," those of other tribes or religions with whom they only share a human appearance.

Particular ergological, social, and religious patterns suggest that the historic Chamacoco tradition is a form of symbiosis between that of a very simple hunter/gatherer (like that of the *canoeros fueguinos* [Fuegian canoe-people]) and a hunter-planter tradition of the Gê from eastern Brazil and the Matto Grosso, dual societies with exogamous patri-clans and incipient agriculture. It is also possible that this tradition may have been influenced by the agriculturists from the Chiquitos plains. Nevertheless, attention is drawn to the contrast between their simple technology and complex social and ideational patterns—dual halves, patrilineal clans, secret male society, initiation rituals, a well-developed theophany, and so on. Although they did have a rudimentary knowledge of ceramics, the Chamacoco lacked permanent homes and a lithic technology. Their material culture was based on a *materia prima* of wood, bone, leather, feathers, rushes, and bromeliad fibers used for braiding and weaving. These technological limitations and the marked climatological oscillations of the

---

[1] Mason 1950, 280–81.

Chaco imposed a seasonal pattern on their social organization that obliged them to concentrate into villages during the wet seasons from September to February and disperse into single-family nomadic units during the dry periods of March to August.

Until the end of the eighteenth century the forefathers of the Chamacoco inhabited the arid zone of Mt. San Miguel and the head-waters of the Verde River located in the northeastern territory of Chaqueña. Cessation of the Mbayá-Caduveo invasions from Mata-grosso, however, allowed them to expand their territory to the western banks of the Paraguay River, from above Bahía Negra to somewhat below Fuerte Olimpo; between 20° and 22° S. latitude. To this territorial belt we must add the southern portion of the hinter-lands extending some forty to fifty kilometers from the coast. Based on their linguistic and sociopolitical organization, the Ishír are divided among four dialectic branches that were created by changing alliances and hostilities between local bands and tribes: (1) the Hório and (2) Ebidóso of the northern territory; (3) the Héiwo in the Fuerte Olimpo sector and (4) the Tomaráho, who inhabit the moun-tainous regions of the interior.

Today there are only about 800 Ebidóso living among the ancient Hório and no more than 150 Tomaráho. Since approximately 1880, the white occupation of the territory not only transformed the Indi-ans into wage laborers for the lumber and cattle industries but also caused an intense acculturation, such as the eradication of traditional rituals boasted by the New Tribes missionaries in 1955. The Tomaráho, on the other hand, inhabited the inhospitable territories of the hinterlands and were able to preserve their ethnic autonomy until after the Chaco War (1932–1935). In spite of the fact that since 1986, they had to join one of the many rival factions of the Ebidóso, their culture shows remnants of many traditional customs (myths and beliefs, the bellicose feathered adornments [for which they are famous], the circular village, the initiatory reclusion of the young, and the complex ritual cycle of the masks, which is celebrated throughout the wet season).

The Cosmovision and Defining of the Sacred

Although the Chamacoco religion does show certain similarities to the geographically and culturally neighboring Ayoreo, Nivaklé, or

Caduveo, as well as the more distant Manassica of the Chiquitos Plains and Kágaba of Colombia, and so on, it is well differentiated from that of other Chaco Indians by its complexity and unique matrix.

The nucleus of their religious contemplation appears to be the contrast between Death (*Tói*) and Life (*Ijípite*). Conceived of as the "strong" and "weak" phases of the same ontological regime based on the experiences of one or the other, which are respectively summarized into "corruption" (*mejné*) and "renovation" (*eicherájo*), as well as the aspects of "disharmony"/"harmony" (*sherwó/óm*) and "unconditioned"/"conditioned" (*eichóso/ábo*) as revealed by the mentioned phenomena, they give rise to the concepts of "power" (*wozósh*), "taboo" (*mejné*), and the onto-temporal articulation of reality and origin. As a result of an incessant expansion of hierophanic meanings for Death and Life, the symbolic extrapolation of the cosmovision ascribed to successive domains of the natural, social, moral, and religious experience also led to the constitution of a stratified mythology and a hierarchical pantheon. These patterns seem to support the hypothesis that, in correspondence to the cultural patterns of the chronological, beyond that of a truly hierophanic level, Chamacoco religiosity includes four additional levels of a more mythological and theophanic nature (table 1).

Life and Death, Purity and Impurity, Cratophanies, Hierophanies, and Fundamental Notions of Cosmovison

While not completely confounding the terms sacred and impure, the Chamacoco, however, do belong to an extensive group of cultures that tend to homogenize the two. In fact, the Ishír equivalent of "unusual power," *wozósh*, primarily refers to the repulsive or negative values of the sacred. Associated with either an undetermined energy, or a discrete and quasi-substantial entity, the power is usually associated with disgrace and impurity. Its empirical and lexical correlation is venom—unexpected with fulgurant effects whose consequences are commonly unfortunate. Some of the immediate associations of power are lightning, pain, putrefaction, sensations of insupportable intensity, and the unusual.

Table 1
Mythological and Theophanic Unfolding of Chamococo Religiosity

	SYMBOLIC	CHRONOLOGICAL	MYTHOLOGIUMS	THEOLOGIUMS
C O R R U P T I O N	PURUJLE: Beings of dreams	Generations with whom direct contact is no longer possible	Forming distinctions between the sacred and the natural order	Idle God: Deities of death and life; Thesmophoric and Jesters, etc.
	POROWO: Ancient beings	Generations with whom direct contact is still possible.	Forming an under- standing of the moral •order, social laws and religious rites	
				AJNABSERO
R E N O V A T I O N	AZLE New beings	Ego's generation and that of Ego's Father.	Extraordinary beings whose behavior is adjusted to the reality of life	DEITIES
	EICHERAXO: Reborn beings	Generation of Ego's Brother (Sister).	Renovation of humanity by a female deity murdered by men.	Deer God

Therefore, located without excessive distortion within the realms of "profane" and "sacred," the revealing of the *wozósh* dynamically ignites reality to life in two spheres that are experientially and con- ceptually distinct. On the one extreme are all the phenomena related to the normal frame of experience. They provoke neither awe nor anxiety and are generally classified as *ié wotísh* (literally, "without power"). On the other extreme, however, are those beings and events that share the features of *ioniak,* a peculiar type of numinous danger linked to the unknown, which unleashes a sensation of *djéjrro* ("fear") within its victims. Therefore the managing of *wozósh* requires the lan- guage of the filthy and the clean. So the possible responses before such signs are either the taboo or the purification. The first term clearly disqualifies Death and decomposition as sources of sacred power. Although the expression *ié éu* (literally, "not to touch") is sometimes used in the usual context of "taboo," the word *mejné* (the most advanced stage of the corruptive process) is more commonly used to refer to prohibitions of this nature.

Together with this concept of *wozósh* associated with the *tremendum* of that which is Holy,[2] there exists a less profiled but parallel notion that is more closely tied with its facient aspect. Putting aside the paradox of the "good venom" obtained from its literal translation, the phrase *wozósh óm* translates rather precisely to the notion of an unusual, attractive, and benevolent power. Associated with freshness, good odor, moisture, and life in general, *wozósh óm* is an efficient agent manifest in fertility and the process of renovation—be it among animals, plants, the astronomical, sociological, or rituals.

Just as "decomposition" (*mejné*)—rational pretext of the avoidance rule associated with *wozósh*—leads to a loss of identity and the form called *purújle*, a feasible correlation for *wozósh óm* is a rebirth or renovation of a being called *eicherájo*. Both lexemes share a similar semantic connection integrated by two dimensions. Thus, the morphemic root /*pur*/ of *purúxle*—apart from designating "Primordial Ancestors" and a qualifier denoting senility and deterioration to the point of being unrecognizable—also links a family of words such as *púrt* (shadow), *puruwó* (memory of ancient events), *purúojle* (dreaming and remembering dreams) or *púruk* (almost forgotten dream experience). In sum, the entities and beings with whom direct contact is now impossible because of a temporal distance (ancestors and the mythical events), the notion of *purújle* alludes to other possible routes of access to this almost invisible horizon: dreaming and the remembering of dreams. In a similar manner, the word *eicherájo*—the passive participle of a verb that encompasses rebirth, renovation, cleanliness, and metamorphosis—possesses, according to the Indians, a certain morphemic relationship with the term *chikéra*, which indicates the action as well as the true states of the dream as the possession (*ochikéreje*) of the ritual actor by a mythical figure.

Finally, the essential complement of Death and Life and the dual distribution of its unfolding are reflected in the structural similarity of the symbols for both. Concomitantly, the image of the body and its processes appears to be the point of symbolic origin. In addition to the coded meaning of febrile, disagreeable odor, infection, inflammation, defecation, or aging, on the one hand, and freshness, propitious odor, health, urine, and infancy, on the other, there is a myriad

---

[2] Otto 1925.

of analogous significance inspired by laterality (left/right), the longi-
tudinal asymmetry of the body (ankle/head), sexuality (disordered/
ordered), or intellectual, temperamental, and cognitive qualities.
According to the accepted norms of symbolic notions, symbols of the
corporal reestablish their meanings in other areas of experience. It is
either about the rules of courtesy, technical instruments, the order or
disorder of the wood for the bonfire, the tastes, culinary techniques,
and the rhythms of the rattle, the flute and ritual vociferation; or the
climate, color, luminescence, orientation, distance, trajectory and the
species of animals and plants.

The notions of "disharmony"/"harmony" (*sherwó/óm*) and "unconditioned"/"conditioned" (*eichóso/ábo*)—principal keys for the characterization of theophanic attributes and functions—are metamorphic
projections of certain sensitive situations. Thus, from the concurrent
images of uncontrollable furor and waves: *sherwó* denotes the loss of
stability and form; *óm*, on the other hand, designates pacificity, con-
ciliation, and the positive agreement between the elements of a set.
In addition, *eichóso*, a characteristic of the individual, distinguishes
the undetermination and absence of ties that singularize the said condition; and the inverse, due to an emphasis in the link, the noun *ábo*
(ova, progeny, child) distinguishes the inalterability of the link of any
given phenomenon with its original source.

It should be emphasized that the language employs various terms
referring to the capacity of a symbol to associate an unknown or distant significance to the literal. In other words, the Chamacoco possess a notion of "symbol" that corresponds to Western concepts of
the same proposed by Kant, Jung, Ricoeur, or Victor Turner. Thus,
for example, the word *ichák*, whose literal meaning refers to the indicators of a determined type of ecological niche, in this sense describes
not only the artificial symbols that commemorate certain mythical
events but also the corresponding ritual gestures.

The Mythological and Theophanic Levels of Religiosity

The Mythology of the Ishír Purújle

No Ishír will deny that these narratives "preceded" the appearance
of the *Ajnábsero* gods. Their dominant axis is the constitution of

diverse ontological domains and the significant marks that identify them. Departing from a "Point 0," which represents the fluidity of forms, intemporality, oscillation of processes, absence of discriminations, or the precariousness of ethical laws, the cosmogonic event is more than an "*ex-nihilo*" creation and should be interpreted as a reordering of the state of preexisting things. The argumental scheme of some of these myths is the following:

Os'iázer, the idle divine. A concept that is practically nonexistent today, it attributes to Os'iázer (literally, "manu-facturer") the creation of the cosmos, humanity, and the etiology of certain animal features such as the testicles of the pig, the locomotion of the birds, and so on). Upon doing so, he became disinterested in his creation and returned to the sky.

The separation of the Sky and Earth and the origin of stars. In ancient times, the Sky was the crown of a cosmic tree anchored in the center of the earth. In this paradise-like place, which lacked day or night, the animals were tame and easily caught; the lagoons never desiccated; and honey lay atop the leaves. By climbing the trunk, the men found food effortlessly. However, when some stingy individuals refused to help a widow, she transformed herself into a termite, gnawed at the tree, and caused it to fall. Those who were in the crown gave origin to the sun, the moon, and the stars.

The separation of the Sky and the origin of color. When the Sky was still very near the earth, a widow adopted an eagle as her lover. But their children killed the eagle and, to escape the vengeance of their mother, they entered the Sky and urged it to distance itself from the earth. However, upon spying the leg of one of them hanging from the sky she pleaded with the birds—who were gray—to mutilate the leg. One bird was successful, and blood of all colors spewed forth. With these colors the woman painted the birds with shades that corresponded to each species. At the end, the brothers transformed themselves into the three stars of the constellation Scorpio, the rest of the leg transformed into shooting stars and, after mourning for the loss of her sons, the widow transformed into the *urutaú* bird (*Aramus guarauna* or "*viuda plañidera*" [Grieving Widow]).

Origin of the anus, and the differentiation of human/animal and the clans. In the beginning humans and animals coexisted in a very

Illustrations of Ajnábsero produced by the Indians

1

Fig. 1. Three illustrations of Shíznimitz; author: Cháleke; tribe: Ebidóso; year: 1973.

Fig. 2. Máo "Black" and Máo "Red"; author: Cháleke; tribe: Ebidóso; year: 1973.

2

3

Fig. 3. Jhó-Jhó and Japérpe;
author: Cháleke; tribe:
Ebidóso; year: 1973.

Fig. 4. Némourt and
Paucháta; author: Cháleke;
tribe Ebidóso; year: 1973.

4

5

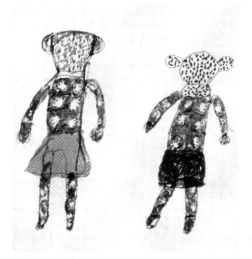

6

Fig. 5. Uakaká Mbaxlút, Uakaká "Black," and Uakaká "Red"; author: Cháleke; tribe: Ebidóso; year: 1973.

Fig. 6. Two illustrations of Hekío; author: P. Vera; tribe: Tomarájo; year: 1988.

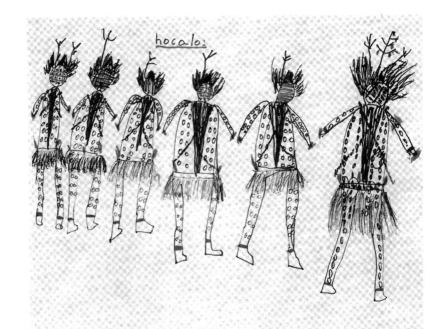

hocalo:

Fig. 7. Hokálo group; author
P. Vera; tribe: Tomarájo;
year: 1988.

Fig. 8. Two illustrations of
Páo; author: P. Vera; year:
1988.

narrow space. As the former had no anus, they could only drink light broths while the latter took advantage of all the other foods. The creation of the anus by a culture hero, however, produced the amplification of space, an ordering of circulation and social ties. As a result, the animals lost their capacity for speech, were separated from the human habitat, and, from then on, became humans' food instead of eating at humans' expense. The people divided themselves according to ethnic identity, and, in commemoration of a previous affinity of some individuals with particular animals, certain species were adopted as symbols of clan exogamy, thereby establishing lines of descent.

Origin of fish and the circulation of water. One day a young man threw his *kumichúk* (club) with such force that it soared far and became lost. For days and days he searched for his club and finally found it stuck deep inside an enormous bottle tree, *Chorisia* sp. When he pulled it out, water spewed from the trunk as well as the first fish. The young man took a few fish and plugged the opening in the tree with the club. Later he showed his people how to eat roasted fish and told them what to do each time they desired more. One time, however, Uatzatzá (Fox) became very nervous and lost the club. He was therefore unable to plug the hole in the tree. This is how the water and fish that were contained therein spilled forth and circulated throughout the world.

Origin of feathered adornments, tobacco, and death. A zeal for cannibalism transformed a father and his son into birds of prey that ravaged the environment. When they were finally killed, their feathers were used to elaborate the first ritual adornments. One man, who had obtained only a few feathers during the distribution, set a trap by opening his legs and arms and waited for birds to draw near. In this fashion he was able to capture some birds until Iínzap—a small hawk who is the Lord of life—made him free them. Later, when the man explained his intentions, some well-formed birds gave him of their feathers. Dichikíor—the carancho bird (*Polyborus plancus*)—then gave him tobacco and a pipe. He instructed him to smoke secretly at night and blow the smoke in all directions to ward off disease. But he also warned the man that he would not die an easy death if he were to be discovered. Although the man did what he was told, he was later discovered by another while smoking in secret and here the purpose of tobacco and its lethal enigma were finally revealed—the man was obliged to surrender the tobacco to the other and died almost immediately thereafter. The same occurred to the successive possessors of tobacco, and, in this fashion, the circulation of tobacco brought on the propagation of death.

Carancho, the origin of death and the land of the dead. Previously, an individual would only temporarily die and after a few days, the "cadaver" would rejuvenate and return to live with its people. During the interim, Dichikíor incessantly visited abandoned village sites, thrusting his lance into the huts. However, one time he did so in a *Jára* "plaza" in the center of a village. Suddenly the ground opened up to expose a path that led directly from the *Jára* and the tomb to the Osépete—the Land of the Dead. From then on Carancho took charge of burying the dead and, with him, began corruption; the age without death had ended. Today, Dichikíor and Iínzap stand to the left and the right side respectively of the entrance to the Osépete. While the former shows the way to those who are definitely dead, the latter procures a return to earth for those dying individuals who still have a chance to recover and continue living.

The qualification of *monejné* as employed by the narratives in question—to which, unlike the "teachings" *aklío*, cannot be attributed absolute certainty nor example—obeys their temporal and thematic penumbra. Although their main characters, the Ishír Purújle, "the invisible people" or "dream beings," look like they lived in an "Age-without-Death" they actually lived in an "Age within Death." The mirage of a paradise implied by certain features of the landscape and the time of origin (*axis mundi*, tame animals, easy feeding, the absence of labor, temporary death, and so on), does not manage to completely cloak its overall mournful tonality. It is not without reason because, beyond the fallacious Eden-like atmosphere, the scene of "Time without Time" continues to survive in the metatemporality of the Land of the Dead, whose inhabitants are replicas of the Ishír Purújle. Therefore the religious rites are more than an "edenic nostalgia" and an intent to recuperate "paradise." They represent a symbolic rememorization of the vicissitudes of the emergence of the physical cosmos and the moral environment of today.

Therefore, from a state of undifferentiation—or at least one of predifferentiation—resulting from a series of successive leaps governed by the opposing powers of Death and Life, there begins the emergence of physical distinctions, social laws, moral norms, and axiological criteria. These orderings are imposed on the cosmology (breaking of the ancient *axis mundi*, the separation of spatial plains, and the appearance of stars, their cycles, and respective trajectories); the physical (colors, odors); the geographic (amplification of habitats, circulation of terrestrial water); the climatological (alternating wet and dry seasons); the zoological (taxonomic and ecological differentiation of species); the anatomical (origin of the year); the sociological (division of clans, sex, and *etarias*); the alimentary (qualification of consumption based on sex and age); the ethnogonical (classification of the tribes and their qualities); the anthropological (constitution of the discourse Life–Death); the theological (theophanization of Death and Life in a pair—Dichikíor and Iínzap—with specific powers); the theodicy (establishing the drama of evil); the soteriological (analysis of the human fallibility); and even on the same aspects of symbolic syntax (emphasis in the recurrence of the typical signs of the phenomena: bird of prey = Life = Iínzap/scavenger bird = Death = Dichikíor).

The Mythology of the Ishír Pórowo and the Ajnábsero Gods

The *Aishniwéhrta* or *Xáu Oso* (the Aishniwéhrta word for "All") or *Or Aklío* ("the Teachings") is the long sacred saga of the Ajnábsero gods. It tells of their emergence from the interior of a *ajpóra* ("wild watermelon," *Jacuratia corumbensis*, a large globular rhizome representing one of the scarce sources of water in the Chaco during the dry season) and the initial appearance of women. Fooled by the women, who concealed the existence of the masculine form; these beings of prodigious capacity and humanoid features—whose reproduction requires the use of masks, corporal paint, and feathered adornments—established the first site of initiation (*Tobích*, or "Place of the Dead") and began their teachings. Later, upon discovering the truth, the women were expelled and the men were initiated, imposing absolute secrecy and the practices of the Tobích. Thus, the creative and thesmophoric actions of the Ajnábsero introduce a revival of the culture: the indoctrination of reason; the transmission of spatial symbolism, the climatological cycle, and the cycle of natural species; the transfer of economic techniques; and the teaching of ethic concepts related to food, etiquette, sexuality, age classes, the principles of exchange, dual relationships, authority, and social organization in general. Some time later, the excessiveness on the part of some deities provoked a rebellion by the men who unsuccessfully attempted to kill them. However, after reestablishing certain equilibrium, Aishniwéhrta—the central figure—revealed to her human husband, Shírre, the key to her vulnerability: her mouth which was hidden in her left ankle. And this is how the men were able to defeat almost all of the Ajnábsero. Once the killing had ended, the goddess transmitted to each of the dead the clan affiliation of his divine victim. In commemoration of the initial events and teachings, she also imposed on the men the obligation to maintain the *Tobích* and initiate the ritual representation of the deities. At the end, Aishniwéhrta and some of her "children" retreated to a stellar place, from which they enforce the observance of their laws. Other Ajnábsero, however, continue living in the waters and chthonic depths.

The apocope of *ajnábsa* combines two distinct concepts: (1) that of the "strange" (*ajnábsa*), whose similar appearance does not involve the essential community which characterizes the "true" (*ejnábsa*) and (2) that of a terrible unleashing (*sherwó*). In other words, this generic denomination expresses the idea of "Terrifying and Terrible Strangers." Depending on Aishniwéhrta (literally, Lightning, Brilliance; or Flower—*ashíni*—Intensely Red—*wehért*—), the Ajnábsero include numerous personalities of both sexes. Although in some cases it deals with individual figures—whose attitudes tend toward the negative (*sherwó*) or the benevolent (*óm*)—and in others (*Ajnábsero eichóso*) whose nature and dispositions are unknown, the majority (*Ajnábsero ábo*) are grouped in sets with a dual segmentation *sherwó/óm* expressed through the chromatic (red/black) contrast. Table 2 reflects the importance of these cosmic categories in the circumscription of taxonomic space in which the divinities are found. In turn, each group of *Ajnábsero abo* depends on a principal personality; its qualifiers—*láta* "mother," for the females, and *mbajlút* "superdimensional," for the opposite sex—appear to translate a certain generic concept of "deity."

With respect to significance, these divinities and their mythology represent a simultaneous retention and expansion of the Ishír Purújle

Table 2
The Taxonomic Space of the Ajnábsero Divinities

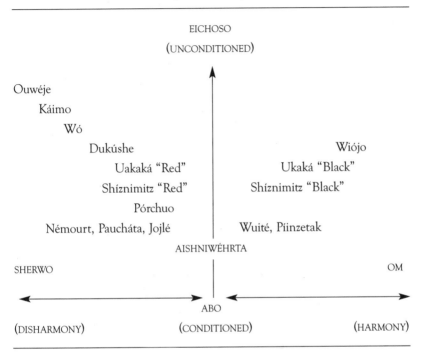

EICHOSO

(UNCONDITIONED)

Ouwéje

Káimo

Wó

Dukúshe   Wiójo

Uakaká "Red"   Ukaká "Black"

Shíznimitz "Red"   Shíznimitz "Black"

Pórchuo

Némourt, Paucháta, Jojlé   Wuité, Píinzetak

AISHNIWÉHRTA

SHERWO   OM

ABO

(DISHARMONY)   (CONDITIONED)   (HARMONY)

mythology, resulting in an exploration of hierophanic meanings produced by Death and Life. It is not difficult to recognize the semantic ties between, for example, the Bottle Tree and the "wild watermelon"; between the areas of competence of Dichikíor and the analogical functions of the Dich'kémzero clan (literally, "the form of Carancho"); between the sovereignty of Life adopted by Iínzap and the similar attributes of certain Ajnábsero (Weicháu, Wiójo, and so on), or between the structural design of the respective narrations, in virtue of which, for example, a good part of the *Aishniwéhrta or Xáu Oso* result in a symmetric inversion of color mythology.

At the edge of the theomorphic process, the essential characteristics of the *Ajnábsero* are their omnipresence and ethic sovereignty. The existence of approximately thirty-five distinct species is undoubtedly associated with the variety of domains in which individual roles are carried out. These roles, to mention a few, range from health, disease and war, or hunting, gathering, fishing, gathering and its astronomical and climatological concomitants, to flirting and female jealousies, and the equilibrium demanded of humans in exchange. However, beyond this diversity, there are certain lines pointing toward the "unique," if not monotheism. This is evident, not only by the existence of various generic denominations (Ajnábsero, Óule, and Debilúbe), but also in the tendency toward functional personifications of the characteristics of the principal divinities under the form of subordinate divinities. For example, the "Daughters of Aishniwéhrta" Aishniwéhrta Abo each represent the "Superdimensional Life" and each of the apocalyptic virtues that goddess possesses).

From a purely phenomenological perspective—in a deliberate absence of any historic-genetic interference—the core of theophanic organization of this class of divinities reveals the coexistence of two distinct modalities. If the typology of predominant deities in traditional societies proposed by Jensen[3]—based on historic-morphologic aspects as well as the intuitions and the subjacent meaning of each one—is to be accepted, then the Ajnábsero are somewhat similar to the uranic gods of the pastoral groups including certain characteristics that relates them to the demi-gods of the paleohorticulturalists. Aishniwéhrta, for example, is closer to the former because of her rudeness and terribleness, the moral nature of her actions and mandates, the omniscience, the omnipresence, the transtemporal remission of her terrestrial actions, the gift as the preferred form of creativity (the similarity between the introduction of life by the uranic gods and of the understanding by the Ajnábsero), and the existence of "prometheus" ties between humans and gods (the robbing of goods and the rebellion against the Ajnábsero). Nevertheless, these are distinguished from them by the lack of cosmogonic and anthropogonic responsibilities, the tendency toward pluralization, and ritual. On the other extreme, the similarity between the Ajnábsero and the demi-gods (made concrete by Erpejlá, *vide supra*) is founded in the observation of their presence toward the end of original time, the motive of the cruel sacrifice of the deities, their ties with the dead and the kingdom of the Dead, their intervention in the genesis of various musical instruments and certain topographical accidents, and the connection of their rites and cult sites with the original events.

---

[3] Jensen 1966.

Mythology of the Ishír Azle

This mythological step is linked to the contemporary ideal existing between its unusual scenes, main characters, and daily circumstances. In this form, the risk of wounding oneself in the forest immediately evokes the destiny of Telérit (literally, "Sharpened Leg"), who, threatened by hunger following an analogous accident, tried of his own flesh, and transformed into a cannibal monster. The list of these extraordinary beings is quite long and includes an expected number of Animal Lords (e.g., Péert: Master of the Wild Pigs; Eintekára: a god of honey). Some of them, such as Xósheta, a Master of Turtles, who simultaneously extends her sovereignty over the rest of the species, associates a marked orgiastic tint and a rich spatial north/south symbolism, which contrasts with the east/west symbolism in the mythology of the Ajnábsero.

The Mythology of the Ishír Eicheráxo and the Renovation

The subject of the restoration of humanity from the quartered cadaver of Erpejlá, a transfiguration of Aishniwéhrta with the appearance of a deer, is one of the chapters of the *Aishniwéhrta or Xáu oso,* whose messages expressly refer to the descending generations.

It so happened that after the massacre of the Ajnábsero, the women discovered the secret of their ritual supplanting by the men. In addition, they continued despising and fooling them in diverse forms. The goddess therefore wished that they would be assassinated together with their children and that no one be spared. Once this drama was over, Aishniwéhrta showed herself again before them as Erpejlá "Deer" (*Mazama* sp.). After coming to live with her one by one, the men killed her, quartered her body and distributed the rest. Sometime later, from the flesh and the blood of Erpejlá, the same women and children that had been killed arose once more. Although they conserved their former appearance, they had lost forever the memory of the past and the motives behind the ritual substitution of the gods by the men.

Thus, the symbolic similarity with Erpejlá is resolved in a unique image through the cosmovisional keys of Life and the sacred codes ascribed to Death. At the heart of this image, the pacificity and the relative capacity of domestication of the deer provide the tangible metaphors of the *ábo* and the *óm*; to the contrary, the ability of this species to change color over the course of time to an intense red—the symbol of the *sherwó*—reproduces the same signs of the ontotemporal curve to which are adjusted human and the sacred processes.

The Sacred Practices and the *Debilúbe Ajmich*

The most common sacred practices are prayer, purification, mourning chants, and shamanic rituals. Before beginning a particular activity, it is common for the individual to direct himself to the pertinent entity and plead for assistance and good disposition. Hunters and widowers are preferred for purification; whether through bathing, separation from a contaminated object, or abstention on the part of the hunter from consuming his prey, these critical circumstances all require a period of isolation and a ritual of reintegration. The obligatory mourning chants (*dukejneré*) of the widowers, act as a cathartic mechanism and constitute a symbolic path through which the ailing individual temporarily assumes the impurity of the dead.

Finally, at the margin of frequency, the only notable quality of the shamanic rites is their variety. Tied to the diversity of cosmological environments and the sacred beings that bestow power on them, there exist at least three classes of magical specialists: (1) the *komzáxo* or *axáne*, characterized by the duplication of powers and the related capacity to call upon beneficial phenomena and conjure the malevolent; (2) the *ajnért*, dedicated more to purely therapeutic practices; and (3) the *enitért* ("furious") or *komzájo naamzóro* ("dark or secret shaman"), involved with sorcery and harm. Parallel to the magnitude of capacity, there exists a gradient from the *komzájo póor áb* (literally, "semi-shaman") who have not yet completed their initiation to the *komzájo díich* or "great shamans."

The truly religious rituals comprise the group called Debilúbe Ajmich, for example, "Feast or Commemoration (ájmich) of the Oúle, Debilúbe, Debilité or Ajnábsero." In consonance with the initiatory reclusion of the boys and the concentration of a great number of actors required in the village to perform the rites, the feast is celebrated in certain years throughout the rainy season. The organization is conducted by the Male Society (Tobích). Their principal functions consist in the coordination of the economic activities to assure the well-being of groups that sometimes consisted of six hun-

Kecht. örmich gut.
a lado del monte.

kecht onota och gut.
a lado del Río

Fig. 9. Indigenous illustration of a ritual competition of Pogóra.
Author: Bruno Barras (in: Cordeu 1989, 557).

dred or more individuals; the gathering of the *materia prima* for the sacred paraphernalia (bromeliad fibers for the masks and cordage, feathers of distinct birds, vegetable and mineral tints for corporal painting, etc.); the initiatory apprenticeship of the young; the public presentation of approximately thirty-five different types of Ajnáb-sero; and the vigilance over violations—in particular, those that pro-hibit women from learning about the occult powers of the feast. However, in addition to certain ball (*Pogóra*) and club throwing com-petitions (*Kumichuló*) that are celebrated simultaneously—involving a dual symbolic analogue—the majority of the scenes acted out by the Ajnábsero are not specific to sex or age.

Although feminine figures are often represented, the ritual actors are usually male. The participation of women is reduced to a few humorous pantomimes in which they play subordinate roles. The act-ing out of certain *Ajnábsero* can only be by an affiliated clan (e.g., the Taxóro clan possesses the monopoly on *Káimo* and *Kaipórta*, while *Aishniwéhrta* must be acted out by a *Dich'kémzero*). However, in the majority of cases there prevails the drive of the individual and his ability for the role. Through the use of masks (simple woven bags of bromeliad that cover the entire face), body paintings of very complex designs (in black, red, or ash) and an extensive gamma of feathered ornaments of excellent manufacture, they mime a corporal image similar to that of the *Ajnábsero*. The reproduction of the segmented dominant distribution in their courtships, their yells and distinctive voices, and their marching and dancing steps all have the same goal.

Most of the presentations, separated by periods of one to five days, occur during the daylight hours. Only the more solemn rituals, cele-brated exclusively in the Tobích, continue throughout the night until dawn. The ritual characterization is also presented here, and actors will commonly help one another, especially with the laborious paint-ing of the body. After the elders approve the garments and the paint, the actors march to the Jára to perform. The performance consists in the singing of characteristic songs, yells, dances around the plaza, and the acting out of the concomitance, be they sacred or not, of practically all of the spheres of the human experience. Upon finish-ing each ritual, the parents usually bring their children to the *Ajnáb-sero* in order that they may rub up against their painted bodies and hopefully acquire their capabilities and healthy powers.

The sequential course of the Debilúbe Ajmich as well as the ritual space in which they take place, are ascribed rich symbolic meaning.

Figure 4
Symbolic Meaning of the East/West Trajectories

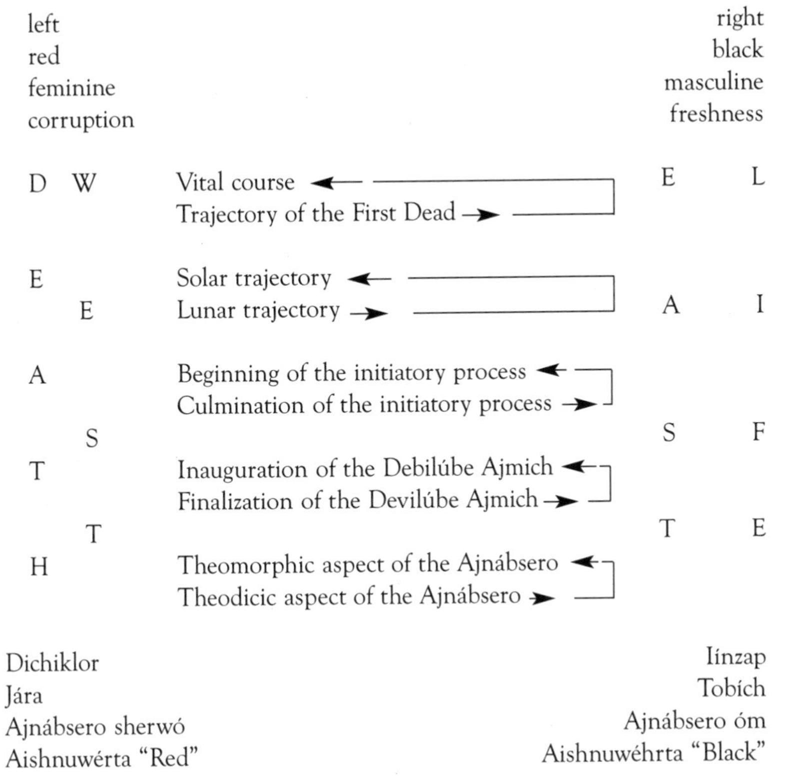

---

left		right
red		black
feminine		masculine
corruption		freshness

```
 D  W      Vital course  ◄─── ────────────┐      E   L
            Trajectory of the First Dead ─►  ───────┘

 E          Solar trajectory  ◄─── ─────────┐
    E       Lunar trajectory ─►  ───────────┘       A   I

 A          Beginning of the initiatory process ◄─┐
            Culmination of the initiatory process ─►┘
    S                                               S   F
 T          Inauguration of the Debilúbe Ajmich ◄─┐
            Finalization of the Devilúbe Ajmich ─► ┘
    T                                               T   E
 H          Theomorphic aspect of the Ajnábsero ◄─┐
            Theodicic aspect of the Ajnábsero ─► ──┘
```

Dichiklor	Iínzap
Jára	Tobích
Ajnábsero sherwó	Ajnábsero óm
Aishnuwérta "Red"	Aishnuwéhrta "Black"

In this fashion, to the inverse of the course of life and the chromatic evolution of the deer—which implies a passage from the pure to the impure—the feast, which began as an "infection" or "inflammation" (*tchorrája*), leads to the renovation indicated by the life-giving breeze which, according to the Indians, begins to blow unfaltered at the instant that the celebrations are over.

The spatial symbolism itself is derived from the condensed mythic geography of the circular village, which is composed of three sectors: (1) the circle of huts, with a meandering easterly path which leads to the Tobích; (2) the Jára, a small round plaza where rites are celebrated (Although the Tomarájo actually use the central circle of the village, the Ebidóso, on the other hand, prepare this circle outside of the village); (3) the Tobích, which is another circular plaza hidden in the forest, sometimes accompanied by a hut where the apparel and ritual implements are stored.

Therefore, as a kind of conclusion: just as Tobích, situated in the east symbolically represents Karcháute, on the banks of the Paraguay River, where the Ajnábsero originated, the Jára located to the west commemorates Moiéxne, the place in the hinterland where the massacre of the gods began and continued along the entire path to the Tobích. Finally, the east and west are two dominant symbols, but in a certain way they are static and agglutinate a good part of the sacred meanings. However, beyond the value of each, the meanings behind the trajectory between both cardinal points provides a second level of symbolic reference. It deals with a dynamic image of the religious meaning of the process and courses shown by the myths and rituals. Finally, it is possible to verify in both spheres the circulation of meanings represented in figure 4.

References

Alarcón y Cañedo, José de, and Riccardo Pittini. 1924. *Il Ciacco e le sue tribu.* Turin: Missioni Salesiane, Società Editrice Internazionale.

Baldus, Herbert. 1931. *Indianerstudien im nordöstlichem Chaco.* Leipzig: Hirshfeld.

———. 1932. "'La Mère Comunne' dans la myhtologie de deux tribus sudaméricaines (Kagaba et Tumerehá)." *Revista del Instituto de Etnología de Tucumán* 2:471–79.

Boggiani, Guido. 1894. "Il Ciamacoco." *Bolletino della Società Geografica Italiana* Serie 3, Vol. 7.

———. 1900. "Compendio de Etnografia Paraguaya Modern." *Revista del Instituto Paraguayo (Asunción).*

Cordeu, Edgardo J. 1984. "Categorías básicas, principios lógicos y redes simbólicas de la cosmovisión de los indios Ishir." *Journal of Latin American Lore* 10, no. 2:189–275.

———. 1989. "Los Chamacoco o Ishir del Chaco Boreal: Algunos aspectos de un proceso de desestructuración étnica." *América Indígena* 49, no. 3:545–80.

———. 1990–91. "Lo Cerrado y lo Abierto: Arquitectura cosmovisional y patrón cognitivo de los tomaráxo del Chaco Boreal." *Scripta Ethnologica-Supplementa* [Buenos Aires] 11:9–31.

———. 1989–92. "Aishtuwénte: Las ideas de deidad en la religiosidad chamacoco." *Suplemento Antropológico (Asunción),* CEADUC, Part 1:

24, no. 1:7–77; Part 2: 24, no. 2:51–85; Part 3: 25, no. 1:119–211; Part 3 (continued): 26, no. 1:86–166; Part 4: 26, no. 2:147–233; part 5: 27, no. 1:187–294; Part 5 (continued) and Part 6: 27, no. 2:167–301.

Jensen, Adolf E. 1966. *Mito y culto entre pueblos primitivos*. México: FCE.

Mason, J. A. 1950. "The Language of South American Indians." *Handbook of South American Indians*, Vol. 6, Washington.

Otto, Rudolph. 1925. "Lo Santo: Lo racional y lo irracional en la idea de Dios."*Revista de Occidente* [Madrid].

Súsnik, Branislava. 1957. "Estudios Chamacoco." *Boletín de la Sociedad Científica de Paraguay y Museo Etnográfico "Andrés Barbero."*

Wilbert, Johannes, and Karin Simoneau, eds. 1987. *Folk Literature of the Chamacoco Indians*. UCLA Latin American Studies 64. Berkeley and Los Angeles: University of California Press.

10

The Sacred as Alienated Social Consciousness: Ritual and Cosmology among the Kayapó

Terence Turner

In this article I present an account of the cosmological ideas and ritual practices of the Kayapó, a Gê-speaking people of the Xingu drainage of Southeastern Para, Brazil. These ideas and practices can be understood as rooted in the practices and forms of consciousness of everyday Kayapó social life. In certain critical respects, however, they also represent ideological distortions of these practices and forms. The essence of these distortions is the representation of the fundamental forms and values of social life as the products of "natural," asocial beings. These monstrous beings, whose deeds are recounted in Kayapó myth, are the prototypes imitated by the feathered and painted dancers of Kayapó communal ceremony. I describe these ideas and practices in the forms they assumed in the period before intensive peaceful coexistence between the Kayapó and the Brazilians, which began for most Kayapó groups in the 1950s. Most of them, however, remain a vital part of Kayapó social and religious life today.

Social Life, Organization, and Values[1]

The Kayapó are monogamous and have a prescriptive rule of matri-uxorilocal postmarital residence. The basic kin group is a bilateral

---

[1] For more complete accounts of Kayapó social organization and values, see Turner 1979a; 1979b; 1984; 1992.

kindred, which constitutes a field of supportive relations but does not act as a group. There is no rule of descent. The traditional form of the village is that of a circle of matri-uxorilocal extended-family houses surrounding a large central plaza, in the center of which stands a men's house. The men's house is traditionally the residence of the age sets of uninitiated youths and bachelors, and the clubhouse of the mature men's associations. These associations, led by chiefs called "chanters," are the main political groups of the society. The mature men's societies and the bachelors also function as units for military and ceremonial purposes, with the chanters serving as war and ritual leaders. Women are also divided into communal age associations, which have important ceremonial, though no political functions. The ceremonies performed by these collective groups are mainly rites of passage, the most important being naming and initiation. These rituals emphasize the importance of extranuclear family relations such as grandparents, maternal uncles, and paternal aunts, and thus stress the incompleteness of the nuclear family as a unit and its members as individuals and their dependence on relations with the extended family and the community as a whole.

The transformations of nuclear family relations produced by these communal rites of passage continually reproduce the extended family. The same communally ritualized transitions also serve as the recruitment criteria of the collective age sets and men's and women's associations, which are of course the groups that perform the ceremonies. The communal institutions constituted by these age- and gender-based associations, in sum, embody the structure of the process of reproducing the extended-family household and of the individual life cycle, articulated as a series of transformations in family roles and household status. The fundamental constituents of Kayapó social structure are thus the processes and relations through which Kayapó society on all its levels, including that of the social person, is continually recreated.

Individual Kayapó are motivated to act toward one another in accordance with these forms because the processes in question produce the commonly recognized forms of social value. Two main categories of value are recognized: "beauty" (*metch*) and what might be called "dominance" or "preeminence" (there is no single Kayapó word or common expression for this value). These modes of value are associated with complementary clusters of social relations. "Dominance"/"preeminence" is an attribute of relatively senior statuses or positions within household or communal group structure. It is prototypically invested in the status and role of wife's parents in relation to that of daughter's husband, the focus of the matri-uxorilocal extended-family household structure, and in the relations between the senior and junior men's and women's age associations. "Beauty," by contrast, is associated with the ceremonial giving of names and other "valuables" (*nekretch*), which, like names, are conceived of as attributes of personal identity. These items get exchanged between indirectly linked relatives such as grandparents and grandchildren, or maternal uncles or paternal aunts and their respective nephews and nieces.

The processes producing these contrasting types of relations and their associated values are of two types, which may be designated "linear" and "cyclical." The first of these is represented by the human life cycle, defined as a linear sequence of successive social ages, which are in turn articulated as stages of the family cycle (i.e., the successive formation and dispersion of families through marriage). This process is linear and irreversible for individual actors, but is continually replicated by successive generations of actors. The second type of process is exemplified by the exchange of identity (names and valuables) between indirectly linked relations (those separated from one another in the linear process of family dispersion and marriage). The ritual exchange between these relatives reverses this separation and recreates a bond of identity between them at a higher, interfamily level. This second process, then, has a cyclical, reversible form, the opposite and complement of the first (linear, irreversible) process.

This bi-axial pattern is fully exemplified in the structure of each extended family household, and likewise by the structure of communal groupings and ceremonies, up to and including the village community as a whole. The same bi-dimensional structure is literally embodied by the individual social person. Each Kayapó man, woman, and child bears upon his or her body a complex system of tokens (body painting, haircut, ornaments) indicating his or her stage of social development in the "linear" series of generational/family statuses. He or she may also wear special earrings denoting his or her relatively "beautiful" or "common" status as the bearer (or, by their absence, nonbearer) of one of the "beautiful" ceremonial names, thus locating him- or herself in relation to the complementary "cyclical" dimension.

It should be emphasized that the two dimensions (linear-irreversible and cyclical-reversible) not only define complementary aspects of social space-time, as explained above, but also and equally modes and sources of power (essentially agency, the capacity to act or to effect changes in a situation). The quality of being an agent as opposed to a patient (that is, ability to act on one's own initiative and thus assert and achieve one's purposes, rather than being obliged to remain passive, unassertive, and thus perforce dependent and subordinate), and the ability to integrate disparate types of relations and attributes in a complete, fully formed social identity, are the two main facets of the Kayapó conception of social agency. They are clearly identified with the two fundamental values of preeminence and beauty, respectively. The same two dimensions also figure as the primary features employed in constructing the various categories of social identity (including the identities of individual actors and the collective identities of segmentary or communal groups).

As a composite structure of space-time, modalities of causality or agency, and features of social identity, this bi-dimensional pattern constitutes what Bakhtin called a chronotope.[2] It serves alike as the underlying framework of space-time and action in the contemporary world and in creation myths. It thus provides a conceptual model for the structure of every level of social interaction, from that of the individual actor through the segmentary kinship group to that of the communal institutions comprising the village community as a whole, and beyond that, at the highest level of abstraction, of the spatial and temporal universe surrounding the Kayapó social world. In all of these respects, this structure, at once a conceptual model and a pattern of social action, comprises a "cosmology." The Kayapó deliberately construct the material form of their society at every level to conform to this pattern, not out of mechanical subservience to a collective cultural model or social norm, but as a pragmatic means of controlling and coordinating the reproduction of the social processes whose forms the pattern embodies, and the values of preeminence and beauty those processes produce for those who participate in them.

Throughout their two-hundred-year history as a distinct Northern Gê people, the Kayapó of Southeastern Para, Brazil, have been in continual contact with a variety of non-Kayapó peoples: other closely

---

[2] Bakhtin 1981.

related Northern Gê groups, non-Gê indigenous peoples like the riverine Karaja and Juruna, and Brazilians and other representatives of Western culture, including early-nineteenth-century slave raiders, explorers, missionaries, rubber and nut gatherers, cattle ranchers and subsistence farmers attempting to settle on their land, mineral prospectors, timber cutters, agents of the government Indian service, journalists, film makers, and last but not least, anthropologists. Until recently, however, none of these non-Kayapó groups were seen as part of the same society as the Kayapó themselves. The autonomous village community remained for practical social purposes the highest level of integration of Kayapó society, and as such constituted the limit of the domain of fully social existence in social consciousness, and the center of social space-time.[3]

The Village as Cosmogram:
The Two Dimensions of Space-Time

The structure of the Kayapó conception of the world in the period when the individual village still functioned as a relatively self-sufficient and autonomous social unit can be most easily grasped from the spatial layout of the traditional village itself. A circle of extended-family houses surrounded an open central plaza, which was the locus of communal ceremony and social activities. In the plaza stood two men's houses, one in the east and one in the west, respectively called the "lower" and "upper" men's houses. The land immediately surrounding the circle of houses was called the "black" or "dead" ground and was conceived of as a transitional zone between the social space of the village and the natural domain of the savanna or forest. In this zone were located the cemetery and various ritual seclusion sites used in rites of passage. The village is thus organized along two intersecting spatial dimensions, one of concentric and one of diametrical (east-west) contrast, the latter also being conceived in terms of the vertical contrast between lower and upper, or in the other pair of terms employed by the Kayapó, "root" and "tip." This

---

[3] For fuller accounts of Kayapo history and the changes in social organization and cosmology that have accompanied them, see Turner 1992; 1993a.

spatial polarity of the village circle is retained in extant Kayapó villages with only one men's house.

The model of cosmic space-time embodied by the ideal village plan can be seen as a model of the process of social production and reproduction, in which the life cycle, defined as a reversible alternation of socialization and death, is subsumed as an ultimately irreversible but infinitely replicated linear process of growth. East is the "root" of the sky, the beginning of the sun's journey, and metaphorically also of the life cycle. West is the "tip" of the sky, the end of the sun's journey, and metaphorically of the human life cycle or the growth cycle of a plant. "Vertical" space thus defines a temporal process, which is linear and irreversible but infinitely replicable. The concentric dimension of space is conceived of as the form of the cyclical, reversible process of transforming natural energy and raw materials into social form (epitomized by the process of socialization) and the breaking down of social forms by natural energy once again (epitomized by death, which is ritually referred to by the Kayapó as "transformation into an animal"). The village is the center point of both dimensions, the focus of social space, which gives way on all sides to the "natural" space inhabited by animals and inferior, non-Kayapó peoples. All levels of social organization, from the village as a whole through the domestic household to the individual person, are conceived of as replicating this same sociocosmic model. The process of social (re-)production is thus recursively embodied in the structure of its products. All levels of the social whole are equally conceived of as products of the single, cyclical, and infinitely replicated process of social production it embodies.

The cosmological terms in which this traditional Kayapó view of the social world was cast left no room for a consciousness of the structure of this integral process of social production as itself a social product. It was, rather, seen as the natural structure of the cosmos. Kayapó society was conceived of both as the central focus of this cosmic process and as the society that most fully conformed to the cosmic pattern. Other, non-Kayapó societies and peoples were accordingly conceived of as both less "social," that is, less than fully human by Kayapó standards, and as less fully exemplifying the "natural" pattern of what a society should be. In concrete terms, this meant that the Kayapó saw them as at once more animal-like (thus, in this sense, more "natural") and less "beautiful" or complete (less fully realized instances of the "natural" pattern of humanity, and thus, in this

sense, less "natural" as well). This pejorative assessment was epitomized in the Kayapó term for non-Kayapó peoples, "*me kakrit*" or
"people of little worth or beauty" (other Ge-speaking peoples, with
their similar social organizations and languages, were sometimes
exempted from the status of "*me kakrit*," and included, with the
Kayapó, in the category of "*me metch*," or "beautiful people").

Beyond and outside the village on all sides, from this Kayapó-
centric perspective, there thus extended a zone of decreasing sociality inhabited by animals and less social, non-Kayapó peoples. The
essential principle of "sociality" in this view is cooperation in the
production of Kayapó social life. Other (usually hostile) Kayapó
groups, ghosts of Kayapó dead, non-Kayapó groups, and animal, fish
and bird species, although recognized as possessing social communities of their own, are conceptually ranged on a scale of declining
sociality, or, what comes to the same thing, of increasingly "natural"
character ("nature" being defined as that which is not produced by
Kayapó but rather produces itself or comes into being independently
of Kayapó society).

Relations of different kinds are possible with members of this
nonsocial category, which permit the incorporation of elements or
attributes of them into the Kayapó social domain, for example,
exchange of ritual paraphernalia, songs, or even whole ceremonies
with other Indian peoples, or trade for manufactured commodities
with the Brazilians; warfare, accompanied by the capture and appropriation of children and possessions; hunting and fishing; the burning and cultivation of forest land to make gardens; and the
appropriation of animal and plant forms, powers, and substances by
shamans and those knowledgeable in curing and magic. Such relations of appropriation of the powers and substance of asocial others
by the Kayapó are counterbalanced by the appropriation of Kayapó
social powers, substance, and life itself by the same others: military
or shamanic attacks by hostile peoples, the infliction of disease and
death by animal and plant agents, attacks by ghosts trying to bring
their loved ones with them into the villages of the dead.

Transactions across the practical and conceptual boundary of
Kayapó society with such asocial beings are articulated upon a concentric, horizontal dimension of space-time. This dimension takes
the concrete form of cyclical, reversible processes involving the transformation of natural energy and raw materials into social form and
the breaking down of social forms by natural energy once again. The

former sort of process is epitomized by the extraction of food from the forest by hunting, gathering, and horticulture and the socialization of human beings, who begin as asocial, animal-like beings; the latter is epitomized by catabolism, the later stages of aging, disease (generally blamed on the inimical influence of "natural" agents such as animals, plants), and death (which is ritually referred to by the Kayapó as "transformation into an animal").

This cyclical, concentrically organized, reversible process, defined within the horizontal plane of space-time, is intersected by a linear process of irreversible development associated with vertical polarity and the two cardinal points of east and west (north and south are not conceptually differentiated or treated as cardinal points). East is the "root" of the sky, also called the "lower sky," and is also identified in temporal terms as the beginning of the sun's journey. West is correspondingly defined as the "tip" of the sky or "upper sky" and the end of the sun's journey. "Vertical" space, like horizontal, "concentric" space, is thus simultaneously defined as a temporal process, in this case one seen as linear and irreversible, but infinitely replicable. It is the form of the human life cycle, the natural growth cycles of plants, the developmental cycles of the family and domestic group, and the series of age sets that form the backbone of the system of communal groups that comprise the highest level of social structure.

This bi-dimensional structure of complementary modes of space-time and social process thus constitutes the framework of the cosmos, defined as the most inclusive, general structure of space-time, causality, and the classification and construction of entities and relations, a structure the basic features of which in one way or another apply to or are replicated by every entity and level of organization constituting part of the whole. Within the terms of this conception, Kayapó society, represented by the individual, autonomous village unit, forms the central, focal point of cosmic space-time. Its outer limits are constituted by the circular edge of the sky, forced to fall to earth when the giant trees upon which they originally rested were gnawed through by a determined tapir in the mythical past. The cosmos, then, is shaped like a dome; more to the point, its limit is the point at which the two dimensions of space time, the horizontal/concentric and the vertical/linear, meet and become undifferentiated. The limit is not only spatial but temporal; it is also the point at which the time of contemporary social existence meets and merges with the qualitatively different time of the mythical past, the point where mythical time flows into the present as the encompassing frame of everyday social time.[4]

Levels of the Cosmos and the Social World

Within the domed space-time of the cosmos as a whole, the region of socially known space and everyday lived time which forms the immediate context of the social community is organized as a micro-cosmic replication of the same pattern. The village, itself circular, is conceived of as surrounded by a transitional zone, called the "black" or "dead" ground, between the village and the fully wild savanna and forest, in which the cemetery and ritual seclusion sites are located. Beyond the "black" zone is the fully "natural" domain of savanna and forest.

At the next lower level, that of the internal structure of the village itself, the same pattern is repeated. The circle of extended-family houses, representing a relatively "natural" level of integration, focused around nuclear family relations, surrounds the central plaza, the locus of the communal ceremonial and group activities associated with full social integration. The plaza itself is divided along the complementary dimension of vertical space, between its eastern ("lower" or "root") and western ("upper" or "tip") cardinal points. Within living memory this vertical dimension was materially manifested in the two men's houses associated with the moiety division, one in the eastern half of the central plaza, called the "eastern center" or the "root center," and the other in the western half, called the "western center," or the "tip center." For historical reasons that I have discussed elsewhere but which are too complex to go into here,[5] the moiety system has broken down, whether permanently or only temporarily is still impossible to tell. All fourteen extant Kayapó villages have only one men's house, called simply "the center," but the eastern and western poles of the diameter of the village plaza, and east and west generally, are still referred to by their "vertical" coordinates as the "root" and "tip" of the sky, or "lower sky" and "upper sky," respectively.

---

[4] Turner 1988.
[5] Turner 1992; 1993a.

The complementary dimension of concentric, reversible space-time is embodied at the village level by the organization and choreography of communal ceremonies, above all the rites of passage for name giving, initiation-marriage, and the induction of boys into the men's house. Even in villages with both moieties present (i.e., two men's houses), the large number of ritual celebrants typically form a single dancing column, or at times a concentric series of arcs of dancers representing distinct men's and women's age sets, and proceed to dance counterclockwise around the periphery of the plaza just inside the ring of houses. Special rites involving the name-receiving children themselves, or those bestowing and receiving special ritual rights or valuables in the ceremony, tend to occur in the center of the plaza. It is also usual for the celebrants of both "central" and "peripheral" groups to move from the village out into the surrounding, liminal "black" zone and beyond into fully "natural" forest or savanna space and back again. Ceremonies, in short, are concentrically organized, stressing the contrast between center and periphery. This spatial contrast is associated with a value contrast of the same form, between "owners of value" (the receivers of names and other special ritual privileges, ornaments, or valuables, associated with the center) and "those with nothing" (the common run of ritual celebrants, who make up the peripheral column of dancers, and the spectators). This value distinction is manifested in the more general social distinction between "beautiful people" and "common people," or those who possess ritual names and valuables and those who do not, respectively (roughly one-half of the total population of a community may fall into each category). Not only this concentric form of contrastive structure, but also the circular movement of the dances themselves, symbolically overrides and neutralizes the linear, irreversible polarity between the eastern and western moieties, men's houses, and cardinal points of the complementary "vertical" dimension.

Although in an abstract sense both dimensions of cosmic space-time are simultaneously present in the conceptual geography of the village, each is thus identified with distinct social groupings and activities, which tend to manifest themselves in complementary alternation rather than in simultaneity. The concentrically organized ceremonies, as I have described, are arranged in such a way as to override and neutralize the structure of moieties and age sets associated with the men's house. The latter, specifically identified with the linear, vertical mode of space-time, is for its part the antithesis of the ceremonial organization. Whereas the ceremonies stress the equal participation of all age sets as segments of the circular column of dancers, all points of which are equidistant from the center, the age-set hierarchy of the men's house and associated women's societies stresses the inequality of juniors and seniors and constitutes the communal organizational basis for the subordination of the former to the latter.

The ceremonial organization, as I have noted, does promote another form of inequality in the opposition of the mass of ceremonial celebrants comprising the peripheral dancing column to the select group of donors and recipients of ritual names and other valuables associated with the center of the plaza. This, however, is an inequality in the degree of "beauty" (analytically glossed as integration, completeness, and finesse in the construction and public expression of personal identity through the requisite set of social relations) involved in the two types of ceremonial roles, not one of relative dominance and subordination, as in the case of the age-set/men's house hierarchy. Kayapó society at the communal level may thus be understood in its own terms as a continual oscillation between two complementary "structural poses,"[6] each associated with one of the complementary modes of space-time and one of the two complementary categories of social value (dominance and beauty).

The oscillation from secular age-set structure to sacred ceremonial organization, however, is not merely a question of shifting vantage points from one mode of space-time or social value to another. A more profound shift in social and ontological perspective is involved, one that puts into question the "social" character of society and its distinctness from the domain of "nature."

From the profane standpoint of everyday social life, as organized at the communal level by the men's house and the age associations of both genders, the distinction between society and nature appears straightforward and clear-cut. Society means the world of the village and the everyday activities of social production, circulation, and consumption. Nature means everything beyond or outside of that, in either space or time: the wild forest and savanna beyond the limits of the village and its surrounding liminal "black" or "dead" zone; or the

---

[6] Gearing.

time of mythical beginnings before the inception of normal social time. In this view, the distinction between social humans and wild animals is clear-cut: the former constitute the social order, the latter the order of nature, and the relationship between the two orders is an external one of ambivalent hostility and interdependence. The substantive associations of the spatio-temporal coordinates of this view are also clear-cut: the center of space and the present moment of time are located in the social village, and within that in its central plaza, as contrasted with its peripheral ring of family households. The social, in other words, is the central, the peripheral the natural.

The shift to the "structural pose" of ceremony brusquely inverts these commonsense values. In the supreme social activity of collective self-reproduction, the central plaza becomes filled with beings covered with feathers, animal teeth and claws, and paint representing species of animals, fish, or birds, performing dance steps and singing songs learned from these or other "natural" beings (and often still phrased in the first person, as if the bird or animal authors of the songs were themselves singing). Around the periphery of this sacred center stand the spectators, ordinary social beings ranged in front of their ordinary social households, witnessing the transference of names derived from fish, birds, or planets, and ritual decorations, songs, or special dance movements derived from similar sources or from alien, non-Kayapó peoples, all of which they accept as the essential, sacred source of the reproduction of their ordinary social institutions and everyday secular existence. The central paradox involved here is not merely that the center has become "natural" and the periphery "social," but that society itself in the most fundamental ontological sense, both as an order of collective institutions and as a communal activity of cooperative self-reproduction, has become "natural," or perhaps more accurately, undifferentiated mixture of "natural" and "social" aspects. Not only ordinary secular space but ordinary secular time appears fantastically inverted; the counterparts of the half-human, half-bird or animal beings dancing in the plaza are to be found only in the mythical time before the creation of the profane social order, that is to say, before contemporary secular time.

Ordinary, "profane" social life, including the cooperative activities through which it is produced and reproduced, remains within the established forms of social relations and the natural world. The same is true of the everyday mode of space-time in which these normal social activities are enacted and experienced. The forms of social relations and institutions, or, in general terms, of the activities that make up the flow of ordinary space-time, are not themselves produced by the activities that merely replicate instances of them. The forms of human existence are therefore not experienced as human (social) products, creations of ordinary human social activity in ordinary social space-time. It follows, from the point of view of the Kayapó actor, that they must be inhuman, extrasocial, and also supernatural products of the creative activities of beings that transcend the limitations of the everyday domains of nature and society, beginning with the distinction between these domains and the mode of space-time in which this distinction has meaning. The ritual creation of social form therefore takes place in the alternative mythical mode of space-time in which the creation of new forms of social and natural existence is possible.

Social Person as Microcosmos

The same configuration of reversible/concentric/cyclical and irreversible/vertical/linear transformations is again replicated at the next lower level, that of the construction of the social person, or, in more concrete terms, the life cycle of the individual. The child begins as a "natural" or animal-like being lacking a separate social identity of its own. It is regarded as still essentially an extension of the animal, natural reproductive powers of its parents, whose social identities provide the only social aspect of its own being. As the child grows, it acquires the attributes of full social personhood along two complementary dimensions. One of these is the linear, irreversible dimension of growth; it learns to stand erect, and the distance from feet to head, root to tip, steadily increases. The second dimension is that of progressive socialization; the child receives names and other ritually valued aspects of identity while still small from its extrafamilial relatives and after that proceeds to acquire increments of social identity in successive rites of passage, which simultaneously mark its induction into communal age groups and its accession to progressively more adult roles within the domestic sphere. This process is concretely imaged as one of regulating the periphery of the physical body in such a way as to convert the expression of the developing energies within its natural core into modalities of social interaction with external social others; in short, a "concentric" organization of social interaction.

The principal medium of concrete imagery through which the two dimensions of growth and development are manifested and coordinated at the level of the construction of the social person is the system of bodily decoration.[7] The peripheral appendages of the body (feet and lower legs, hands and forearms, and head) are painted red to accentuate and activate the individual's capacity to interact with others in surrounding social space, while the core of the body (trunk, upper arms, and thighs) is painted black to suppress the direct expression of the "natural," psycho-physical powers of the individual. At the same time, the head is differentiated from the feet through a series of specific treatments designed to accentuate and regulate the social capacities of the person located in the head: the organs of seeing and hearing (in Kayapó thought, the active and passive modes of understanding), and the mouth, as the organ of speech.

In rites of passage, states of mourning, and grave illness, the normal socializing treatments of the body may be reversed or undone. The whole body may be painted a single color (black or red), thus effacing the differentiation of core and periphery; and ornaments that betoken the individual's previously obtaining social condition may be stripped away, to be restored or replaced by others, upon the termination of the ritual or transitional state. Hair of the head, otherwise left long, may be shaved off, and the individual may be enjoined from speaking at all, or at least in anything louder than a whisper. The visual and verbal aspects of personhood associated with the head, the "tip" of the vertical dimension of the person, and the distinctive criteria of vertical development, are thus suppressed. The concentric contrast between the social and natural zones of the individual actor may, in sum, be reversed, while the vertical contrast between head and feet is neutralized.

When the individual takes part in ceremonial activity as an ordinary celebrant, the code of bodily adornment is again altered to express the transformation of ordinary social identity involved. The most striking aspects of this transformation are the "natural" materials, above all feathers, that constitute the rich variety of Kayapó rit-

---

[7] Turner 1993b.

ual costume. Resplendent capes of macaw plumes, feather head-
dresses, armlets, leg-, lip-, and back-ornaments of many shapes and
sizes, and the coating of the body with green parrot breast-feathers,
are among the more striking of these decorations. There are also
animal-hoof belts and leg-rattles, animal tooth and claw necklaces,
and other appurtenances utilizing animal and plant materials in their
recognizable natural forms. The total effect is to efface the profane
social identity of the individual and supplant it with a sacred, "natural" (or transcendentally natural-social) identity. This inversion of
the cosmic connotations and attributes of personal identity through
the medium of bodily adornment obviously replicates, at the level of
the individual, the parallel inversions of the village and kindred-
household levels that have already been described.[8]

Sources of Power, Social Agency, and Social Identity

To sum up, the same pattern, comprising two complementary modes
of transformative or productive activity embodied in two complementary dimensions of space-time, manifests itself at all levels of the
structure of the universe, from the framework of cosmic space-time
through the layout of the village, the personal kindred and the segmentary extended family household, down to the construction of the
social person and the individual life cycle.

In my analysis of the form and content of this process, I have
sought to emphasize the continuity and reciprocal interdependence
of its material aspect as social action and its symbolic aspect as social
consciousness. In the most general terms, the process is articulated
as the interplay of two complementary tendencies or movements: an
irreversible, finite, but continually replicated linear process, and a
reversible, cyclical, potentially infinite one. The former is articulated
in terms of the construction and deconstruction of social form in the
individual life cycle, while the latter corresponds to the integration
of successive life cycles through the perpetual alternation of socializing and naturalizing transformations. Both the linear and reversible

---

[8] Turner 1991.

modes of this process constitute different levels or modes of the more fundamental dialectic of social production and disintegration, the continual conflict between the appropriation of natural substance and energy through transformation into social form and the decay of social form into the relatively disordered state of nature, as in the breakage of manufactured objects, aging, disease, or death.

What appear at first as distinct, complementary processes, each with its distinct mode of space-time embodied in separate sets of representations, thus reveal themselves, upon analysis, as complementary modalities of a single, totalizing process of social activity. This global process comprises Kayapó social production, including the reproduction of the relations of which the various parts of the productive process are constituted. As modalities of production and reproduction, the two movements have specific material extensions in space and time. These extensions, as in all activity, assume the reciprocally relativized forms of space-time. As modes of material activity, they equally imply definite concepts of agency (specifically, the nature and sources of the power to act and of the causal aspect or efficacy of action). As a set of schemas of interaction, they likewise imply a set of actor identities (pragmatically constructed as nodes of social relations).

Cosmology as Ideology:
Ritual as Fetishized Production

This system of social relations, ideas, and values, then, is no mere symbolic configuration, metaphorical figure, or abstract semiotic structure of binary oppositions, but the dynamic organization of the material process of producing and reproducing the social world, including the actors and the principal segmentary groups of which it is composed. As a (re-)productive process that is itself its own ultimate product, its structure is embodied in the social entitites and relations that act to produce it and are in turn produced by it. All levels of social organization, from the community as a whole to its individual members, are conceived of as formed simultaneously through the same process, which is in turn conceived of as instantiating the encompassing form of the natural universe. The form itself, its structural dimensions and their associated meanings and values, is therefore seen as outside the domain of social activity, even while it constituted the encompassing framework of that domain: in a word, as "natural" rather than social. The cultural formulation of the structure of this process as the paradigm of the general structure of the cosmos thus manifests the fetishization of social consciousness of the form as the encompassing natural frame of social activity. The pragmatic enactment of the form thus simultaneously reproduced the form itself and the alienation of the consciousness of the social nature of the form.

The paradoxical corollary of this fetishized view is that full participation in this fundamentally "natural" process of social production becomes the criterion of full sociality: in other words, of being fully human. The essence of the fetishistic inversion of social consciousness involved is that society is seen as imitating and reproducing a "natural," cosmic pattern rather than as producing that pattern as the form of its own process of reproduction. An effect of this inversion is that the exploitative nature of the focal relation of social production, the domination of married daughters and sons-in-law by parents/parents-in-law, is obscured. In the fetishized view, social actors acquire socially valued qualities like "beauty" and "dominance" in proportion as they fulfill, and thus identify themselves with, the natural pattern embodied in social institutions. Elders of both genders are seen as more fully embodying the social relations comprising this pattern than juniors and are therefore more highly esteemed, in terms of the two principal dimensions of social value, than the latter. Values, in other words, are seen as inhering directly in individuals and the statuses they hold, rather than as deriving from the social process through which those persons and statuses are constructed. The material social reality that the subordination of the juniors and dominance of the seniors is produced by the reproduction of the uxorilocal relation within the extended-family household is obscured by the fetishized appearance that the relation itself, and the hierarchical distribution of valued status attributes which it defines, is "natural" and thus not socially produced.

A further result of the same deformation of social consciousness is the distortion of the relation between the structure of society and that of the individual actor, and indeed between the formal aspect of structure-as-product and the dynamic or operational aspect of structure as constructive activity. From the fetishized point of view, the formal pattern of the process of social production is reified as an independently existing object, that is, as a static structure, which is then seen to constrain activity to conform with its own preexisting form. The material reality, as I have argued, is precisely the reverse: the structure of society is primarily a structure of activity, which reflexively objectifies itself as an object of production, that is, as a product. The structure, that is to say, does appear in one aspect as a static pattern or object, but only in the *a posteriori* sense of a goal to be achieved through activity, postulated as a part of the activity itself, or as a product of the completed activity, which thus embodies and presupposes the activity, not as an *a priori* form, itself inactive, which somehow constrains action to conform with itself—for example, as a "model of" and "model for" it. As social consciousness, the latter view has the result, as we have seen, that society becomes seen as an ahistorical form, which cannot itself be conceived of as a product of the activity of human agents. Social activity is rather understood as the reproduction of a received, socially uncreated pattern. The social actors themselves, by the same token, are symbolically constructed according to the same pattern, ostensibly as reflections of the same universal, presocial form, rather than being understood as constructing themselves through the pattern of their interactions with social Others.

The inversion of social consciousness of which I have been speaking is not an intra-psychic process, lacking empirical manifestations and accessible only to abstract analysis. It has a material social form, that of collective ceremony, which is the focus of the most intense collective fascination of the Kayapó with themselves and their society. Ceremonial performance implicitly involves a shift of subjective perspective, from the internal vantage point of a member of society (the perspective of profane, everyday existence), to the external vantage point of a creator of the forms of social organization as such.

Such an external perspective on the constitutive forms of society as a whole can only, given the fetishized limits of Kayapó social consciousness, be that of the transcendental, social-natural beings of the mythical border regions of social time and space, or (which comes to the same thing) social life and death.[9] At the moment when the Kayapó collectively organize themselves to reproduce the forms of their social order, and thus in a material sense to assume the role of

---

[9] Turner 1985.

producers of themselves and their social world, they are therefore ironically obliged to exchange the character of social beings for that of asocial, quasi-natural monsters, dancing around the village plaza covered with feathers, palm-fronds, and animal teeth.

That the highest, cosmic level is *not* manifested in two inverted forms is indicative of its special relationship to the lower levels, as an abstracted representation of their common structural features that lacks any material referent of its own (that is, any specific process or level of social activity). As the abstract concept of the whole, the vantage point that permits of no higher, external vantage point, this highest-level, cosmic structure embodies the unconscious irony of Kayapó social consciousness and frames its ideological deformation. The projection of the structure of society as the structure of the natural cosmos implies the naturalization of that structure, and thus the denial of the social character of society. The implication that the structure of society, as a "natural" form, is therefore external to society itself, paradoxically confronts the reality that, *qua* structure of society, it is nevertheless at the same time internal to it at all levels of organization. Society, in sum, comes to be seen as including and encompassing its "natural" structure at the same time that it is encompassed by it. The structure itself, as an abstract form, thus transcends the distinction between the "social" and the "natural" as distinct zones of relations or vantage points on reality. It can therefore have no distinct "social" and "natural" transformations, only its single, transcendental, ambiguously undifferentiated social-natural mode of being.

That every level of Kayapó "cosmology" below that of the highest, most abstract conception of the form of the cosmos as a whole, has two reversed formulations, in which the dimensions of social space and time, the character of agency and the construction of actor-identity assume inverted forms as the producers rather than the products of material social existence thus emerges in its full theoretical significance as a concrete manifestation of the ideological character of Kayapó social consciousness, or, which comes to the same thing, Kayapó "religion."

One attribute of ideological consciousness, as defined above, is alienation, defined as the double inversion of the subjective and objective aspects of action, in which the subject perceives its own contribution only as object and imbues the object with the properties of subjective agency. The pivoting back and forth in the Kayapó system between the "sacred" and "profane" structural poses or transformations of each of its levels of structure save the highest manifests the complementary interdependence between the alienated and unalienated aspects of Kayapó social consciousness, the "sacred" transformation representing the former and the "profane" the latter. "Alienation" in this sense takes two complementary forms: first, the "naturalization" of the basic structure of society itself, so that it comes to be regarded not as a historical product of human action, but as a form determined outside of historical time by some nonhuman agency; and second, the reification of the form, or its conception as a self-existing object independent of, and prior to, the actors who have in reality produced it. These two aspects define the tension between the "sacred" and "profane" modalities of the Kayapó conception of the world.

References

Bakhtin, M. M. 1981. "Forms of Time and of the Chronotope in the Novel." In *The Dialogical Imagination*, edited by M. Holquist.

Turner, Terence. 1979a. "The Gê and Bororo Societies as Dialectical Systems." In *Dialectical Societies*, edited by D. Maybury-Lews. Cambridge, Mass.: Harvard University Press.

———. 1979b. "Kinship, Household and Community Structure among the Northern Kayapó." In *Dialectical Societies*, edited by D. Maybury-Lewis. Cambridge, Mass.: Harvard University Press.

———. 1984. "Dual Opposition, Hierarchy and Value: Moiety Structure and Symbolic Polarity in Central Brazil and Elsewhere." In *Differences, Valeurs, Hierarchie: Textes Offertes à Louis Dumont et Reunis par Jean-Claude Galey*, 335-70. Paris: Editions de l'Ecole des Hautes Etudes en Sciences Sociales.

——— 1985. "Animal Symbolism, Totemism, and the Structure of Myth." In *Natural Mythologies: Animal Symbols and Metaphors in South America*, edited by G. Urton. University of Utah Press.

———. 1991. "We Are Parrots, Twins Are Birds: Play of Tropes as Operational Structure." In *Beyond Metaphor: The Theory of Tropes in Anthropology*, edited by J. Fernandez. Stanford: Stanford University Press.

———. 1992. "Os Mebengokre Kayapó: De communidades autonomas a sistema inter-etnica." In *Historia dos Indios do Brasil*, edited by M. Carneiro da Cunha. São Paulo: Companhia das Letras.

———. 1993a. "De Cosmologia a Historia: Resistencia, adaptacao e consciencia social entre os Kayapó." In *Amazonia: Etnologia e Historia Indigena*, edited by Eduardo Viveiros de Castro and Manuela Carneiro da Cunha. São Paulo: Universidade de São Paulo.

———. 1993b. "The Social Skin." In *The Body as Social Text*, edited by C. Burroughs and J. Ehrenreich. Iowa City: University of Iowa Press.

11

Fragments of Southern
Tehuelche Religiosity and Myths

Alejandra Siffredi

The Aónikenk, or "Southerners"—terms used to denote the southern Tehuelche, who are also referred to as Patagonians in the classical literature—inhabited that region of the Argentine Patagonia which is circumscribed to the north and south by the Chubut River Basin and the Strait of Magellan, and to the west and east by the base of the Andean Mountains and the Atlantic Ocean respectively. Together with the southern Tehuelche and the Ona of Tierra del Fuego are the peoples of the so-called Tehuelche Complex, whose languages have been assigned to the Araukan-Chon family. Owing to the geographically peripheral habitats of the Aónikenk and the Ona, the trials of the historical era were felt relatively late. Nonetheless, they were equally responsible for the annihilation of these three ancient hunter-gather societies and, to a lesser degree, the agro-pastoral traditions of peoples such as the Araucanians.

Advancing from Chile in successive waves, the Araucanians managed to dominate the Pampa-Patagonian region during the nineteenth century, and the Tehuelche—a name of Araucan origin meaning "wild people"—experienced to varying degrees the effects associated with the adoption of the horse and acculturation under the Araucanians. Even if we were to accept the northern Tehuelche society of hunter-gatherers as having become one of mounted hunters,[1] at least three factors would have made improbable a similar change in lifestyle for the Aónikenk: (1) the horse was incorporated

---

[1] Wilbert 1984, 2.

only during the first third of the eighteenth century; (2) the availability of relatively few horses (due in part to a lack of grazing lands) and the use of them for subsistence activities and transportation meant that horses were only vaguely associated with economic and military power and inter- or intratribal hostilities; and (3) the continued hunting of *guanaco* (llama) and *ñandú* (rhea) required seasonal migrations between the base of the Andes and the Atlantic coast in increments of only fifteen kilometers, a distance equivalent to that which could previously be made on foot.

These circumstances, however, did not prevent the Aónikenk from adopting a considerable variety of innovations and customs since the eighteenth century. Among the changes were the consumption of mare flesh and new types of personal property (herds of horses and weavings and silver ornaments of Araucanian manufacture); expanded expeditions—often ethnocentrically confused with an increase in nomadism—such as the celebrated traversing of Patagonia from the Strait of Magellan to the mouth of the Río Negro that was accompanied by the English sailor George Musters in the years 1869-1870;[2] and a concurrent amplification of intratribal and interethnic relations which brought to the regional markets suppliers of feathers and furs (especially fox and llama) and consumers of alcohol, tobacco, herbs, and sugar. As this trend generated a growing and irreversible economic dependence, it is probable that the indigenous participation in commercial networks was a fundamental factor in the acculturation of the southern Tehuelche during the nineteenth century.[3]

In addition, a movement known as the "Araucanization of the Pampa" greatly influenced the progressive retreat of the Tehuelche until their final defeat in Languiñeo, Barrancas Blancas, and Shótel Káike at the beginning of the last century. Their defeat by the Araucanians marked the political and military domination of the latter and promoted an escalation of biocultural mestization resulting in Araucanian preeminence. In the minds of the present-day Tehuelche, their defeat of almost one and a half centuries ago represents the beginning of their oral history.[4]

The final genocide, definititive subordination, and complete dis-

---

[2] Musters 1871.

[3] Palmero 1986, 157-71.

[4] Escalada 1949, 246.

articulation of the remaining bands were the consequences of the Conquest of the Desert led by the Argentine army during the National Consolidation movement toward the end of the last century. The image of a "population void" transmitted by the expression Conquest of the Desert, rather than reflecting reality, portrayed national aspirations to control the frontier and the prejudice that "desert" (no-man's land) was any territory not occupied by people of European origin. Thus the obsession to "clean up" the Patagonian region through the elimination of its indigenous population became the orienting philosophy of their endeavor.[5] This policy soon led to the arrival of "colonial" ranchers, the seizing of Indian territories, the fencing-off of lands, the confinement of indigenous survivors to reservations, and the educating of Indian children in Salesian schools.

A major part of the ethnographic data used for my research was obtained from two field trips to a reservation in the Province of Santa Cruz during the summers of 1965 and 1967. At that time the population of Aónikenk origin was estimated at two hundred individuals of which only about seventy could express themselves—to varying degrees—in their own language and Spanish, and an even smaller number also spoke Araucanian.

Our knowledge of Aónikenk religion is fragmentary because of the genocide and ethnocide alluded to earlier and a reluctance on the part of the indigenous people to communicate with foreigners. Nevertheless, between 1950 and 1975, a considerable corpus of mythographic data describing the already classic "cycle" of the cultural hero Elal was saved from oblivion. Until well into this century, the Indians displayed deliberate reservation in and even open rejection to the sharing of their mythology with the whites for fear of cultural sanctions of various sorts. One example of how native social control discourages individuals from divulging religious information is through public contempt that marks them as traitors and treats them as "skunks." The metaphor of the informant as a skunk is based on the analogy of the repulsive odor emitted by this animal when surprised, which gives away its presence.[6]

My own communicative experience was not particularly difficult, although I did perceive various moments of intentional silence. I was

---

[5] Martínez Sarasola 1992, 284.
[6] Llaras Samitier 1950, 180.

not always sure whether my only informant, Doña Luisa Mercerat de Zapa, who had a small Patagonian hut next to her home, where she would go to sing, weave traditional coats of *guanaco* leather and converse with me, was divulging a minimum and fragmented version of the cycle of Elal[7] because she was trying to elude me, or whether her silence reflected a partial or total absence of knowledge.

Taking into account that the agony of the sociocultural experience associated with colonial ranchers may have reinforced these reserved attitudes[8] leads one to think that they may reflect an intentional strategy or resistance designed to protect their religiosity from the whites.

The Gods

Based on an ethnocentric prejudice anchored in the notion of religion that privileges the ties between humans and a "unique" god, travelers, evangelists, and researchers, either consciously or unconsciously influenced by the idea that the authenticity of the religious phenomenon is based within a monotheistic framework, attempted to discover local images of a supreme god or indications of a unique divine being among the Aónikenk.[9] From these weak notions arose an equally prejudiced discourse that argued of the general disappearance of a religious system among the Tehuelche. For example, during the initial phases of my research,[10] I suggested the possible identification of a celestial deity called Kóoch, or Sky, with the figure of a "high god" whose subtle profiles I attributed to two processes: (1) the atomization of such attributes as omnipotence, creativity, or the uranic features of other deities with specific functions; and (2) the almost complete replacing of Kóoch by Elal, a deity assimilated into a religious form more accessible to the daily experience and therefore more practical.

According to some myths Kóoch was responsible for the original creation and the regulation of natural elements. Kóoch has since

---

[7] Bórmida and Siffredi 1969–70, 224.
[8] Wilbert 1984, 3–4.
[9] Musters 1871, 202; Escalada 1949, 237; Llaras Samitier 1950, 176.
[10] Siffredi 1969–70, 247–50.

become inactive and distant in his relationship with humans, which leads me to think of him as a *deus otiosus*, an idea that also fits into the "unique" concept. Kóoch coexisted with other deities, though without a specific hierarchy, but practice of the cult appears to have been developed without explicit reference to Kóoch. Thus, for the Indians, far from being a central or unique form of the divine, he is fundamentally a mythological entity.[11] Worth mentioning is a masculine personification of the sky whose names denote expressions equivalent to "the noble," "the ancient," or "the enduring"; these may allude to Kóoch's role as trustee of the body of laws governing social life that were bequeathed by Elal. In a sense this characterizes Kóoch as the judge of the dead who evaluates the deceased by comparing their actions during life to the ideal ethic which is centered on the qualities of valor, ingenuity, sharing, hospitality, and reservation toward strangers. Furthermore, according to the cultural principle of complementarity between the sexes, Kóoch is assisted by the goddess Seecho, whose function is that of verifying the presence of a special tattoo on the left forearm of the deceased. This mark allows the dead access to the other world, a place devoid of poverty, disease, and evil located over the eastern horizon. On the other hand, according to their beliefs, the absence of the tattoo authorizes Seecho to cast the deceased into the sea.[12]

There has also been an attempt, guided by the phantom of monotheism that tries to identify dominant divine figures in the myths based, for example, on an uncritical acceptance of certain recurring indigenous references to Elal as "our true god." This serves only to place ethnographers in harmony with a religious code that is familiar to them: the Kadde-Christians and in a broader sense all white people—whom they have incorporated in part as a consequence of Salesian evangelization.

It is worthwhile inquiring into the identity of these gods that are so distantly related to the ritual gestures. Some of the names point to the order of nature: Kóoch, the sky, the visible celestial bodies such as the Keenguenkon-Keenguenken pair, the Moon goddess and the Sun god, about whom there are episodes in the Elal Cycle that describe their metamorphosis from human beings into astral bodies;

---

[11] Wilbert 1984, 8.
[12] Siffredi 1969–70.

Karuten, the thunder, represented as an indigenous male of a vengeful nature who roams the lower sky producing violent meteorological phenomena; Joóshe, the tornado, personification of the freezing wind from the Andes who lives in a cave.

Distinct from the above are the names of other gods that refer to the "order of culture." They constitute the foundation of society through a body of laws and prescriptions bequeathed in mythical times. So Elal—apparently the personal name of the mythical hero—represents the original transformation of the true culture because the constitution of the sociocultural is contemporary not to the Aónikenk but to a mythical time that predates them. Upon completing his mission, Elal returned "to the Land Without Evil," for which there are no messianic-type narratives.

Elal is not, however, perceived as a god who is distant, abstract, or detached from a relationship that unites human beings with the divine. In fact, the deep rootedness of incest prohibitions in daily life bequeathed by Elal was observed in a comment made by Doña Feliciana Velázquez when she narrated an episode about an incestuous act attempted by the maternal grandmother with Elal, for which she was transformed into a mouse:[13] "My grandmother stamped on a mouse she saw because it was through her fault [incestuous attempt], that her powerful grandson [Elal], who was raised by her, had fled." On the other hand, although quite covert, there is evidence of ties with Elal through rituals such as an exclusively female body of sacred songs that are transmitted from mother to daughter. I have suggested also that the repeating and canonical form of the orations sung by the heads of bands before initiating hunting expeditions appears to contain some prayers directed to Elal, inventor of weapons and hunting techniques.[14]

The Sky of Elal

The narrative itinerary of the diverse versions of the Elal Cycle contains notable coincidences. In all of them a uniting thread is provided by key moments in the life cycle of the hero: his fantastic birth;

---

[13] Bórmida and Siffredi 1969–70.
[14] Siffredi 1987, 14:363.

his childhood prowess; his childhood battles against undefined and superior entities over whom he prevails; his frustrated loves and the failure of his only marriage, which ends with the establishing of the social order through the delegation of goods, rules, and institutions, followed by his final departure to the Land Without Evil.

Without disregarding the logical virtue of indigenous discourse, and limiting myself to the eight versions of the Elal Cycle that I personally obtained, the present interpretation of the corpus is based in the cultural categories of space, time, and social relations.[15] These categories are intertwined because the concept of time is modeled after the perception of the natural and social environment. The spatial concept predominates in the discourse, as indicated by references to the physical—for example, a distance traveled on foot or horseback, speed of travel, places associated with key moments in the life cycle, the nature of social relationships, and the quality expressed in series of interactions. These eminently qualitative interactions become objective in the episodes of the Elal Cycle as determined spatial settings or scenes from which one can distinguish a prior state from a later one, thereby permitting the restoration of a sequence.

Recognizing the broad nature of the aforementioned categories, I selected six recurring themes of the narrative and grouped them into two contrasting series in order to operationalize them in function of the situation. The first series contains signs of chaos and the senseless. The second contains signs of distinction and meaning. Processual images are inserted between the series in order to show indispensable mediations and to identify particular aspects of both. The grouping of the first series refers to "spatial distance," "the previous," and "sociological reserve," while that of the second represents their opposites. In addition, the assembling of the two series also takes into account the spatial positioning and identification of the narrators, who define themselves as true Aónikenk, different from the northerners, whom they call Pénkenk. It is true that the cultural frontier between the two populations—which coincides geographically with the basin of the Santa Cruz River—is more clearly visualized in archaeological than in ethnographic terms.[16]

Within the first series the "spatial distance" indicator refers to a

---

[15] Bórmida and Siffredi 1969-70.

[16] Hernández 1992, 63.

mythical scene on the Senguerr River, which forms part of the traditional habitat of the Pénkenk. It also alludes to the mediations of the hero between the "above" and the "below"; "the previous" alludes to the channeling of a primordial chaotic and untested reality by the undetermined and fluid nature of beings and things; "sociological reserve" refers to the predomination of coded relationships in terms of kinship based on mutually dependent and hierarchically positioned roles. This configuration allows for a reduced number of dyadic relationships of the type grandmother/grandchild, father/son, father-in-law/son-in-law that determine a restriction in interactive networks.

Imagined as a small extension of land completely surrounded by a motionless sea, the Senguerr River valley represents a primordial microcosm because it shows physical evidence of divine activity: springs, particular topographical features, and petroglyphs that identify the faraway scene of the heroes' fabulous birth and young life.

Elal incarnates the conjunction of antinomical situations. The father was one of the chthonic monsters engendered by Tons—the darkness—which in original times instilled panic in the people because he would devour them. The pregnant mother, one of the clouds created by Kóoch, is shredded and eaten by the father of Elal, while his maternal grandmother rescues the neonate and takes charge of raising him. Two accounts of these events spark the indigenous memory: a spring, arising from the quartered cadaver of the Cloud marks the birthplace of Elal and is known today by the toponym Agua Linda. Further, the red sunrises that are regularly observed from any given elevation reinforce the memory of the shedding of the prototypical blood.

Elal's young acts of valor constitute mediations between the "above" and the "below," between a chaotic "before" and a more harmonic "after," and between the natural and the cultural. For example, the mediation with the "below" is evidenced in the successive battles of the hero against his father and paternal uncles. They are perceived as giants among humans and minerals, whose main feature is their invulnerability, except for their heels, where Elal finally destroys them. Upon their death they become petrified and, in their immutable forms of rocks and fossil remains, lend proof of the primeval chaos.

Elal's mediation with the above occurs in the episode of his journey to the celestial habitat of Sun and Moon, his future parents-in-

law. The divine couple displays an open hostility toward him by sub-
jecting Elal to a series of mortal tasks before giving him the hand of
their only daughter. Elal successfully completes the tasks but takes
the luxury of abandoning her soon thereafter and permanently con-
fines his in-laws to the sky. A rock with the imprints of his feet—probably the petroglyphs of the "footprint" style (2500 B.C.E.) in southern
Patagonia[17]—marks the site where he ascended to the sky. Events
such as these identify the distinction between the divine and the
human through the ceasing of communications between the above
and the below that is characteristic of origin myths.

On the level of social relations, the failure of the marriage with
the daughter of Sun points to the risks and "absurdity" of an
exogamy that is too loosely defined. The abhorrence of incest is
expressed in the following episode, where the grandmother of the
culture hero intends to seduce him only to end up as a mouse con-
demned to living underground.

This particular episode constitutes an indispensable mediation
between the series because it marks the point of inflection for both.
In effect, from the incestuous situation, which is the condensed symbol for "sociological reserve" and "primordial disorder," one detects
a systematic inversion of the indicators of the first series. Thus, the
second series now includes "spatial proximity," as represented by the
familiar scene of the region to the extreme south of the continent
which the Aónikenk claim as theirs; "the after," summarizing the
processes focused on the consolidation of a differentiated reality; distinguishing the constitution of the social; "sociological receptivity,"
basically referring to the linking of different protagonists through
various systems of relationships. These dynamics bring about a tendency toward the amplification of interactive networks and finally
those of the sociability.

Thus, the "distance" from the scene of origin is contrasted by the
"accessibility" to the experience that the new scene represents. For
example, one episode about the creation of the Aónikenk territory
recognizes its steady emergence from the primordial sea, which was
forced to the east by the well-aimed arrows of Elal. At the same time
the arduous journeys of the hero between the east and west—which

---

[17] Gradín 1971, 114.

foreshadowed contemporary seasonal migrations—confer upon the habitat a known and varied physiognomy that alternates between mountains, forests, mesas, rivers, valleys, lakes, and islands.

In harmony with this spatial configuration, the "after" indicator pits the homogeneity of primordial time—which figures as continual life, the uninterrupted summer, or the primordial sea—against periodicity, which supposes the installation of laws that regulate the cycle of death and reproduction, the seasonal alternation inherent in rhythmic productions, and the regularity of the oceanic movements.

For example, an anthropogonic narrative referring to the origin of the Aónikenk as an inversion between a preexisting humanoid generation and the sea lions also includes motifs that allude to periodicity through the individualization of species, which become more subjected to the cycle of reproduction and death, in accordance with the mythical notion that generating life implies generating death.[18] In concrete terms, until the social is consolidated, Elal urges the perennial and still undifferentiated beings not to initiate sexual relations. However, the transgression committed by the sea lion prompted the individualization of species and the origin of copulation, marriage, reproduction, and death.[19]

At the same time, the indicator "sociological receptivity" translates to an extension of the interactive networks made possible by the diversification of social relations with respect to those that predominate in the space-time scene of the Senguerr River. Anchored in kinship, social relations result in dyadic ties of a hierarchical order, contrastable to the relations of companionship, cooperation, competition or rivalry between pairs (more horizontal and varied) which are initiated between the actors of the episodes that occur in the familiar habitat.

It is not a coincidence that these episodes, where the constitution of the social adopts a key position, invariably take on the form of a "commission," an association that groups different protagonists horizontally linked in diverse manners into a situation of negotiation. In the heart of this political institution, which foreshadowed the male counsels at the level of a local group, Elal assumes less of an authoritarian role than that of a *primum* between pairs because the entire

---

[18] Waag 1980.
[19] Siffredi and Cordeu 1970, 9.

discussion concerning decision making is that which frequently permits the reaching of an agreement.

For example, one version of the origin of seasons[20] presents Elal as a band leader united in counsel with his followers—the cockroach, the puma, the mountain lion, the armadillos, the hare, and the rhea—to negotiate the duration of winter, a subject of opposing opinions until two proposals are drawn up. The first, supported by the rhea, asks for a long winter, while the second, proposed by the hare, suggests a short winter. Based on the reasoning put forth by Elal concerning the subsistence difficulties represented by the cold, hare's proposal gains greater acceptability until he suddenly shouts "three months" and flees to his burrow in order to escape his pursuing opponent who wanted a continuous winter.

Still remaining to be answered is how they become cognizant of the constitution of the social through two principal routes. One question we have to ask is why the narrative described above puts animals into motion as Elal's only co-protagonists. Keeping in mind that the Aónikenk was a hunting society, it is not unusual that animals adopt protagonistic roles in their mythology. However, this event does not occur in the primordial scene but rather in the familiar scene where the daily interaction with Elal seems to be the way to understand the constitution of the social because it is this class of interaction that is associated with the achievement of attributes and forms of human-specific relationships. Another way to express the same is that society finds its foundation in the body of rules and mandates bequeathed by Elal. These are included in the narratives concerning the origin of the sexual division of labor, marriage, and procreation, and the culinary significance of fire.[21]

Also associated with the constitution of the social is the vision of the "other," which permeates the narrative about intercultural contact that I outline below.

The Expression of Contact in the Elal Cycle

The narrative of the Elal Cycle is not dissociated from the historical dynamics witnessed by the Aónikenk, whose great lines were sum-

---

[20] Bórmida and Siffredi 1969-70, 217.
[21] Bórmida and Siffredi 1969-70.

marized in the introduction. Inscribed in the problematic ties between myth and history, the expression of intercultural contact is modeled in this narrative according to two nonexclusive processes: incorporating history into myth and incorporating myth into history. The first implies an absorption of historical events into mythical structures in such a way that they become anchored in an original past.[22]

The oldest version of the Elal Cycle[23] contains a yet unexplored episode about intertribal contact that offers an interesting example of incorporating history into myth. Although the identity of the "other" remains implicit, it can be deduced from the mention of the stone ax and the spear, which, as insignias of the warrior, are unmistakable features associated with the Araucan culture of the eighteenth and nineteenth centuries. The account assimilates the bloody confrontations of the Aónikenk with this "other"—as we saw happen at the beginning of the last century in the region of the Senguerr River—which leads to a reorganizing of the chaotic scene of the origin. Characterized as "an epoch of violent transitions in which the order of things was altered," a key sign of the reigning confusion is Elal's loss of the divine attributes, both before Sintalk'n, the personification of the Araucan warrior (considered omnipotent and astute), and before the giant cannibals of the primordial time, who are reborn larger and more immeasurable than before.

However, in contrast to some representations of the interethnic contact, those that come from this episode connote a reversible process, indicated by the recuperation of the powers of Elal leading to the defeat and death of his opponent. It is worthwhile noting that the inconsistency between the mythical elaboration and the actual result of the historical dynamics, as we saw, implied that the Tehuelche were forced to accept the political-military dominance of the Araucans during the major part of the past century.[24]

On the other hand, the mythical genesis of white domination presents this process as irreversible when constructed in terms foreshadowed by the unequal relationship inherent in a situation of interethnic friction. In this sense, the narrative in question could be identified with a recurring form of indigenous interpretations con-

---

[22] Turner 1988.
[23] Lista 1894, 16–26.
[24] Hernández 1992, 226.

cerning contact with the whites in mythologies from the lowlands of South America that Turner has called "origin myth of inequality."[25] For example, the dynamics alluded to above are seen in an account that ascribes the differences between Indians and whites to an unfortunate distribution of the animals in primordial times caused by the trickster fox. Even if what Elal projected were in reverse, the result of this distribution would show that the autochthonous fauna remain with the Aónikenk and the cattle of European origin with the white colonists.

According to the same account, the incorporating of myth into history could coincide in the same corpus with the inverse process.[26] The incorporation of history into myth brings together distinct modes of contemporary historical consciousness.[27] Thus, the consequences of the capricious conduct of the trickster demonstrates the discerning of a decisive historical event in the process of contemporaneous sociocultural change. I refer to the commercial hunting associated with the insertion of the Aónikenk into the regional markets as providers of prized skins. We see in the corresponding section of the account: "So Elal told his fellowmen: What the Fox did was fine: he freed the animals; in a few more years he will not come through here again, they will hunt him with dogs and traps and his skin will become valuable, let him pay for the fault he committed when he frightening the herd of horses over there. And this is how it was: now for that deed his only worth is his fur. . . ."[28]

Therefore, whether the Aónikenk incorporate the destructuralizing impact of contact on the level of mythical elaboration—with both the Araucans and the whites—and the conflicts derived therefrom is limited to a moral reflection. Evidently, sociocultural annihilation could account for the absence of messianic myths and revival practices already revitalized (maybe a strategy of hiding the beliefs is an exception), and compensated in part for the mythohistorical reflection about the significance of alcoholism, the appropriation of their ancient hunting grounds or the subalternation.[29] Also in the context

---

[25] Turner 1988, 266.
[26] Bórmida and Siffredi 1969–70, 219.
[27] Turner 1988.
[28] Ana Montenegro de Yebes 1967.
[29] Bórmida and Siffredi 1969–70, 224.

of the Elal Cycle, the great penury of the Aónikenk is reflected in the final impotence of the once powerful deity.

References

Bórmida, M., and Alejandra Siffredi. 1969-70. "Mitología de los Tehuelches Meridionales." *Runa* 12, nos. 1-2:199-245.

Escalada, F. 1949. *El complejo Tehuelche*. Buenos Aires: Coni.

García Marquez, G. 1989. *Crónica de una muerte anunciada*. Buenos Aires: Sudamericana.

Gradín, C. 1971. "Al propósito del arte rupestre en Patagonia meridional." *Anales de Arqueología y Etnología (Argentina)* 26:111-16.

Hernández, I. 1992. *Los indios de Argentina*. Madrid: MAPFRE, 1992.

Lista, R. 1894. *Una raza que desaparece: Los indios Tehuelches*. Buenos Aires: Coni.

Llaras Samitier, M. 1950. "Primer ramillete de fábulas y sagas de los antiguos patagones." *Runa* 4:170-99.

Martínez Sarasola, C. 1992. *Nuestros paisanos los indios*. Buenos Aries: Emecé.

Musters, G. 1871. "On the Races of Patagonia." *Journal of the Anthropological Institute of Great Britain and Ireland* 1, no. 11: 193-206.

Palermo, M. 1986. "Reflexiones sobre el llamado 'complejo ecuestre' en la Argentina." *Runa* 16:157-78.

Siffredi, Alejandra. 1969-70. "Hierofanias y concepciones mitico-religiosas de los tehuelches meridionales." *Runa* 12, nos. 1-2:247-71.

———. 1987. "Tehuelche Religion." In *The Encyclopedia of Religion*, edited by Mircea Eliade, 14:363-66. New York: Macmillan.

Siffredi, Alejandra, and E. Cordeu. 1970. "En torno a algunas coherencias formales de las antropogonías del Chaco y Patagonia." *Relaciones de la Sociedad Argentina de Antropología* n.s. 5, no.1:3-10.

Turner, Terrance. 1988. "Ethno-Ethnohistory: Myth and History in native South American Representations of Contact with Western Society." In *Rethinking History and Myth*, editing by J. Hill. Urbana: University of Illinois Press.

Waag, E. 1980. "Mitología tehuelche." *Revista Nacional de Cultura* 7:85-101.

Wilbert, Johannes. 1984. "History of Tehuelche Folk Literature Studies." In *Folk Literature of the Tehuelche Indians*, edited by J. Wilbert and K. Simoneau, 1-13. Los Angeles: UCLA Latin American Center Publications.

Contributors

ALFREDO LÓPEZ AUSTIN has a doctorate in history from Universidad Nacional Autonoma de Mexico (UNAM). He specializes in the history and culture of Mesoamérica, and currently he is researcher emeritus of the Anthropological Research Institute in UNAM. He is professor in the School of Philosophy and Letters at the same university. He has published fifteen books and co-authored six books. Among them are *La Constitución Real de Mexico-Tenochtitlan* (1961); *Hombres-Dios* (1973); *Cuerpo Humano e Ideologia* (1980; English 1988); *Los Mitos del Tlacuache* (1990; English 1993), *El conejo en la Cara de la Luna* (1994; Japanese 1993; English 1996); *Tamoachan y Tlalocan* (1994; English 1997; French 1997). As co-author with Leonardo López Luján, he has published *El Pasado Indigena* (1996; Italian [Jaca Book] 1998; English 2001), also with López Luján, *Mito y Realidad de Zuyuá* (1999).

DAVÍD CARRASCO is currently a Neil L. Rudenstine Professor of the Study of Latin America at Harvard with a joint appointment in the Department of Anthropology and the Divinity School. He was a professor of history of religions and director of the Raphael and Fletcher Lee Moses Mesoamerican Archive at Princeton University. He received his Ph.D. in the history of religions from the University of Chicago, where he worked with Mircea Eliade, Charles Long, and Paul Wheatley on symbolism of sacred space and the formation of the Ecumenopolis. Among his publications are the prize-winning *Quetzalcoatl and the Irony of Empire: Myths and Prophecies among the Aztecs; Religions of Mesoamerica: Cosmovision and Ceremonial Centers; To Change Place: Aztec Ceremonial Landscapes; and Waiting for the Dawn: Mircea Eliade in Perspective*. He is presently editor in chief of the forthcoming multi-volume *Oxford Encyclopedia of Mesoamerican Cultures*.

PETER VAN DER LOO is a Dutch citizen, born in Indonesia. He has studied in Holland, where he obtained his doctorate in history of religion and comparative science of religion from Leiden University. He specializes in Mesoamerican religions and the Borgia codices. He has lived for several years in Mexico, where he has conducted field and library research. He has published several scientific books and articles. Currently he teaches at Northern Arizona University in Flagstaff, Arizona.

MERCEDES DE LA GARZA is a graduate in History from the Universidad Nacional Autonoma de Mexico, where she teaches and conducts research on Maya Civilization. She directed Centro de Estudios Mayas for thirteen years. She created and currently coordinates the Program for Graduate Studies in Mesoamerica, and the certification in theory and history of religions from the School of Philosophy and Letters at this university. In 1995 she won the Universidad Nacional Prize; she was director (1997–2000) of the National Museum of Anthropology. Her research focuses on the history and theory of religions. Her books have been published in Mexico as well as in other countries. She is author of numerous articles and twelve books, among them El Hombre en el Pensamiento Religioso Náhuatl y Maya, UNAM, IIF, Mexico (1978); El Universo Sagrado de la Serpiente entre los Mayas, UNAM, IIF, Mexico (1984); Aves Sagradas de los Mayas, UNAM, Facultad de Filosofía y Letras (FFyL), Mexico (1995); Tratto di Antropologia del Sacro, Jaca Book-Massimo, Milano (1997); Rostros de lo Sagrado en el Mundo Maya, Paidós, Mexico (1998); Sueno y Alucinación en el Mundo Náhuatl y Maya, UNAM, IIF, Mexico (1990; translated into French and English).

JUAN M. OSSIO graduated in history and anthropology from the Pontificia Universidad Catolica del Peru and from the Universidad Nacional Mayor de San Marcos and earned his doctorate at Oxford University. He is an Honorary Professor of Universidad San Antonio Abad del Cuzco and a member of the Peruvian Society of History, Tinker Visiting professor in Chicago University, and detentore in exchange with John Simon Guggenheim. He has published Ideologia Mesiánica del Mundo Andino (1973); Los Retratos de los Incas según el Padre Fray Martín de Murúa (1985); Violencia Estructural: Antropologia (1990); Familia Campesina y Economia de Mercado (with Oswaldo Medina, 1985); Parentesco Reciprocidad y Jerarquía en los Andes (1992); Los Indios del Perú (1992); Las Paradojas del Peru Oficial (1994).

ROBIN M. WRIGHT studied anthropology at Stanford University (M.A. in 1974 and Ph.D. in 1981). In 1996 he was awarded Livre Docencia in Religion from Universidade Etadual de Campinas. Currently he is Associate Professor of Anthropology at UNICAMP and director of the Center for Research in Indigenous Ethnology. He has done extensive fieldwork primarily in the Brazilian Northwest Amazon since 1976 with the Baniwa Indians. He has published extensively on the history and religion of the Indians of the Northwest Amazon, indigenous advocacy, and the history of indigenous peoples of Lowland South America. His most recent works include *Cosmos, Self and History in Baniwa Religion: For those Unborn* (University of Texas Press, 1998), *Transformando os Deuses: Os Multiplos Sentidos da Conversao entre os Povos Indigenas no Brasil* (UNICAMP, 1999) and *Waferinaipe Ianheke: A Collection of Baniwa Myths* (FOIRN/ACIRA, 1999). He has just completed a major collection on the anthropology of assault sorcery and Amazonia (with Neil Whitehead, Duke University Press, 2002), and is organizing a volume on pentecostal religions among South American Native Peoples (UNICAMP, 2002).

TOM ZUIDEMA is Professor Emeritus of the Center of Advance Studies of the Anthropology department of the University of Illinois, Urbana, USA. After studying humanities and social sciences of Indonesia, he has specialized since 1950 in anthropology of South America with particular interest in the ethnohistorical study of the Inca empire and its capital, Cuzco, in addition to the socioanthropological study of modern Andean peoples. These interests led him to pay special attention to Andean religion (myth, rituals, and the calendar) and art (including Inca, pre-Inca, and colonial art). At the moment he is finishing a book-length manuscript on Inca astronomy, the calendar, and calendrical rituals.

EDGARDO JORGE CORDEU, an Argentine anthropologist, has a bachelors degree in anthropological sciences and a Ph.D. from the University of Buenos Aires. Currently he is professor of Systematic Anthropology III (Symbolic Systems) in the School of Philosophy and Letters at the same university. He is a head researcher for the National Research Council of Science and Technology (Consejo Nacional de Investigaciones Científicas y Técnicas) of the Argentine Republic. He has conducted research on religion, mythology, and cognition of the Toba and Chamacoco (mainly Ebidoso and Tomaraho) in the Gran Chaco. In addition to the titles contributed in his bibliography, one list of his main contributions appears in Wilbert and Simoneau (editors), 1987; and in Cordeu 1999 *Transfiguraciones Simbólicas: Ciclo ritual de los indios tomaráxo del Chaco Boreal*. Quito, Abya Yala, Biblioteca Abya Yala No. 63, p. 339.

TERENCE TURNER is professor of anthropology at the University of Chicago. Since 1962 he has done extensive field research among the Kayapo of Central Brazil. His numerous writings about them cover such areas as social organization, myth, ritual, history, politics, inter-ethnic contact, and aspects of cultural, social, political, and ideological change. He has also made ethnographic films about the Kayapo with the British broadcasting company and Granada Television, and for the last seven years has been directing the Kayapo video project, in which the Kayapo have been filming their own culture and relations with the Brazilians.

ALEJANDRA SIFFREDI, an Italio-Argentine anthropologist, holds a doctorate from the University of Buenos Aires. Currently at the same university she is professor of American Ethnology and director of the Ethnology and Ethnography Section in the Institute of Anthropological Sciences. She is also a researcher for the National Research Council of Science and Technology (Consejo Nacional de Investigaciones Científicas y Técnicas). In the last thirty years she has conducted extensive research in indigenous towns of Patagonia and the Gran Chaco. In 1960s she recaptured the forgotten mythology of the southern Tehuelche, producing many articles. Since 1970 she dedicated herself to the intensive study of Charote culture and cosmology. Starting in the 1980s she began to focus on the Nivaklé of northern Chaco, publishing profusely on social structure, symbolism, and ritual. Her recent research corresponds to topics such as myth dynamics, ethnicity, and the relations between cosmology, indigenous knowledge, and ecology.

LAWRENCE E. SULLIVAN is director of the Harvard University Center for the Study of World Religions and Professor of History of Religions at Harvard University. He has served as president of the American Academy of Religions and as national lecturer for the American Council of Learned Societies. He is associate editor of the sixteen volume *Encyclopedia of Religion* published by Macmillan Publishing. His book *Icanchu's Drum* won Best Book Awards from the Association of American Publishers in the American Council of Learned Societies. He formerly taught on the faculty of the University of Chicago. His most recent published volume is *Enchanting Powers: Music in the World Religions* (1997).

Index